The Morning Offering

Daily Thoughts for Orthodox Christians

ABBOT TRYPHON

ANCIENT FAITH PUBLISHING
CHESTERTON, INDIANA

The Morning Offering

© David M. Parsons (Abbot Tryphon)

Scripture quotations are taken from the New King James Version, © 1979, 1980, 1982 by Thomas Nelson, Inc. Used by permission.

Published by:
    Ancient Faith Publishing
    A Division of Ancient Faith Ministries
    P.O. Box 748
    Chesterton, IN 46304

ISBN: 978-1-936270-98-9

Printed in the United States of America

Cover photo by Abbot Tryphon

30 29 28 27 26 25 24 23 22 21   13 12 11 10 9 8 7 5

Introduction

Having taught in a small college before embracing the monastic life some thirty-six years ago, I still have a special place in my heart for young people. As a regular guest lecturer on area college and university campuses in the Puget Sound region, I am often greeted as Gandalf, something that brings me great joy.

It was with these young people in mind that I started writing these short essays in the form of a blog, desiring to give them an inspirational message to jumpstart their day. However, the audience for *The Morning Offering* blog has grown to include people of all ages, and many thoughts here are addressed to parents or to anyone who wishes to deepen his or her spiritual life.

These articles are not meant to be scholarly in nature, but simple inspirational reads over a morning cup of coffee, or, as is the case with us living on Vashon Island in the Puget Sound, something one can read while waiting for a ferry.

Abbot Tryphon

Resolve to Exercise Virtue

When we make New Year's resolutions, we pledge ourselves to positive change in the coming months. We decide we're going to lose weight, and we set a loss of a certain amount as our goal for the coming year. We promise ourselves we'll be more frugal in our spending and set aside more of our income for savings. Our children will be more central in our weekly allotment of time, with family time coming before personal recreation. The yard work will not be put off in the coming months, and that major kitchen remodel will actually be put on the front burner.

A better plan would be to pledge ourselves to exercise virtue during the coming year. Doing this means disposing ourselves to do good habitually and firmly. We pledge ourselves not only to perform good acts, but also to give the best of ourselves to others. Virtuous people tend toward the good with all their sensory and spiritual powers and also pursue the good, choosing to do it through concrete actions.

A Good Place

S miles are contagious. Ever notice how a room brightens when some- one walks in who is always smiling, always happy, always extending a warm greeting to others? What better gift can you give another than a sincere smile?

Many years ago, I was hiking on a trail deep in an Oregon forest when I came upon a young man sitting on a log. The trailhead was some four miles from that spot, and I was surprised to find another person, alone, that far into the forest. He had been deep in thought, so I apologized for startling him. I commented on the beauty of God's creation and asked if he'd like to share a sandwich and some coffee. I sat down on the log next to him, opened my backpack, and handed him half of my lunch.

After a moment, he turned to me, showed me a revolver, and told me he'd come to that remote spot to kill himself. When he saw me appear with a long beard, long hair, and dressed in my long black robe, he thought I might be an angel sent by God. He'd been praying that God would for- give him for what he was about to do.

I assured him I was indeed flesh and blood, and no angel. But I also told him I had been sent by God with a message. That message was that he was loved and that his period of despair would soon pass.

He handed me his revolver, which I placed in my backpack, and we had a long conversation about his life.

I've long wondered about the direction he must have taken after that encounter in the forest so many years ago. I've also wondered what might have happened if I'd continued on that trail without stopping to greet him, without offering a smile and a shared sandwich.

When we put aside ourselves and put on Christ, we become God's messengers.

JANUARY 3

Divided Loyalties

"No one can serve two masters; for either he will hate the one and love the other, or else he will be loyal to the one and despise the other. You cannot serve God and mammon."

Matthew 6:24

As you begin the new year, be mindful of where you place your priorities. Are you of Christ, or are you of the world? Do you serve God, or do you submit to this temporal world, which shall one day come to an end?

Do you think you can divide your loyalties in this life, serving your spouse or boss during the week and serving God only on weekends or perhaps just on major holy days? Do you think of God only when in church or with religious people? Are you disconnected from your spiritual life because you've compartmentalized it? Jesus says this is impossible, because "no one can serve two masters" (Matt. 6:24).

Are you overly concerned about money, your popularity, or the home you own, or do these things take a back seat to Jesus Christ? If God is your Master, you will be able to say honestly that none of these worldly things is anywhere near as important to you as your relationship with Christ.

Christ said, "Therefore do not be like them. For your Father knows the things you have need of before you ask Him" (Matt. 6:8). If we serve only God as our Master, all else that we need will be provided.

JANUARY 4

The Best Basis for Our Priorities

The Apostle Paul taught in 1 Timothy 3:15 that the Church is the "pillar and ground of the truth," and it is to this Church that the Apostles entrusted the Faith "once for all delivered to the saints" (Jude 3) as its guardian and protector. Thus, the Church's services, liturgies, prayers, and sacraments are all essential if we are to be authentic as people of faith.

St. Athanasius the Great said, "In accordance with the apostolic faith delivered to us by tradition from the Fathers, I have delivered the tradition, without inventing anything extraneous to it. What I have learned, that I inscribed, conformably with the Holy Scriptures."

It is through this Tradition that we bind ourselves to Christ, serving only Him. All else must be secondary. When the Lord says, "You cannot serve God and mammon," He is referring to things of a material nature (Matt. 6:24; *mammon* is the Aramaic word for "god of wealth"). He asks us all to declare whom we serve: God or mammon? And the way to determine whom or what you love the most is to see where your loyalties lie. When you face a choice between God and anything else, what is your choice? Do you choose to attend church on Sunday, or do you choose to sleep in? Do you prioritize your life around your relationship with God, or do sporting events, vacations, family outings, entertainment, or friends take center stage? Do prayer, reading the Bible, serving others, financially supporting the Church and its mission, and giving alms serve as your central theme, or do you choose personal gain and pleasure as central to your life?

JANUARY 5

Political versus Spiritual Authority

Priest, bishops, and others who serve the Church are often tempted to think their parishioners should adhere to their political ideals. This temptation can lead to the alienation of some members of their flock, especially the young.

Our society has seen great changes, and the moral and spiritual authority of the Church cannot be compromised by attempts on the part of her clergy to enforce a political litmus test on her faithful. There is room within the Orthodox Church for a great many political views, and it is best that the clergy help the faithful find their way by sticking to the preaching of the Gospels. This allows the message of the Gospels to work transformation within the heart and conscience of each believer.

The Church can never be about membership in one political party, nor can Orthodox Christians be expected to put aside views that differ from that of the Church. Being a thinking person does not disqualify anyone from membership in Christ's Body. The healing that comes within the sacramental life of the Church is for everyone, and each of us falls short of the ideals that flow out of the gospel message. Forcing anyone to cast aside opinions can actually drive a person from the very arena where healing can take place.

No one political party or human philosophy is flawless. Truth can be found in many places, and the Church, if she is true to her calling, should be the guiding light for each of us, regardless of our political allegiances. His Holiness Kirill, Patriarch of Moscow and All Russia, in an address to the Holy Synod of Bishops, said, "The Church must have no political means of exercising an influence on those in authority. The Church 'loses public confidence' if it becomes a political player. The Church only has one way to influence the powerful and the powerless, the rich and the poor, the educated and the simpleminded—to preach God's word."

Let us not, in our zeal for upholding the truth, become a stumbling block for those who have not yet been fully integrated into Christ's Church.

The Saints: Our Living Helpers and Friends

According to St. Symeon the New Theologian, vigil lights are placed before the icons of the saints as a way of showing that without the Light, who is Christ, the saints are nothing. It is only as the Light of Christ shines on them that they become alive and resplendent.

The saints show us what a glorious destiny we have in God. Through the example of their lives, they point the way to our becoming "partakers of the divine nature" (2 Peter 1:4). The saints, as the cloud of witnesses in heaven, are present in the divine services, worshiping the Holy Trinity with us. They, as our friends, intercede before the throne of God on our behalf, having won the good fight, and we are encouraged by the memory and example of their lives as we struggle on our own path to God.

It has been said that there are two kinds of people in the world: sinners who think they are saints, and saints who know they are sinners. Saints are Christians who let God's light shine through them and whose lives have been transformed by the power of the Holy Spirit.

We venerate the saints as we seek their intercession with God, but we adore and worship only God in Trinity: the Father, the Son, and the Holy Spirit. We venerate the images (icons) as well as the relics of the saints and martyrs. Yet, according to the decisions and canons of the Seventh Ecumenical Council, this veneration relates not to the icons as such, but to their prototypes—to the persons they represent.

The interior walls of our temples are adorned with icons of the saints as a reminder that we are surrounded by a cloud of witnesses—the saints—and that the Church Militant (here on earth) is not separated from the Church Triumphant (in heaven). In Christ, death does not divide us, for the saints are not dead, but alive in Christ Jesus.

Glory to Jesus Christ, who is glorified in His saints.

JANUARY 7

Godly Friends and Spiritual Progress

It is easy to feel trapped by our bad habits. Growing as Christians is often fraught with failure, and we find ourselves stuck. Our spiritual progress feels more like a treadmill; we are seemingly moving forward, but the scenery remains the same.

If we have friendships that keep us from growing, perhaps it is time to leave those friendships behind. Back in the 1960s, I often hung around with a group of friends at a coffeehouse in Berkeley, California. We'd talk about the books we were going to write—but all we did was talk. One young man shocked the rest of us one day when he announced he was no longer going to come to the coffeehouse. He'd decided it was a waste of time. He told us he wanted to go to medical school and was therefore planning to put all his energy into completing his college degree with the best grades he could possibly get. We all tried to convince him that he could accomplish all that without abandoning the coffeehouse scene. But that was the last evening he'd ever join us.

His decision haunted me, for deep down I knew he was right. I was feeling increasingly unfulfilled, both spiritually and intellectually. Within six months I made the decision to move to Portland, Oregon, for a fresh start.

For us as Christians, it does make a difference whom we hang out with. If you have friendships with individuals who are simply not interested in things of a spiritual nature, you will find yourself wasting precious moments in your journey to God. Having friendships with fellow Christians is the only way we can keep ourselves centered in Christ. Build a stronger relationship with Christ by spending time with people whose values are the same.

If you waste your time with people who are only pursuing worldly pleasures, you'll end your life doing the same. The time God has allotted us must not be squandered.

JANUARY 8

Watchfulness: The Guarding of the Heart

Watchfulness was described by Elder Ephraim of Philotheou as "the axe which shatters the large trees, hitting their roots. When the root is struck, it doesn't spring up again." Attention to our thoughts is an important tactic in spiritual warfare, and it is necessary if we are to have weapons that are stronger than those of the enemy.

St. Paisios of the Holy Mountain tells us about some of the consequences of not being watchful.

> When our soul lives carelessly without watching over its thoughts, it will consequently fill up with dirty and sly thoughts. As a result, people start developing psychological problems which gradually pile up. . . . Some people, while they are found in this situation and come face to face with the problem itself, they do not realize it, and thus are unable to humbly confess to their spiritual father their fall. Instead, they look for a "secular" solution and consult a psychiatrist, who will inevitably prescribe medication. . . . The only solution is to become aware of the problem and confess it to a spiritual father and then humbly follow his advice.[1]

Watchfulness and the Jesus Prayer are weapons that mutually reinforce each other, as constant prayer goes with watchfulness and attentiveness of the intellect. A Christian life without watchfulness is doomed to failure.

JANUARY 9

Finding the Lost Sheep

The work of the Church is to seek out the lost sheep and bring them into the fold. The modern mission of the Church is to go out into the community and find those who are lost. Many who were previously Orthodox, but who never made a personal commitment that ensured they would remain in the Church and grow strong in their faith, are out there waiting to be found. Those who've been lost to the Church demonstrate the clear reality that it is not enough to practice the externals or to know how things should be done; we must know why we do what we do and why we believe what we believe.

It is not enough that we fill our churches with people if they are not believers. Our people must be made strong in the faith if they are to withstand the secular assaults that are gaining influence in our modern world. The traditions and ceremonies of the Church are meaningless until people have taken in Christ for themselves. The Lord said, "Do not marvel that I said to you, 'You must be born again'" (John 3:7). Belonging to the Church without understanding the teachings of the Church and making them our own is simply not enough.

The clergy fail in their service to Christ's Church if they do not instruct the faithful. Metropolitan Meletios of Preveza and Nikopolis said, "This is the work of the Church: to help man to become aware of his eternal vocation, to draw near to a higher power, to Christ our Savior." Too many clergy fail to look for opportunities to interact with people, to be missionaries in our own homeland. The people of the Western world have abandoned Christianity in droves, making it imperative that the Church reach out with a renewed missionary zeal.

JANUARY 10

Losing Parishioners

Even those who are members of the Church are in danger of becoming lost sheep if they are ill-prepared for a secular and atheistic society that is increasingly Christianophobic. As priests, we dare not let even one parishioner leave the Church without doing everything we can to bring her back into the fold. Priests must do everything in their power to seek out those who've stopped coming to church and to love them back into the life of the Church. Christ Himself demonstrated, as the Good Shepherd, the need to leave the ninety-nine sheep and go out and find the one who has left the fold.

Young people, especially, are turned off to the inauthentic. They can see when their parents or even their priests are simply going through the motions of religiosity. They will not commit to a life that demands sacrifice if they do not see it lived out in the lives of their elders. Priests must reach out to young people with Orthodoxy, even going to college and university campuses. We must not cheat today's youths of the knowledge of Christ.

I, like so many of my brother priests, weep with sadness when I see our youths turn their backs on the Church. I recall an encounter with an Orthodox man. He approached me with a request for a blessing, while his grown son stood by with a smile and pleasant small talk, not asking for a blessing himself. This fine young man, gifted with a wonderful heart and a good mind, was estranged from the Church. I wanted to grab them both by the scruff of their necks and usher them before the royal gates of the temple.

There are times I've probably given too harsh a sermon or been parental when I should have been more accommodating. All I can do, in the aftermath, is pray for those lost sheep and keep my heart opened wide with the love of Christ. Just like a father in the flesh, I must leave the door open and not be too harsh. That's no easy task.

Community: The Essential Element

Christianity is a communal faith, one that requires its followers to be actively involved with others. The Church's worship is communal, and salvation itself is a corporate act, one that necessitates interaction with others. One is not saved in a vacuum but as part of the corporal life of the Church.

Your salvation must be as much a concern to me as is my own. My relationship with Christ is not about me but about us. Our sins are not just against God but against the Body of Christ, the Church. Our love of God cannot be salvific if we do not love others, for St. John the Evangelist said, "If someone says, 'I love God,' and hates his brother, he is a liar; for he who does not love his brother whom he has seen, how can he love God whom he has not seen?" (1 John 4:20).

Given the communal nature of the Church, it is alarming to see increasing numbers of people isolating themselves from others. Many have turned to the internet as the primary source of interaction with others, finding "friendships" with people they will never meet in person. Social interaction in the central square, as seen in traditional villages where the café life and the church are the primary sources of interaction, is the way to prevent increasing estrangement.

It is thus imperative that we guard against the temptation to spend too much time in front of the computer and too little time with others. The sight of young people sitting in coffeehouses together, yet apart, is troubling. Text messaging, communication through email, and countless hours on Facebook lead to the furtherance of an isolation that is murdering the soul. As humans, we are meant to be together, for it is in our lives together that we grow in mind and spirit. It is in community that we learn to love God. For friendships to be limited to online conversations is a tragedy of major proportions, one that will ultimately be the ruin of society.

The Idolatry of Self-Esteem

Among the contributors to self-worship is a form of idolatry associated with self-esteem. It is easy to fall into, since our society has placed a great deal of emphasis on the need for self-esteem. The modern religion of psychoanalysis has promoted self-esteem as though it were the modern equivalent of enlightenment. The priests of this modern, humanistic religion have made millions selling self-esteem, resulting in a society given over almost entirely to image.

Our children have been deprived of childhood, focused as they are on the acquisition of an image promoted by pop culture. Little girls have been sexualized by a society that has allowed them to be influenced by the music and fashion industries. Parents and teachers have been almost powerless in combating the horrid influences that have torn childhood innocence away from our little ones.

Little boys have not escaped the insidious warping of childhood innocence as they are immersed in a society that has become hypersexualized. The whole of society has entered into such a hedonistic state as to be largely untroubled by the cultural changes of the twenty-first century. Image has become all-important to many people, with plastic surgery, face lifts, and tummy tucks becoming the new normal, as large numbers of people have suddenly become dissatisfied with their faces and bodies.

Self-esteem displaces the role of humility—so valued a hallmark for a well-adjusted, good person—and pride enters the heart. This demon of pride can be driven away only by intense prayer and by not doing or saying anything that contributes to a sense of self-importance. The self-esteem that gives rise to pride seals us to the fate that cast down the highest of the angels. Let us turn quickly away from pride and not ally with it, lest we surrender our life to others and our substance to the merciless (see Prov. 5:9).

When Guilt Destroys Us

The conscience is a gift God has bestowed on us that tells us when we have sinned against Him and against our neighbor. It calls us to turn from our sin and to seek to change the patterns of behavior that have caused us to sin.

This tug by our conscience can be counterproductive if we make no effort to change our behavior. It can also be counterproductive if we simply give in to despair and resign ourselves to our sinful behavior, as though there were no cure for our illness. The sense of guilt is meant to aid in the fight to turn around our bad behavior.

When we have sinned, and our sins are tormenting us, at that moment we must seek out Christ, for only His sacrifice for our sins is eternal and living. When we lay our sins before the face of that sacrifice, we have nothing to fear, for we recognize that we cannot be saved by our own efforts.

If we simply surrender to guilt, we find nothing but destruction, and our conscience will have been of no benefit whatsoever. And victory will not be ours.

Self-Reliance

Since the foundation of our monastic community some twenty-seven years ago, our holy brotherhood has been working toward becoming as self-reliant as possible, given the age we live in. Though most of humankind, since the beginning, has had no choice but to depend on planting gardens for vegetables, harvesting trees for cooking and heating, and raising cows for milk and cheese, chickens for eggs, and pigs for sausages, we live in a time when being totally self-reliant is impossible for most. We are now dependent on others for much of our food and fuel.

When I was a child, most people in our neighborhood raised their own chickens and rabbits for food, grew large vegetable gardens, and even baked their own bread. Today, most people purchase packaged food that requires little preparation. A "homemade" cake only requires adding eggs and water to a mix, popping it in the oven, and frosting it with icing out of a plastic container. I would guess most people have never made a cake from scratch or kneaded their own bread, and few know how to grow a vegetable garden. Fewer yet have taken eggs from the nests of their own chickens. In short, we have become a nation of dependents.

At our monastery, growing and canning our own vegetables, baking our own bread, harvesting our own honey from our beehives, making our own cheese, and brewing our own mead has given us a real sense of self-reliance. I can't imagine what it would be like to revert back to depending on a local grocery store.

This has also opened the door to an awareness that, as Christians, we would not want to sacrifice our dependence on praying together and working together toward the common goal of living fearless lives of faith in our Lord Jesus Christ. Our connection as members of the one Body of Christ, the Church, is a crucial interdependency.

After Meeting Christ, We Have a Choice

In the story of the Magi, three wise men, having seen a star in the east, travel to a desert cave, where they find the Child, laid in a manger by His Virgin Mother.

This encounter with the Messiah filled them with life-transforming grace; they were no longer the same. Although they had agreed to return by the same route and to report the whereabouts of the Child to King Herod, their encounter in the cave made them true believers, convincing them that the One they had beheld was truly the Son of God, the Messiah.

They knew they had two roads back to their own country. One would lead to destruction, and the other would lead to the Kingdom of God. The way to Herod would be the worldly path; if they had chosen it, that would have meant that having met the Christ, they had experienced no change in their hearts, and they remained of the world. The other way was the way of Christ, by which they could return to their own country as changed men. This narrow path to the Kingdom of God was revealed to them, for they had encountered the Savior of the World.

We too face a choice of two paths having met this Christ. One leads to destruction, and the other leads to the Kingdom. The first is the way of sinners, leading to Herod, while the other way leads to Christ, which allows us to return to our own country as changed people. Let us turn away from the path to Herod, ruler of an earthly power, and travel to the everlasting dwelling of our heavenly country.

God Alone Provides Satisfaction

The lifeless things of this world offer no spiritual satisfaction, yet we often sell ourselves to things or people by giving them power over our hearts. It is easy to feel abandoned or hurt by those to whom we've given power. If we need affirmation from others, we risk empowering demons to use our personal needs to keep us from focusing on that which is eternal.

Our need for affirmation from others can also distract us from focusing on God. Ownership of our heart should be reserved for God alone, for evil spirits use whatever means they can to make us feel abandoned, discounted, or unloved by anyone we've allowed to own our hearts. We can easily be distracted from our service to God if we allow ourselves to become envious of the recognition others receive. Recognition for a job well done can be nice, but not if it comes at the price of losing our soul.

God's love must be sufficient, for only our relationship with Him has lasting and eternal value. Sometimes we have to pull ourselves back from others and enter into the silence. This self-imposed exile is the spiritual retreat that helps us focus on what we have in God. Then our relationships with others become healthy, fulfilling, and life-giving.

Our Struggle for Peace

In an age when we are forever witnessing wars between nations and civil wars within nations, peace seems to be about as possible as the alchemy that turns metal into gold. Peacemakers struggle to find peaceful solutions for the conflicts between nations, political parties, religions, neighbors, and even within families. But when peace comes to one part of the world, war breaks out in another part. War always seems to have the upper hand, while peace seems to be only the dream of pacifists and poets.

In the 1960s, many hoped peace was about to reign in our world, for pop philosophers and hippies thought they were ushering in a new age. In preparation for this Age of Aquarius, young people grew their hair long and wore flowers in it, and they embraced a lifestyle they thought would last forever. The musical *Hair* touted this ideal, and a whole generation "tuned in, turned on, and dropped out."

When the Soviet Union imploded and the Cold War ended, many believed war would be no more. The West no longer had an enemy. Yet it didn't take long for all to realize that peace was still beyond our grasp, and wars between nations and peoples continued. We were no longer at war with communism, but with Islam or other ideologies. So peacemakers still struggle for the cause of peace, but on different fronts.

We Christians have always had the acquisition of peace as a central theme in our corporate prayers. The Liturgy of St. John Chrysostom contains petitions for peace throughout. The priest even prays for "an angel of peace and a guardian of our souls," as an angel of peace, our personal guardian angel, was assigned to each of us as at the moment of our baptism.

Peace Begins at the Cross

Peace is such a central theme in the life of the Church that the nine-teenth-century Russian St. Seraphim of Sarov said, "Acquire peace, and a thousand around you will be saved." The personal acquisition of peace begins with repentance, that moment when we have a change of mind and decide to follow the path to wholeness.

Peace is not just an idea, but an active force for change. When we pray in the Liturgy for "peace for the whole world," we are praying not just for this world but for the entire cosmos. We are praying for peace for people, peace for animals, peace for plants and rocks, peace for the sun and moon and stars. When we pray for peace, we realize that it is a gift of grace from heaven, and this peace is beyond comprehension, for it is the peace of Christ. It is "the peace of God, which surpasses all understanding" (Philippians 4:7).

True peace is bound up in the sacrificial offering of Christ on the Cross. Peace is interdependent with sacrifice. The services of the Church bring us into the atmosphere of peace, for this peace comes from God. Peace can enter the world only if it takes root in the hearts of humans, and this peace requires sacrifice. The transformation of the cosmos begins with you.

Entering into Silence

All Orthodox Christians are aware of the importance of prayer, fasting, and almsgiving in our journey to God. Prayer is our way of communicating with God on a daily basis. Fasting days (Wednesday and Friday) are called for throughout the church year. As Christians, we are also obligated to give alms to the poor, as demonstrated throughout the New Testament. And all three of these practices are at the heart of the fast of Great Lent.

Yet we often overlook the great spiritual practice of entering into silence as a way to discover ourselves and deepen our experience with God's presence.

Not more than a hundred years ago, most families had silence as an everyday experience, for at the end of the day, they nestled into warm corners of their parlors and their kitchens, often reading books or simply watching a crackling fire. Along with this quieting down, silence was part of every evening. Orthodox families were especially cognizant of the need to spend quiet time on the eve of the Sunday Liturgy, as well as during great feasts of the Church. They knew this silence served as a preparation time for receiving Christ's Body and Blood.

Keeping silence by turning off radios and television sets, muting music, and turning off computers and cell phones is a splendid way to allow everyone in a family to experience the silence that allows us to listen for the voice of God speaking in our hearts. Refraining from conversation, music, and all forms of entertainment for just an hour or two helps open us to an experience of God that has become foreign to most Americans.

Silence is the means by which we may access and deepen our relationship with God as well as develop self-knowledge. St. Theophilus, Patriarch of Alexandria, placed the virtue of silence on par with the faith itself in a synodal letter from AD 400. "Monks—if they wish to be what they are called—will love silence and the catholic faith, for nothing at all is more important than these two things."

Remember, this invitation into the silence is not for monks only.

Enduring Trials

Many are suffering job loss, illnesses, mortgage foreclosures, and all kinds of strife and hardships. Yet if we look at these difficulties in light of eternity, this time of trial is nothing. The Apostle Paul wrote, "For I consider that the sufferings of this present time are not worthy to be compared with the glory which shall be revealed in us" (Rom. 8:18).

God's desire that we all come to the knowledge of the truth—and be saved—is real. His love for us is all-consuming, and nothing that happens in our lives is without value in this journey to eternity. Our God does not send anything our way that is beyond our ability to withstand, for His grace is sufficient for us. Suffering has a salvific role, for it is in suffering that we are able to take up our cross and follow Christ. Without ascetic struggle, we remain unchanged, for transformation of self is then unattainable.

God desires all to be saved, yet this gift of salvation has to be accepted by the believer, since God will not force salvation on us. As we freely receive the gift of salvation, suffering allows us to remember that this world is transitory and that we need God. When we turn to God during periods of struggle, we grow in our faith, coming one step closer to deification, where we are united in our humanity to God's divinity. This transformation takes place when we embrace repentance as a way of life, placing ourselves before God's mercy.

There is nothing a person can do to earn salvation, for it is a gift from God. Yet to be saved, we must work together with God in a synergy whereby our entire being, including our will, effort, and actions, are perfectly conformed with and united to the Divine.

We are familiar with suffering, but we will do anything we can to avoid it, forgetting that Christ told us if we follow Him, we have to take up our cross. Without suffering, the Cross cannot be embraced.

JANUARY 21

Being Ready to Meet the End

Increasingly Christians have been talking about the coming of the Antichrist. Events around the world have created a sense of doom among many believers, who see the economic downswing, the rise of Islam, extreme climate change, and the breakdown of societal norms as precursors to the end times.

It is important to remember that Christians in the first century were prepared for the end of times and the Second Coming of Christ. And we should be too. We are struggling against the principalities of darkness, just as God's people have been struggling since the Fall of humankind. Yet the hour for the return of Christ is not to be revealed, for only the Father knows the time and the hour, as Christ Himself told us.

None of us knows when our own end will come. At sixty-seven, I am more aware of my ultimate end than ever before. I've had increasing numbers of friends depart this life, some after illnesses, some without warning. All of us must be prepared to give account for our lives before the Lord at any given moment. We cannot expect to have time to repent, for most of us will meet our end without warning.

Whether these are the end times or not, we must live in preparation for that final moment of accountability. In the end, Christ will triumph over evil. That is a fact. For now, we must fight the battle, that we too may triumph over evil. This life is full of spiritual warfare.

Where Do We Lay Blame?

A humble and spiritually active man, when he reads the Holy Scriptures, will refer everything to himself and not to another.

St. Mark the Ascetic

We all have a natural tendency to lay blame on others, when in truth we must blame only ourselves. When facing our own sins and shortcomings, it is easy to put the blame on others, yet our faith tells us that spiritual progress can come only with the acquisition of a humble and contrite heart. As long as we put the blame on others for our shortcomings, we remain stagnant on the spiritual path. The saints give a clear witness that progress toward holiness comes when we look only at our own faults.

It is far more comfortable to see the wickedness of others, for in focusing on them, we can forgo the all-important work of changing our own behavior and allowing the Holy Spirit to transform our fallen nature. Focusing on others' shortcomings allows our self-serving pride to grow stronger. So we remain puffed up and wallow in unfounded pride.

When we keep our attention focused on our shortcomings, we keep vigilant until our last day, guarding our souls until the final judgment. When we take our eyes off our faults and focus on our neighbor's sin, we deprive ourselves of precious time for repentance. Since we do not know the day or hour of our last breath, we must treat every moment as though it is our last.

Be Not Troubled about Many Things

E very day can bring about an event or problem that makes us feel
unsettled. If we want to keep unrest at bay, it is important that we
prayerfully receive everything with the knowledge that God is watching over us and that all will be fine in the end. Spending time worrying
accomplishes nothing, for worrying simply keeps our attention in the
wrong place.

If we keep our focus on Christ, knowing that He is with us in both
times of trouble and moments of celebration, we can peacefully receive
all that befalls us. Knowing that even difficulties and hardships are vehicles
used by God for our salvation, how can we despair?

When we serve the Lord, we shall not be "troubled about many things,"
but will always keep in mind the one thing that is needed (Luke 10:41–42).

On Making a Good Confession

Following His glorious Resurrection, as He appeared to His disciples, our Lord Jesus Christ said, "If you forgive the sins of any, they are forgiven them; if you retain the sins of any, they are retained" (John 20:23). From that moment in history, the Church has seen confession (or repentance) as one of the Holy Mysteries (or Sacraments) of the Church, through which the penitent receives the divine forgiveness of Christ for sins.

The Lord Jesus Christ bestowed His authority upon the Church to forgive sins. The priest or bishop, as His representative on earth through his ordination, prays to God for the salvation of the penitents who repent of their sins, and God forgives through the priest. The Mystery of Holy Confession is holy because it connects God and His children, with the priest acting as the bridge. To make a good confession, it is necessary to prepare carefully, asking God to grant grace sufficient to make a thorough examination of our conscience.

Sometimes we get so bogged down with regret, we fail to move on and grasp the moment. The wonderful thing about confession is the ability we are given by our loving God to receive absolution and to move into the present moment. The past is forgiven, and the future is filled with hope. We must not occupy ourselves with the past nor with the future. All that is important is the present.

JANUARY 25

Eternity Is a Very Long Time

God reveals Himself to us if we seek Him out, and He remains invisible to us only if we refuse, out of pride and self-absorption, to let Him enter our lives. If you desire the knowledge that is yours for the asking, simply make it known, and God will open the way for you. Do not let the distractions of this world and pleasures that are of a transitory nature keep you from casting your eyes toward God.

It is sad how many people spend their lives in pursuit of material pleasures, job success, and entertainment but give little thought to things that are of eternal importance. What we do in this life does have an impact on what we will face when we stand before the Lord. When we are called to give an account for ourselves, it will not be enough to explain to God that we lived in a great house, raised good children, and gave time to the charity of our choice if we did nothing to further our relationship with Him.

Eternity is a very long time, and this life we have been given is a very short time. Lest we waste it, we must bring our focus back to what really matters. Dinner and a movie with friends is a tragic waste of time if we have not given equal time to God.

If you are feeling spiritually dry, you can only look to yourself to find the reason. God has done His part; you must do yours.

The Saints and the Poor

The Orthodox Church is very clear in her teaching regarding the poor. Our Lord Jesus Christ taught us by His example as the great *philanthropos*, and we can do nothing less than follow. He commanded us to love and serve the poor and the hungry. He told us we must care for the sick and suffering, and that we must visit those in prisons and clothe the naked.

The Church's liturgical hymns and seasons are filled with the commemoration of saints who were known for their love of the poor. St. Basil the Great of the third century established Church-sponsored hospitals and mental institutions. St. Nicholas of Myra distributed money to those in need. St. John the Almsgiver was one of the most charitable patriarchs of the Byzantine Empire. St. Joseph of Volokholamsk emphasized the ancient monastic tradition of hospitality and care for the poor, and St. Elizabeth, a grand duchess of Russia, established hospitals for the poor and destitute. The newly canonized saint Mother Maria Skobtsova created soup kitchens and established houses of hospitality in World War II France.

These holy saints provide unique examples to the rest of us of what it means to be Christian. They showed forth the light of Christ by following His example of love for the poor, giving of their talents, time, and money to those in need. Orthodox Christians hold up the saints as exemplary people whose lives are worthy of emulation. They show us the way to live out the Gospels and point out the way of Christ.

The Divine Flame Will Consume You

At the very moment you decide to turn to God, your heart begins to be warmed by the action of the Holy Spirit. It is kindled with the divine flame, which will consume you completely and will melt everything of a fallen nature within you. Once this flame of divine love has been actualized within your heart, do nothing that would allow it to be extinguished.

Cooperate with the fire of God and let it completely consume you. Put all your effort into this spiritual transformation, which begins in your heart. Let nothing else take center stage over this action by God, which is meant to save you and make you complete.

From a little flame, this fire will burn in your heart, and nothing of your fallen nature will be able to withstand it. It will transform your whole being, for the action of the Holy Spirit will take you into God's Kingdom, which resides within you.

The Importance of Frequent Communion

Eternity is an everlasting banquet that takes place in the heavenly realm. Every time we participate in the Divine Liturgy, we are transported into a place where there is neither time nor space, and we participate in that very banquet. As we receive the Holy Mysteries (Christ's Body and Blood), our brokenness in both body and soul are treated with the healing medicine that we so very much need.

God is everywhere present and fills all things. There is nowhere He is not. Hellfire is none other than the fire of God, burning those who are unloving and unresponsive to His invitation to commune with Him. God does not send anyone to hell, for we sentence ourselves. Eternity with God necessitates a transformation of our souls, that we may be purified in order to be engulfed by God's uncreated light. Our fallen nature cannot withstand the presence of God without having been purified.

The Eucharist is the very medicine God designed for this transformation. Our response should be one of humble submission to this invitation to commune with the God who created us. Holy Communion is meant to be the agent that changes us, making us whole. The Holy Mysteries give us life. Frequent confession and communion are the means we have for change.

The Eucharist is both mystical and symbolic and is understood to be the genuine Body and Blood of Christ, precisely because bread and wine are the mysteries of God's true and genuine presence and His manifestation to us in Christ. This defies analysis and explanation in purely rational and logical terms, precisely because it is a mystery. The Eucharist is a mystery of the Kingdom of heaven, as is Christ Himself. It is "not of this world," as Jesus tells us (John 18:36).

St. John of Damascus said, "If you enquire how this happens, it is enough for you to learn that it is through the Holy Spirit. ... We know nothing more than this, that the word of God is true, active, and omnipotent, but in its manner of operation unsearchable."

God's Grace Lifts Us from Despair

Many people sail through their life thinking happiness is something they have created for themselves. They think good fortune and success in work and play are things they've brought about, either through struggle or by pure luck. And when they experience difficult times or the loss of things that brought them comfort, they despair.

Sometimes it takes the loss of this established order to enlighten our darkened hearts to the reality that only happiness that is of an eternal nature will never be lost. For someone who has been so enlightened, nothing can take away from the comfort and security she experiences that are based in faith. God's grace fills her very essence with such peace that nothing—even loss of worldly comforts—can bring about despair.

How can we possibly despair when we know that the God we worship in the Trinity and who has created us and our world is our co-suffering Savior? He has showered us with such an abundance of grace that no hardship that comes our way can detract from the peace and joy we have experienced in our life in Him.

Compared to this grace-filled life, all else is but folly. Grace has liberated us from the temporal nature of earthly happiness and has taken up residence in our hearts, from which springs forth the healing that transforms us. This grace makes us whole, and our sickness disappears as though it had never been.

JANUARY 30

The Fear of Loss

Some people fear commitment because it can bring loss. They fear the
other person will either leave them or be lost in death, so they remain
aloof from a possible relationship. Some put on a façade of indifference
for fear of rejection, depriving themselves of happiness. They become the
ultimate losers, for the happiness that comes in a committed relationship
evades them.

When you refuse to become vulnerable by giving yourself over to a
committed relationship, you deprive yourself of one of the most fundamental aspects of what it means to be human. When you fear loss, you are
hard-pressed to live a life of courage, for it is in living with courage that we
are able to participate fully in life and become fully human.

Grieving the loss of a relationship, either by death or breakup, is just as
important to the maturation of our heart as having a long-term relationship, for in grieving we allow ourselves to stay connected to others, and we
remain open-hearted to what God has for us. If fear of loss disables us, we
may not be able to risk having anything that really matters. By throwing
courage to the side, we deprive ourselves of the touch and the intimacy
that help us open our hearts to all God has in store for us.

Grieving is the way you can heal from loss and, in turn, be open to
relationships that can make your life more complete and more fulfilled.
Many people do not allow themselves to grieve, so they deprive themselves
of relationships that can lead to spiritual growth. You grow stronger if you
allow yourself to grieve when you've experienced loss, for grieving is one
of the most fundamental of life skills. It is the way the heart can heal from
loss and go on to love again and grow wise.

If we refuse to love another for fear of loss, we remain closed off, not
only from others but also from God. "He who does not love his brother
abides in death" (1 John 3:14).

Gathered around the Hearth

Sometimes our monastery's electrical power goes off during a storm. On one such occasion, our community huddled around our gas fireplace, and our kerosene lanterns and candles provided light. We were reminded that a hundred years before, this would have been the norm. Prior to electricity and central heating, most families gathered in parlors, spending evenings reading, sewing, and conversing. The notion that everyone would retreat to bedrooms, kitchens, or dens, separating themselves from other family members, was unthinkable.

I can remember, as a child (this really dates me), sitting with my brother and my parents, listening to radio dramas. Before television, families would gather for evenings in the living room, where children would build with Lincoln Logs or play board games with their parents.

Evenings spent together as a family not only build a bond between parents and their children, but also serve as important times in which to share family values. But the old saying, "A family that prays together stays together," is often forgotten.

A Catholic family that lived next to us had a small family chapel, complete with an altar, statues, and candles. Every evening they would gather to pray the rosary. That chapel left a permanent imprint on my mind, even though I was only six years old.

Family meals are also important for building strong moral and spiritual foundations in children. Sitting around the dinner table is a great time for parents to develop strong bonds of trust with their children. Family members that disperse throughout the house for the evening are likely to function as autonomous entities, and family bonds are unlikely to develop.

The domestic church, which has been such an important part of Orthodox Church tradition, cannot be developed in a family where meals, prayer, and social life all take place in separate parts of the home.

Key Ingredients of a Lasting Faith

Faith is a gift from God that can grow only if we cooperate with the grace that gives birth to our faith in the first place. If we idly sit by and expect God to do all the work, we find that our faith is not able to sustain us during times of great trial and difficulty. Prayer, fasting, church attendance, spiritual reading, and frequent confession and communion are all key ingredients to a lasting, sustaining faith.

Immersing ourselves in the sacramental life of the Church, reading the Holy Scriptures on a daily basis, and making it a practice to keep to a prayer rule are all tried-and-true means of deepening our relationship with Christ. These practices also serve to bring a family closer together, for they are building blocks of loving spousal relations and create the stability and familial support that help children thrive.

Run from the Praise of Others

Pride is the mother of all sins, for it blinds us to our faults, puffs up our egos, and makes us think we are better than others. Pride makes us think we don't need to change. We are blinded, thinking that we are good and that God must be pleased with us. We are steeped in the sin of self-importance.

Rather than allowing us to be brought down by our sinful pride, God allows humiliating experiences to prepare our hearts for true transformation. When we are blinded to our faults, God allows things to happen that put down our ego and remind us that we are but sinful creatures in need of His mercy. The praise of others should be avoided, but when we are belittled by others, we must give glory to God, for it is in such difficult and humiliating times that we make the most progress.

St. Isaac the Syrian said, "It is a greater miracle to be able to see your sins than to be raised from the dead." When we suffer humiliation and are brought down, we must see this as a gift from God. Such moments are by far the most spiritually profitable, for they can lead the soul to a state of humility and godliness.

Others' praise can lead to our spiritual death, for such praise can be like poison for us. When we embrace humiliation or the disdain of others, God's grace can abound. Pride is put to death when we embrace humiliation. The saints ran from the praise of others, and we should follow their example if we wish to be saved.

FEBRUARY 3

Dressing for Church

The Church is our home, a place where we should feel comfortable and at ease. It is also God's house and a temple set aside for worship of the Holy Trinity. Although times have changed and we have become a very casual society, this attitude cannot be allowed to influence the way we dress to worship God.

Our way of dressing for church should reflect our desire to offer our very best to Christ. If we were invited to the wedding of our boss's daughter, we'd make sure to show respect to our employer by dressing our best. Does God deserve anything less?

Just as we want to act in ways that demonstrate the centrality of Christ in our lives, our dress should show forth the modesty that is befitting a Christian. We should wear clothes that are modest, especially when worshiping in God's house.

In our monastery's temple, we keep the ancient practice of removing our shoes before entering, recalling God's direction to Moses, "Take your sandals off your feet, for the place where you stand is holy ground" (Ex. 3:5). We ask that no one wear shorts or T-shirts when entering the holy grounds of the monastery. As is proper in all Orthodox churches, we ask visitors to prevent distraction by not wearing clothing with slogans or showy clothing that is best reserved for elegant events. Both men and women should avoid wearing clothing that can be distracting to other worshipers.

We want to keep our focus on the divine services, so we must not be the cause of distraction for our fellow Christians. Christ should be the focus of our worship, not our outfits. Church is not the place to show off the latest fashion or the results of our hard work at the fitness center.

FEBRUARY 4

When Despondency Seizes Us

The renowned Russian saint Seraphim of Sarov (1759–1833) said of himself, "I don't know anything." These words were remarkable coming from a hermit who was the most sought-after spiritual adviser of his age, with even the tsar seeking his counsel. Yet St. Seraphim recognized that he was but a funnel, so anything good that came out of him was from God.

As a priestmonk, I am often tortured with the knowledge that I am a poor example to others and that I fall short—daily—of living out the image of Christ in me. Yet I am compelled to live every day with joyfulness of heart, no matter what. I am also compelled to preach, teach, write of the things of the Lord, and try to trust God, no matter what. I try, as best I can, to remember the words, "Rejoice in the Lord always. Again I will say, rejoice!" (Phil. 4:4).

I also try to remember the words of St. Basil the Fool for Christ, whose holy relics reside in the cathedral in Red Square that bears his name. He said, "Winter is cold, but paradise is sweet." Like St. Anthony the Great, I cry out to God, "Where are You?" all the while floating in a river of grace. I want to be a friend of God, yet I often feel like the eagle chick who has been pushed out of the nest by its mother.

I am comforted by the counsel of St. Seraphim, who instructed his spiritual children with these words:

> *When despondency seizes us, let us not give in to it. Rather, fortified and protected by the light of faith, let us with great courage say to the spirit of evil: "What are you to us, you who are cut off from God, a fugitive from heaven, and a slave of evil? You dare not do anything to us: Christ, the Son of God, has dominion over us and over all. Leave us, you thing of bane. We are made steadfast by the uprightness of His Cross. Serpent, we trample on your head."*

Do Not Allow Anger to Take Root

Most people, when angered by someone, think the best way to deal with it is by avoiding the person who offended them. The problem with this approach is that it allows the anger to take root in the heart, where it can fester as a sinful passion. Because anger is a sin, it cannot be conquered by avoiding the person who made us angry. It must be rooted out by love, and this requires us to reach out to the offender.

The Scriptures tell us, "If your enemy is hungry, feed him; / If he is thirsty, give him a drink; / For in so doing you will heap coals of fire on his head" (Rom. 12:20). The only way we can do battle with the passion of anger is by setting aside our petty egos and reaching out to the offender.

We must realize that the anger we feel is not really about the person who has offended us, but about the sin that lurks in our own hearts. If we were not plagued by the passion of anger, we would not have become angry to begin with. If we are to conquer the sins that have taken root in our hearts, we must return only love and kindness to the person who has offended us. By doing so, we sow the seeds of Christ's love in both of us.

The Opposite of Anger Is Not Permissiveness

There are times when it is necessary to distance yourself from someone who is angry. For example, too many women—either out of fear, or for economic reasons, or for the sake of the children—remain in abusive relationships. This is clearly a situation that does not require the abused to remain living with the abuser out of Christian charity, for to do so could prove dangerous. Likewise, if you, out of a desire to help an abuser, simply offer love but do not call him to account for his behavior, you could be guilty of lending support to it.

Taking vengeance must not be our response to an abuser, for this disregards the fact that he is in danger as well—spiritual danger—for he must be called to repentance. Yet we must not be permissive. The person struggling with anger does not need you to be his enabler, and codependent relationships have the potential of being spiritually destructive for both parties. As long as our response to someone's anger is itself devoid of anger, we are safe. We must cultivate a strong sense of right and wrong as well as a desire to oppose evil, not out of passion, but out of righteousness.

It is also important for me to state clearly that if the anger is accompanied by a history of violence, that requires the abused to remove herself (and any children) from the dangers of living with such a person.

Our Lord drove out the moneychangers from the Temple in righteous anger. Likewise, you have the right to defend yourself, your children, and your home from those who would steal from you, abuse you with insults, or betray your friendship. Such people need not be allowed to remain in your life.

Why We Need Our Church Community

Christianity is a communal religion, one in which even the concept of salvation is corporate. It is not about being saved in some vacuum, all by yourself. Your salvation and my salvation are connected. As St. Seraphim of Sarov said, "Acquire the Holy Spirit, and a thousand around you will be saved." After all, the whole of the cosmos is being transformed in Jesus Christ.

Our unity as the people of God is based in the unity of the Holy Trinity. This is why we Orthodox Christians don't simply wake up on a Sunday morning and decide which church we'll try. We are part of a community of believers in which we grow spiritually together, as a family, with those who know us well. Like all families, ours is not perfect. There are some members of this family that irritate us and some that we gravitate toward more than others.

One of the central, most important attributes of this family is accountability. If you are flitting from one parish to another, it is easy to simply miss church altogether. Who will know? Weekly attendance at our chosen parish is a way of keeping ourselves accountable.

Imparting the Faith As a Missionary People

Two Byzantine brothers, Ss. Cyril and Methodius, brought Orthodox Christianity to the Slavs in the ninth century. The brilliance of Eastern Orthodox missionary outreach, as opposed to that of the Latin Church, was in the use of the vernacular. These great saints, who became known as the Apostles to the Slavs, left the Slavs with a liturgical language that was understandable to them. The services were no longer imparted in the Greek language—as though it alone was sacred enough to be used in the Divine Liturgy—and this helped them understand their new faith.

The first missionary monks to North America came to a land where Orthodoxy had never been. Their encounter with the native peoples was one of mutual respect. They did not greet their new neighbors as pagans, but as a people whose experience with God was limited but held to certain truths that were, by their very nature, Orthodox. Sharing with these peoples, the Orthodox monks came to know that the native Alaskans did not worship totem poles, but used them as tools for passing on family and tribal history. The monks honored the indigenous peoples, befriended them, and, most important of all, treated them as God's children.

As Orthodox Christians, we are duty-bound to share our faith with others. Christ is for everyone, but with all the bad press Christianity has been getting during the past decade, it is especially important that we approach evangelism in light of the historic Church. The missionary mind of the Orthodox Church must be rekindled in our time. Parishes must not remain enclaves of Greeks, Russians, Bulgarians, Palestinians, or Serbs. The doors of the churches must be opened wide, welcoming all, in keeping with our Orthodox tradition and history.

What Does the Lord Require of You?

As we explore how to live as Christians, we look to those who leave an impression of goodness, kindness, and humility; they are examples of what we would like to become. Those saintly people, by their example, exude the humbleness of the Lord, and love seems to be palpable when we are in their presence. Such people don't just appear, for their traits aren't naturally found in humans. Such humility and kindness are developed over time, sometimes from childhood, for these people have sought out the grace of God and have made every attempt at giving back the love and goodness they've received from the Father of lights.

Such people desire to become more like Christ daily. The humility of the Lord becomes their personal standard, for they are quick to forgive, quick to grant justice, and ready to be kind to everyone who comes into their presence. They do not fabricate such sweetness of soul, as though they were politicians running for office, for it is the Lord Himself who dwells in them, and it is Christ in them who is full of justice, kindness, love, and mercy.

> *He has shown you, O man, what is good;*
> *And what does the LORD require of you*
> *But to do justly,*
> *To love mercy,*
> *And to walk humbly with your God? (Micah 6:8)*

Hearts Are Changed When We Live Our Faith

Many of us have made the mistake of trying to convert our friends and relatives to the Orthodox Church, only to be disappointed. We've found a great treasure, and we wish to share it with those we love, and we are confounded and disappointed when they don't see what we have seen. The best way to share the treasure that is Orthodoxy is to live Orthodoxy. Living a serious and loving life of commitment to Christ and our Orthodox faith will bring about many a change of heart in those who are outside the Church established by Christ Himself.

Most importantly, I believe, we must remember that our own conversion was effected, not by debate and persuasion, but by the Holy Spirit. It is the Holy Spirit that brings people into the Faith, not we. A true missionary, in the Orthodox sense, is not one who buttonholes others and preaches to them, but who lives the Faith. When we are immersed in our Orthodox faith, and our commitment to growth in the Lord is strong, the grace of the Holy Spirit abounds, and it transforms all those around us.

Partake Often of the Source of Life

There is the true story of a priest-monk—the renowned Starets Alexis of Goloseyevsky Hermitage—who was conducting the revesting of the relics of St. Theodosius of Chernigov. The starets (elder) became tired, fell asleep, and saw before him the saint, who told him, "I thank you for laboring with me. I beg you also, when you will serve the Liturgy, to commemorate my parents, the Priest Nikita and Maria."

Startled by the request, Starets Alexis asked, "How can you, O Saint, ask my prayers, when you yourself stand at the heavenly throne and grant to people God's mercy?" St. Theodosius responded with these words: "Yes, that is true, but the offering at the Liturgy is more powerful than my prayers."

As a priest, I am a servant of the altar and a slave of Christ. I take this role very seriously. Heaven, the ultimate goal of all Christians, is the eternal Kingdom wherein the Heavenly Banquet (the Eucharist) is eternally celebrated, eternally offered, in worship of the Holy Trinity.

As Orthodox Christians, we find life in this celebration, for the Eucharist is not only an offering to God, but the source of life for us. Christ said, "Whoever eats My flesh and drinks My blood has eternal life" (John 6:54). It is not a symbol or a memorial of something that took place in the past, but a place where we meet eternity. Within the celebration of the Divine Liturgy, we enter into the heavenly Kingdom, where the Church Triumphant (in heaven) unites with the Church Militant (on earth). We enter into the communion of saints!

I am a proponent of frequent Communion, as are the fathers of the Holy Mountain of Athos, because we need the Eucharist. It sustains us, encourages us, fortifies us, heals us, transforms us. The early Christians received whenever they gathered together, for they knew the communal participation in the eucharistic banquet was life-giving.

A Grateful Heart Is Fertile Ground

When you strive to interact with members of your family, friends, coworkers, and all others with respect, humility, and dignity, you lay the groundwork for the abundance of grace needed to quicken your heart for the things of God. The soil is prepared for the planting of seeds that allow you to respond to God's grace, for a grateful heart is fertile ground for the things of God.

When you open your heart to others with gratitude, the path is prepared for a relationship with Jesus Christ. And the indwelling of the Holy Spirit fills you with the power to live a life that is transformed by God's grace. You are filled with heartfelt gratitude for all God's gifts, and inner peace is yours.

The preparation for sowing the seeds of the love of God begins with responsive gratefulness. The Apostle Paul wrote, "Remember that you do not support the root, but the root supports you" (Rom. 11:18). Any relationship with God must begin with a grateful heart and then be cultivated by kindness and goodwill toward others. When you are grateful, you respond toward God and others by enacting other virtues.

The cultivation of deepened appreciation and heartfelt gratitude for others quickens the soul to feel the inner need to freely and thankfully respond to God's invitation to commune with Him.

What Do We Do about Our Youth?

Young people are filled with ideas, dreams, and goals, and their youthful exuberance is full of hope and vitality. When they bring this to the table, they begin to replace the present generation as leaders of this world.

What will they receive from us that will enable them to be the very best leaders for the future? I believe the most important gift we can impart to them is the gift of faith. And the best way to impart this gift is by loving them, respecting them, and, most importantly, demonstrating the truth of our faith by living it. If they don't see Christ in us, but only posturing, they will see nothing they want. They must see us as a people changed by our relationship with Christ. They must see Christ in us, loving them, and reaching out with respect and hope. They must see us as prayerful people.

It is not enough to be regular church attenders. If our Orthodoxy does not extend beyond the door of the temple, we will fail our youths. If our Orthodoxy is no more than an "ethnic preservation society," they will not want what we have.

The day of reckoning is upon us, and we must step up to the challenge. Nothing new is happening in our present age that has not happened in ages past. And, just as men and women brought past generations out of darkness and despair, so too this older generation must come forth with hope and faith, bringing the light of Christ to an age that is fast losing hope.

Since many of our young are being forced to drop out of college due to economic hardship and are facing bleak prospects for their future, they must see hope in us. The only hope for this world is to be found in Christ, so now is the time for a new age of faith. Only in Christ will the world find true wealth and lasting peace.

Let the light of Christ shine forth throughout the world—in us! Let our young see the joy of Christ in us, lighting the way to true happiness and everlasting prosperity. Let them see hope in us.

God Is Not a Prosecutor, but a Physician

The Scriptures, the works of the early Church Fathers, and the liturgical texts of the Church all attest to the fact that the ancient Church did not teach that Christ's Incarnation was intended to be a propitiation of divine justice. Rather, Christ came as a physician intent on bringing healing to fallen humankind. Christ's Incarnation brought the whole of human nature together with His divine nature for a cure. His spiritual medicine brings healing, removes the stain of sin that had introduced death to the cosmos, and makes everything whole.

This condescension of God, who took on our human flesh and joined His divinity to us, cannot be seen in legalistic terms, but must be seen from a medical perspective. We are ill. Our sin is not about law but about illness. In our fallen state, we've departed from communion with God, and Christ's death upon the Cross was accomplished, not because the Father demanded blood, but because He desired to heal us and to restore life to His creatures, who've inherited death from our fallen forefather, Adam. That Christ assumed our human nature made possible the cure.

The Lord Jesus Christ established His Church as a hospital of the soul, and within her walls we are given the medicine to bring about the healing we so need. God does not desire suffering or our blood, but only that we be restored to the image He intended for us. This loving Father is not our prosecutor, but our physician.

When We Look into the Face of Another

E ven small towns across our country are now home to people from Ghana, India, Pakistan, Mexico, and China, to name but a few. We have communities of Sikhs with their colorful turbans as well as women wearing the *hijab* living among us. Our children attend schools with students who are members of religions that are relatively new to American shores, and the racial makeup of our country is changing. Now that we are witnessing increased conflict in the Middle East, we are tempted to look toward new immigrants with suspicion or even fear.

As Christians we must make sure the present strife in our world does not become the vehicle for the virus of hate to enter our hearts. The most difficult commandment Christ gave to His disciples was that we must love our enemies. If we translate that directive into the simple task of being nice to the crabby old man next door, we will have missed the point. Jesus said, "But I say to you, love your enemies, bless those who curse you, do good to those who hate you, and pray for those who spitefully use you and persecute you" (Matt. 5:44).

Whom do we see when we look into the face of another? It is Christ! It is either Christ glorified or Christ crucified. That we have all been created in the image and likeness of God means we are all His children and therefore brothers and sisters to one another. That some of our brothers and sisters have chosen to be our enemies in no way lessens the truth that we are all the children of Eve, charged by Christ to love each other. If we are of Christ, we must follow His commandments.

Avoid the Old Man

At the moment we commit ourselves to a life in Christ, change takes place. We begin walking the path of repentance, putting off the "old man" and putting on Christ. The waters of baptism began this change, and the life-giving waters of regeneration make us new creatures. This moment of conversion begins with a negation: the turning away from the worldly passions that dominated our previous lives. We deny our old selves. We turn away from our old ways and commit ourselves to allowing Christ to change us.

We do not remain static but move forward in a dynamic way, moving into a life in Christ and availing ourselves of God's grace. At that point we are no longer in a negative mode, fighting off the old self, but entering into a positive state: the joy of an encounter with the living God.

The old self is to be avoided, and we remember our old ways only in order to avoid the things that kept us separated from God. We move forward, away from everything that was a source of death.

Losing Religion and Replacing It with Nothing

According to Professor Mark Silk of Trinity College in Hartford, Connecticut, "The real dirty little secret of religiosity in America is that there are so many people for whom spiritual interest, thinking about ultimate questions, is minimal."[2]

Increasing numbers of people are concerned only with new cars, mortgages, entertainment, or their favorite rock band or football team. Even people who regularly participated in the life of the Church have shrugged off their obligations to God, preferring to sleep in on Sundays. They even begin to question their faith, having withdrawn from the abounding grace that had previously sustained them. They begin to question whether the Church is relevant to them, or even if God exists.

Having become minimalists in the area of religion, they slowly sink in the quagmire of secularism and ultimately the atheism that follows. Surrendered to the hazardous behavior of absenting themselves from the grace-filled Mysteries of Christ's Church, they sink into the mud of a life devoid of meaning, surrendering themselves to material pursuits. Ultimately they find that life hasn't been very fulfilling, and they wonder why.

A few years ago, after a hip replacement, I decided I needed to strengthen my body to give support to the other hip and to fight off the arthritis that was starting to weaken my knee joints. I was surprised at how quickly my muscle tone returned, and I remembered the truism that muscles have memory.

The soul is like that. Just as muscles rebuild themselves when we make the effort to exercise, so too the soul is quickly restored to health when we avail ourselves of the healing grace that abounds within the Church.

As you continue this new year, why not make a resolution to commit yourself to a reformation of your life? Commit yourself to regular church attendance and keeping the fast periods, to spiritual reading, and to prayer. Usher in a new year of enlightenment, where the Son of Righteousness reigns in your life anew!

Lives Transformed Impart the Faith

That the Orthodox Church possesses the totality of apostolic truth is a given, yet if in our weakness as believers, the obviousness of that truth is invisible to others, we will have betrayed that truth. If in our weakness we fail to be an image of Christ, and love and joy appear to be absent, visitors to our temples will see only ritual, and the beauty of the mystical theology of our faith will remain invisible to them.

For Orthodoxy to be seen as different from other faiths, love and joy must be manifested in our lives, and others must know we are of Christ by the transformed lives we lead. They must see in us the impact this faith has had on our souls. A faith that does not lead to transformation, but only rests in beautiful temples and forms of worship, will not impart the sublime theology that is rooted in our relationship with Jesus Christ.

St. Clement of Alexandria said, "When the pagans hear from our mouths the oracles of God, they marvel at their beauty and greatness. But when they discover that our actions are not worthy of the words we speak, they turn from wonder to blasphemy, saying that it is a myth and a delusion."

FEBRUARY 19

Holy Tradition Supports Proper Bible Interpretation

Many evangelical Protestants see Holy Tradition as standing in direct contrast to Scripture, relegating it to "the traditions of men." However, there are numerous references in Holy Scripture to Holy Tradition. For example:

> *Inasmuch as many have taken in hand to set in order a narrative of those things which have been fulfilled among us, just as those who from the beginning were eyewitnesses and ministers of the word delivered them to us, it seemed good to me also, having had perfect understanding of all things from the very first, to write to you an orderly account, most excellent Theophilus, that you may know the certainty of those things in which you were instructed. (Luke 1:1–4)*

It must be noted that in this instance, the oral word preceded the written word, hence becoming Holy Tradition. In John 20:30–33, it is revealed that "Jesus did many other signs in the presence of His disciples, which are not written in this book," and in John 21:25 we read, "There are also many other things that Jesus did, which if they were written one by one, I suppose that even the world itself could not contain the books that would be written." One of my personal favorite passages regarding Holy Tradition is found in 2 Thessalonians 2:15: "Therefore, brethren, stand fast and hold the traditions which you were taught, whether by word or our epistle."

Holy Tradition does not stand apart from the Bible, but supports the proper interpretation of the Bible. It emanates from Christ Himself and is expressed by the Apostles, the Holy Fathers, and the Church. The Fathers, in fact, are the very guardians of the Apostolic Tradition, for they, like the Apostles before them, are witnesses of a single truth—the truth of the God-Man, Jesus Christ. Since Christ is one, unique, and indivisible, so also is the Church unique and indivisible. The Church is the incarnation of the incarnated God-Man; it will continue through the ages and even throughout eternity.

Be Still and Know That I Am God

G reat and Holy Lent is considered by most to be the forty days before
Pascha when we give up certain foods (dairy, meat, eggs, fish) and
give more attention to almsgiving. This season is also a time when we try
to replace entertainment, nights out with friends, and worldly pleasures
with increased time attending the divine services. Lent is also the time
when we increase our spiritual reading, consulting with our priest or the
proprietor of our local Orthodox bookstore for suggestions of books to
accompany our Lenten journey.

I would like to suggest another element—one that is important but
seldom talked about. During the forty days of the Great Fast, why not put
aside the noise of this world and discover the value of silence?

When radio was first introduced on the American scene, an important
element in daily living was lost forever. No longer was silence a part of
everyday life. With families gathering around the radio, listening to shows
or music that were far from edifying, the loss for the human spirit was
great. In the present "information age," we are seeing even less silence, for
not only do we have televisions blaring from the moment we walk into
our homes, the internet has introduced noise of a different nature, on command at any time. Hi-tech gadgets fill our waking moments with music,
shutting out the sounds of nature—birds chirping, the sound of wind, the
lapping of waves on a beach.

The Psalmist David tells us, "Be still, and know that I *am* God" (Ps.
46:10). Silence to the noise of this world opens our ears to the whispers of
the Lord, who speaks to us from within. Silence should not be feared, but
sought out and embraced like a lover.

Whose Recipe Is It, Anyway?

One of the most powerful reasons for embracing Orthodoxy is that it holds to the evangelical and apostolic doctrine of the ancient Church. In an age when everything is up for change, there is a certain security and stability when one institution (the Church) stands firm in her apostolic authority and refuses to allow popular culture to influence her rightful role as hospital for the soul.

We know from the very foundations of the Church, set down in the Gospels and in the apostolic canons, that the Church exists not to judge, but to make whole those who would enter into her gates as into a hospital. Yet the Church is also aware that sin is not really a private matter, for even private sins have an effect on the whole cosmos. Therefore, the Church continues to bear witness to the commandments of God, the hope that is found in the Gospel of Christ, and the forgiveness and healing that can lead to wholeness.

The Church may seem to be irrelevant for our times, a view that has caused many denominations to alter foundational teachings in order to please a more liberal society. This has led numerous denominations to ordain women as clergy, perform same-sex marriages, and bow down to modern views on abortion that have lead to the deaths of millions of innocents.

Like all Orthodox clergy, I teach by my presence in a modern and fallen world that my faith is an ancient one and that change is not necessary, for the faith of our fathers is just as effective in bringing about the healing of the soul as it was in ancient times.

The sad state of American Christianity has as its basis a constant attempt to conform to an ever-changing society. With each change, there is less and less of authentic, ancient Christianity to be seen. This could be compared to using an old family cake recipe, dropping one ingredient or replacing another with each passing generation. In the end, is it really great-great-grandmother's cake recipe, or is it something else?

FEBRUARY 22

Forgiveness Is the Cure

O ur Lord Jesus Christ told us: "Judge not, and you shall not be
judged. Condemn not, and you shall not be condemned. Forgive,
and you will be forgiven" (Luke 6:37). In the Our Father, the very prayer
Christ gave to His disciples after they asked Him to teach them to pray, we
say the words, "Forgive us our debts, as we forgive our debtors." These
strong words make it clear that we are to forgive others if we expect God
to forgive us.

St. Tikhon of Zadonsk, in his book *Journey to Heaven,* says,

> *Do we forgive our neighbors their trespasses? God also forgives
> us in His mercy. Do we refuse to forgive? God also will refuse to
> forgive us. As we treat our neighbors, so also does God treat us.
> The forgiveness, then, of your sins or unforgiveness, and hence
> also your salvation or destruction, depend on you yourself, man.
> For without forgiveness of sins there is no salvation.*[3]

Throughout His ministry, Christ emphasized the need for us to be
willing to forgive others, for if we expect to be forgiven, we must nurture
a forgiving heart. If we hold grudges and remember wrongs, we poison our
souls, and love has no place in us.

Elder Samson of Russia said, "The drunkard, the fornicator, the
proud—he will receive God's mercy. But he who does not want to forgive, to excuse, to justify consciously, intentionally. . . . That person closes
himself to eternal life before God, and even more so in the present life. He
is turned away and not heard."

As we are quick to forgive our neighbors, so God also forgives us in
His great and loving mercy. If we refuse to forgive, God too will refuse to
forgive us. Our salvation depends on our willingness to forgive others, for
without forgiveness of sins, there is no salvation.

Put Aside Resentment

The decision to forgive another person a wrong done to us begins when we let go of resentment and thoughts of revenge. Forgiving someone does not mean we forget what they did to us, for that may be impossible. The memory of the hurt may always remain with you, but when you decide to forgive the person who wronged you, the grip of resentment is put aside. When you forgive someone, it is even possible to find yourself filled with compassion and empathy for the person, for an act of forgiveness opens a heart to God's grace.

When we forgive people, we are not denying their responsibility for hurting or offending us, nor are we justifying their act. We can forgive them without approving or excusing their transgression against us. The act of forgiving another opens our hearts to the peace that brings closure to hurt and pain, and it opens us up to the love and peace that comes from living a life without resentment.

If we find ourselves struggling to forgive, it is a good reminder to recall hurtful things we've done to others and to remember when we've been forgiven. It is especially good to recall how God has forgiven us and to call upon Him to give us the grace needed to put aside our resentment and truly forgive the other person. Being quick to forgive and putting aside all thoughts of revenge will open our heart to a joyful and peaceful life.

Finally, if we pray for those who've offended us, we open the door to all kinds of possibilities. When we ask God to help the person who has been unkind and hurtful, our own hearts receive healing, for when we've forgiven others, grace abounds.

As Peter wrote, we should do good to others, "not returning evil for evil or reviling for reviling, but on the contrary blessing, knowing that you were called to this, that you may inherit a blessing" (1 Pet. 3:9).

FEBRUARY 24

Submitting to the Will of God

Pride keeps us from living according to the will of God, and it causes us to focus only on self. Without submission to God, we wallow in the dankness of our fallen world, and our true self remains dormant. We cannot submit to God without humility, and when we do, we gain true freedom and are able to be triumphant over the powers of darkness that attack us. "Therefore submit to God. Resist the devil and he will flee from you" (James 4:7).

Our submission to the will of God begins when we submit as children to our parents and as adults to lawful authority, be it civil or ecclesiastical. The Apostle Peter wrote, "You younger people, submit yourselves to your elders. Yes, all of you be submissive to one another, and be clothed with humility, for 'God resists the proud, / But gives grace to the humble'" (1 Pet. 5:5). Submission to lawful authority builds humility, for self-will is by necessity set aside.

Submission begins with trust. We trust that God loves us and that our submission to His commandments will return us to our inheritance, which is God's Kingdom. In our submission, we permit His grace to transform our fallen nature and return us to full sonship in our Father's Kingdom. In submitting to the will of God, the Lord Himself begins to lead us, and we are healed of our sickness and made whole.

When we submit to God, our soul is filled with the Holy Spirit; His Kingdom is actualized in our heart; and we become living tabernacles of the Most High. The soul that submits to the will of God fears nothing. And whatever should happen, it says, "It is God's will." When the body is ill, such a person thinks, "God has seen fit to send me this illness for my salvation; otherwise I would not be ill." When such a person is persecuted, he is not disturbed, for he knows that God is with him. And so his soul remains at peace.

Prayer, Fasting, and Almsgiving

Jesus Christ called for a thorough conversion of our heart and mind, and a complete turning away from the old man (our fallen nature). The main act that begins this conversion is *metanoia,* a thorough change of mind. This happens when we become aware that we have sinned and that we are in need of God's forgiveness, and we resolve, with His help, to submit to Him.

When we go to confession, a priest sometimes gives a penance, which is a spiritual discipline that can aid in our journey to God. Penances are often in the form of disciplines meant to help increase the time we spend in prayer, fasting, and almsgiving. These three disciplines help us deepen our relationship with Christ and aid in the acquisition of the Holy Spirit. Sometimes we are asked to do akathist hymns, where we seek the aid of saints or the Holy Virgin as we struggle to go deeper in our spiritual quest. We might be given extra periods of fasting, so that in depriving ourselves of food, we will be able to see deeper into our hearts and be rid of the dirt and grime that resides within us. Other times we might be asked to perform acts of charity as a way of moving beyond ourselves.

Disciplines that focus on increased prayer, fasting, and almsgiving, along with immersing ourselves in the Holy Scriptures, help us in our quest to live a life in total submission to Christ. These three aid us in the acquisition of the Holy Spirit and help us to live our life for Christ.

Prayer, fasting, and almsgiving are not ends in themselves but exercises that help in spiritual warfare against the demons that would bring us down. They help us in our attempt to repent and to have a thorough change of mind (metanoia). This repentance does not mean that we must feel sad, but that we strive to put off all pride and selfishness, and replace the ego with love, joy, peace, patience, gentleness, goodness, kindness, meekness, and self-control.

FEBRUARY 26

The Trainer and the Spiritual Director

Just after my graduation from college I moved to Portland, Oregon, where I worked at various jobs, including waiting tables, bartending, and working as an orderly in a trauma center. All these jobs contributed in important ways to my ultimate vocation as a priest and a monk. (I'll leave it to you to figure that one out.)

Shortly after my move to Portland, I decided I wanted to work out at a local weightlifting gym. After asking around, I discovered Loprinzi's Gym, a Portland institution to this day. Being a skinny college grad, I felt somewhat intimidated as I walked into a gym filled with Olympic-style weightlifters. But one of the trainers approached me and offered to help me get started. Grateful for the direction, I began what was to be a mainstay of my physical exercise for years to come. I didn't stop weightlifting until I became a monk, and I have always regretted the decision to stop.

The day I walked into Loprinzi's Gym, another young man walked in for his first try at weightlifting. But he was too prideful to accept direction from anyone. Some six months later, my trainer quietly pointed to the other young man and said, "Since he has been his own trainer, he sees only his front side, so his muscle development is concentrated in his upper arms and chest. His back muscles and legs are underdeveloped."

I share this story because of the saying in Orthodoxy, "The man who is his own spiritual director becomes the disciple of a fool." When we embark on the spiritual path, we need the direction and foresight of someone experienced, for there are all sorts of traps ahead, including pride.

St. John of Kronstadt wrote:

> *A priest is a spiritual physician. Show your wounds to him without shame, sincerely, openly, trusting and confiding in him as his son; for the confessor is your spiritual father, who should love you more than your own father and mother; for Christ's love is higher than any natural love. He must give an answer to God for you.*[4]

Heavenly Worship Must Enter into the Heart

The beauty of Orthodox worship is meant to lift us up and connect us to the heavenly worship that is eternally taking place before the throne of God. The description of heavenly worship found in the Book of Revelation is clearly an image of the Divine Liturgy. The beatific vision granted to St. John revealed the connection between the eucharistic service we celebrate here on earth and the heavenly banquet that awaits us in eternity. The beauty of the Orthodox Divine Liturgy is but a foretaste of what awaits us.

When we stand in worship, it is important that we take in the words, making them our own. Merely observing the services is not worship, for we must enter into worship with our hearts, giving attention to the Word of God that permeates the whole of the services. We must breathe in the Word of God, letting the action of the Word take root in our hearts. The Word of God is a living word that imparts God's grace.

The Word, whether read formally from the readings of the Epistle and the Gospel or prayed in the liturgical texts, is meant to transform us and make us a holy people. The Word must enter into the heart, for it is then that regeneration takes place.

Abbot Nazarius said, "Strive as well as you can to enter deeply with the heart into the church reading and singing and to imprint these on the tablets of the heart."

Looking at the Sins of Others

When we take our eyes off our own failings, shortcomings, and sins, we notice the failings of others. As the sins of others get our attention, our focus turns away from our own struggles with the passions, and we begin to fall further into sin, our eyes having turned away from the Lord. When our focus is no longer turned toward the conquering of our passions, our hearts become vulnerable, and we begin to expend our energy on picking apart our neighbor. Their sins become the hot topic with our gossiping friends, and we fall further into the rottenness of our sins. Regarding this, Abba Sisoes asked, "How can we guard the heart if the tongue leaves the door of the fortress open?"

If we are to take ourselves out of the mire of sin and, with Christ's help, be transformed and made whole, our eyes must never look at the sins of others. St. John Cassian said, "A person cannot be disquieted or concerned about other people's affairs if he is satisfied with concentrating on the work of his own hands."

As we approach Great and Holy Lent, let us refocus ourselves and prepare for the struggle ahead. Let us make this Great Fast the most profitable of all, with the goal of acquiring a humble and contrite heart. If we focus on our own failings only, we will find this Lenten season to be the most profitable of all, and we will be lifted up by God. Our celebration of Holy Pascha will then be the most glorious of them all.

Remember, the Great and Holy Fast was created for us as a time for repentance, renewal, and the restoration of heart, mind, and body. Let us keep our spiritual eyes on Christ and be open to the healing of our soul that comes for us through this very Christ Jesus, whom we worship and adore.

Are We Flatterers or Faithful Citizens?

The Byzantine court was filled with sycophants busying themselves with building alliances that would help them rise in status and influence. Many emperors were tricked into believing these sycophants were their friends and could be trusted, but they were being played. The sycophants were quick to change allegiances should a better opportunity arise, and many an emperor was betrayed by those he had thought could be trusted.

In the end, the whole of the empire suffered. These people were not true citizens of the empire. They focused on their own advancement, putting self before the empire. In the end, the emperor would be betrayed, and the empire would have suffered yet another round of intrigue.

True loyalty is never based on blind obedience, for such a system only serves to promote sycophants—and in the end, everyone suffers. The emperor who did not tolerate flattery but sought out true advisers ruled in peace and harmony.

As we prepare to enter into the Great and Holy Fast, let us reexamine our own relationships. Are we sycophants, or do we speak from the heart, without thought for self-promotion? Are we true friends to those with whom we share our lives, or are we always thinking only of ourselves? Do we really desire to be loving people, or are we only focused on our own needs? Are we like the emperors, surrounding ourselves with people who tell us only what we want to hear, or are we ready to receive the feedback that will actually help us grow spiritually?

Let us humbly approach the Savior during the Great Fast, seeking the transformation that is ours through His divine grace and, through His mercy, we will be made whole. Let us not be flatterers and betrayers of others, but true friends, putting ourselves last. Let us love God above all and others as ourselves. And with God's help, let us make this Lenten journey the most spiritually profitable of them all.

MARCH 2

The Preeminence of Love in Obedience

Obedience is a central theme in the history of salvation. Without obedience to God's commandments, there can be no salvation, for the *nous* (the eye of the soul) must be healed before we can be made whole. The role of obedience is so central, in fact, that we must submit ourselves to God's will before the healing process can begin.

Obedience has often been misunderstood, for many associate submission with enslavement. For many, obedience is a relic of the past, when people had to bow before kings.

Consider that love is the root of good parents' expectation of obedience from their children. Age and experience give parents an advantage, for it equips them with the needed tools to guide and protect their child. Experience lets parents know it is never a good idea to leave church attendance up to their children, just as no responsible parent would ever think of asking their children if they'd be interested in pursuing an education. Parents know that church attendance forms children into adults with a spiritual grounding that will serve them well.

Obedience also plays a role in our spiritual development, in our willingness to seek out spiritual guidance and to try to follow the direction we are given. The husband and wife who are obedient to one another find true freedom in their mutual submission, for in surrendering their self-will, they open themselves to the grace of God and healing of the nous can take place.

The obedience of a monk to his abbot and to the rule of the brotherhood also leads to a freedom he cannot enjoy when he wallows in self-will. Likewise, the obedience a priest gives to his bishop is ultimately liberating, for in surrendering himself in obedience, the priest gives himself over to God's will. The bishop, abbot, husband, or parent whose position is God-ordained must rule with love. Intimidation and coercion have no place in the life of any Christian, and the husband, priest, abbot, or bishop who rules without paternal love betrays the love of Christ, whose example we are called to emulate.

Pride: The Enemy of Faith

*Jesus answered and said to them, "This is the work of God, that
you believe in Him whom He sent."*

John 6:29

The necessary element for salvation is faith. Faith alone will save us,
for only faith brings us into communion with God. Faith is a free
gift, for nothing we can do can save us. No good works can save us. Being
good people will not save us. Only faith in Christ will bring us into everlasting life.

The enemy of faith is pride, for pride destroys faith. Pride makes us
believe we do not need God. It also leads many into the abyss of atheism,
for it makes us believe there is nothing beyond ourselves. Pride leads us to
believe that we are all-important and that nothing exists beyond ourselves.
Once pride takes hold, our heart grows hard, and faith grows cold and dies.

Repentance is the cure for pride, and only through repentance can we
rekindle the grace that brings life to our faith. Humbling ourselves before
God and giving ourselves over to divine worship brings us back into the
natural relationship that was preordained for us before the Fall, and faith
grows as grace abounds.

The Church Is Like a Forest

Growing up in Northern Idaho, I was surrounded by mountains and forests. I don't remember a time when forests did not tug at my heart and fill my imagination with thoughts of adventure. My parents took my brother and me on annual camping trips to a state park on the far northeast side of Lake Pend Oreille. There my dad made us small toy canoes, complete with sails, out of birch bark.

As a high school student, I regularly went hiking in the mountains around Sandpoint, Idaho, with my best friend (now a professor of theology and philosophy in Scotland). Jim and I would climb to the highest point of a given mountain and pray together. We could understand the Prophet Moses' meeting with God on Mount Sinai, for we too felt the presence of God on the mountain.

When we first cleared the land to build the monastery, we cut down as few trees as possible, desiring to have the buildings appear as though cupped in the hands of God. We even named our forest after St. Seraphim of Sarov, who sought solitude in a forest. Our forest not only provides needed solitude but also gives us oxygen.

Monks have always had a special place in their hearts for forests. Coptic and Ethiopian monks have been known to plant trees on desert mountains on which monasteries have been built; they call these places "holy forests." Russian monks sought their solitude in the Northern Thebaid, forests that became their desert.

Our temples are like forests in many ways. When we enter into an Orthodox temple, we are encompassed in the living presence of God, and our spiritual lungs are filled. We breathe in oxygen for the soul, and the forest that surrounds us is none other than the cloud of witnesses, the saints, who join us in worship before the throne of God. The oxygen we breathe in is God's grace, which flows out to all who seek the safety and sanctuary that await us in God's holy temple.

Authentic Christian Charity

The Church, if she is to be authentic in her Christian witness, must grapple with the challenges of society, starting with its most marginalized sector. If the Church does not teach with a loud voice that fasting is about more than refraining from certain foods, she is failing in her duty to preach the fullness of Christ's gospel. The Church's ministry must include service to the poor and downtrodden, for her role does not stop with her liturgical services, but begins there. St. John Chrysostom teaches that fasting without accompanying good deeds is like a ship going from port to port without cargo.

The newly canonized St. Sophrony of Essex wrote:

> *A man is not saved by having once shown mercy to someone, although, if he scorns someone but once, he merits eternal fire. For "hungered" and "thirsty" is said not of one occasion, not of one day, but of the whole life. In the same way "ye gave me meat," "ye gave me drink," "ye clothed me," and so on, does not indicate one incident, but a constant attitude to everyone. Our Lord Jesus Christ said that He Himself accepts such mercy from His slaves (in the person of the needy).*[5]

St. John Chrysostom, perhaps the greatest preacher of all time, told us:

> *Do you wish to honor the Body of the Savior? Do not despise it when it is naked. Do not honor it in church with silk vestments while outside it is naked and numb with cold. He who said, "This is my body," and made it so by his word, is the same who said, "You saw me hungry and you gave me no food. As you did it not to the least of these, you did it not to me." Honor him then by sharing your property with the poor. For what God needs is not golden chalices but golden souls.*

MARCH 6

Prayer: The Remedy for Gloom and Despondency

Depression is one of the plagues of the modern age, overtaking many with its insidious poison and ravaging many a life. The pain and suffering that come with deep depression can infect those who surround the sufferer, for the depression of one person can spread like mold on stale bread. Psychiatrists are kept busy writing prescriptions, and drug companies rake in the money, selling a "cure." Families are destroyed, marriages come apart, and young people drop out of school—all because of depression.

Although there are certainly cases where depression is caused by imbalances in the chemical makeup of the body, it is far more common for depression to be the result of the sickness of the soul. The cure, in this case, is to be found in the life of the Church. Giving oneself over to the pursuit of God and increasing the time we spend in prayer and worship can gradually transform depression into joy.

St. John Cassian wrote, "But first we must struggle with the demon of dejection who casts the soul into despair. We must drive him from our heart. It was this demon that did not allow Cain to repent after he had killed his brother, or Judas after he had betrayed his Master."

The Orthodox periods of fasting are perfect times to confront the spirit of depression, for increased attendance at the Church's divine services and time spent in private prayer contribute to the healing of the soul, taking our minds off our problems and turning our hearts toward the things of God. Spiritual reading, frequent confession, and the reception of the Holy Mysteries all bring the healing the soul longs for.

MARCH 7

Caregivers Must Care for Themselves

My dear mother was diagnosed with dementia in 2003. Soon after the diagnosis, I moved her from Coeur d'Alene, Idaho, into an assisted living place on Vashon Island, where I could be involved in the supervision of her care. Almost from the beginning, she needed me to be with her as much as possible. I spent hours every day by her side, taking her on drives around the island, treating her to lunches in the Chinese restaurant, and bringing her to the monastery for services.

Increasingly, people of my generation are being called upon to be caregivers for parents, siblings, or other family members. It is important that caregivers not sacrifice their own spiritual and social needs. They must not feel guilty or feel they are betraying their loved one when they step out with friends for dinner and a movie. They should not feel they are abandoning their responsibility by attending the divine services or partaking in a Bible study.

As a priest, I must tend to my own needs if I am to minister to others. When we allow ourselves to be depleted spiritually and emotionally, we do a disservice to those we serve. When we are depleted, the person in our care ultimately suffers, for a caregiver (or priest) who becomes resentful can slip into being abusive without even realizing it.

Many organizations provide in-home care so caregivers can take a break. Whether you are a caregiver or in some other service to others, be sure to take care of yourself, lest you become ineffective in your service.

Be Quick to Embrace the Prodigal Son

Some people abandon themselves to sin in order to cover up their lack of self-esteem. In their need for intimacy and acceptance, they seek out worldly pleasures, thinking these will fill the void that has kept them from happiness. In their desperate search for love, they are unable to form lasting friendships, and they spiral down, failing to achieve what will satisfy them. Substituting carnal pleasures for true intimacy, they fall further into their brokenness. Falling ever more deeply into the abyss of the self-serving ego, they are estranged from true joy and lasting peace.

These people are in need of mercy. And what is the Church, if not the place where they can be healed? If we who form the Body of Christ see ourselves as inspector generals and seek to expose their sins and shortcomings, we deprive ourselves of the grace that comes from being merciful. If we, in our pride and self-serving ego, become like the elder brother of the prodigal son, protesting our Father's embrace of our returning lost brother, we become lost ourselves.

What are we to do when we see the sins of others? What is our response? The Great and Holy Fast is a time for repentance and forgiveness. If we expect God's mercy, we must be quick to be merciful to others. We must be blind to their sins and shortcomings and look only at our own brokenness. For it is in reconciliation, not punishment, that we find God and love of neighbor. We must rejoice when one among us has repented, and like the father of the prodigal son, we must be quick to run forth with arms open for an embrace.

When we are brought down by the acknowledgment of our own rottenness, we can begin to overlook the shortcomings of others. When we focus on God, we do not see the sins of our neighbors. We learn not to react, not to resent, and not to lose our inner peace.

Godparenting Is an Awesome Responsibility

The institution of godparenting (sponsoring) dates back to the first century of the Christian Church. Anyone approaching baptism, infant or adult, is required to have a godparent. In the case of an infant, the godparent speaks for the child, answering the questions posed by the priest during the baptismal service.

But it doesn't stop there! The godparent is charged by the Church with the duty to make sure the newly baptized is instructed in the teachings of the Church, remains a frequent communicant, and remains active in the Church. In the case of a child, the parents entrust their child to the godparent, knowing that the godparent will actively support the child within the life of the Church. Should something happen to the parents, it is traditionally the godparent who makes sure the child continues to be taken to church and remains Orthodox.

Because baptism has been called illumination, as it brings us out of the darkness of sin and into the light of Christ, the role of the godparent is critical. The godparent must ensure that the light of Christ continues to shine in the soul of the godchild. Thus, this role of godparent is an awesome responsibility, and it is not to be considered a one-day event. If you've been asked to be a godparent but are unwilling to see this as a lifelong vocation, please decline the honor.

On Choosing a Godparent

Because of the awesome responsibilities of godparenting, great care must be taken when choosing a godparent. The Church does not allow anyone to become a godparent who is not Orthodox, for how can one who is not a pious, active Orthodox Christian give witness to living a life immersed in the Orthodox faith? The godparent must be a person of high moral character and able to inspire the godchild to fulfill the baptismal vows.

When the newly baptized approaches the holy chalice for the first three consecutive Sundays following baptism, it is the godparent who accompanies her to receive the Holy Mysteries. Therefore, the godparent must be a frequent communicant. Additionally, godparents must be active in the life of the Church, supporting the Church with their tithe, keeping the fasts, and otherwise living in all piety and holiness.

The person chosen to act as a godparent must be willing to honor a commitment to the newly baptized for a lifetime and willing to help nourish the spiritual life and development of the child throughout his life. Thus, it is a bad idea to pick someone as a godparent simply because she is a good friend. Godparents are duty-bound to continue giving support to their godchild, even into adulthood. They must remember to honor their godson or goddaughter on special occasions, such as a birthday or name day. They should be a part of the godchild's life during the great feasts of the Church, such as Pascha and Nativity. They should commemorate the anniversary of the godchild's baptism by giving her a Christian gift, such as a Bible, prayer book, or icon.

Everything should be done to strengthen the bond between the godparent and the godchild throughout the ensuing years. They can take each other out to a restaurant for dinner or receive Communion together when possible (if living in different cities). Time should be allotted to cultivate a unique spiritual bond, and the godparent should assist the godchild's parents whenever possible, especially when doing so enhances the godchild's commitment to the Orthodox faith.

Keeping the Great Fast for the Right Reasons

The Lord condemned the Pharisee, not because he fasted, but because his motivation was based on pride. The Pharisee wished to be seen by men, and he had no fear of God. He dared to stand before the Lord in pride and arrogance, while the publican stood afar off, beating his breast, begging for the Lord's mercy. Whereas the publican saw his sins and repented, the Pharisee stood before the Lord in arrogance, thinking he was better than other people. He did not desire to commune with God, but to be honored by others.

As we enter into the Great Fast, let us imitate the publican, who saw himself as the worst of sinners and begged God's forgiveness. Let us keep the fast, not to be seen by others, but to make way for the Lord. Let us shun meat, dairy, and fish because we love God and desire to be drawn closer to Him, emptying ourselves of earthly pleasures.

Let us embrace the fast as an opportunity for self-limitation, abstinence, and self-emptying. Let us bear the cross in self-crucifixion, dying to self as we put on Christ. We dare not think we are Christians if we refuse to fast, for bearing our cross is the only way we can be true followers of Christ.

Let us embrace the fast, knowing that "fasting appears gloomy until one steps into its arena. But begin, and you will see what light it brings after darkness, what freedom from bonds, what release after a burdensome life" (St. Theophan the Recluse).

Finally, let us be mindful that, as St. John Cassian wrote:

> *Fasts and vigils, the study of Scripture, renouncing possessions*
> *and everything worldly are not in themselves perfection . . . ;*
> *they are its tools. For perfection is not to be found in them; it*
> *is acquired through them. It is useless, therefore, to boast of our*
> *fasting, vigils, poverty, and reading of Scripture when we have*
> *not achieved the love of God and our fellow men. Whoever has*
> *achieved love has God within himself, and his intellect is always*
> *with God.*

Denying Self-Absorption by Putting on Christ

We are bombarded with thousands of messages, some subtle and some not so subtle, that impact the way we interact with others and the way we relate to God. Much of what we glean from these messages is narcissistic in nature, estranging us from one another.

We become so self-absorbed that we fail to live authentically as Christians, being peacemakers, working toward justice; we fail to forgive those who've wronged us and are not compassionate toward those in need of mercy and charity. St. Macarius the Great said, "Those who hear the word ought to give proof of the work of the word in their own souls."

If we wear a cross around our neck, make the sign of the cross perfectly, keep the fast periods, but have not the love of the poor, we have gained nothing. St. John the Evangelist told us that we cannot love God, whom we've not seen, if we do not love our neighbor (1 John 4:20). If we do not give alms to the poor and speak out for human justice, we will have gained nothing. If we do not treat everyone with respect and love, and show mercy to all, we have not Christ in us.

We must put on Christ with the rising of the sun and with its going down. Christ must be in every word we speak and in every action of our heart. He must reign supreme in our lives, that all may see Christ in us, just as we must see Christ in every person with whom we come in contact. "It is no longer I who live, but Christ lives in me" (Gal. 2:20).

Resentment Makes the Soul Sick

Some people insist on holding on to resentment, often inventing situations in their minds that never happened, justifying their bad behavior, and putting the blame on others. They see themselves as the abused party and are quick to take offense. Rarely are they able to have healthy relationships, for they are, in reality, abusers. Their world centers on themselves, and any attempt by others to appease them only contributes to their antisocial behavior. Such behavior betrays a deep spiritual and psychological illness, one that is not easily healed.

People like this feel empowered by making other people uncomfortable, and normal attempts at rapprochement often end in failure, for such people are always looking for ways to continue their control over others. Their illness is difficult to heal, for their pride and deep-seated sense of superiority make repentance difficult; they simply don't see themselves as having a problem.

The cure for the illness of the soul is to be found in the life of the Church, where her sacred Mysteries (the Sacraments), her Scriptures, and her divine services are the source of the healing the heart so craves. Forgiveness Sunday Vespers is but one of the sources that can begin the process of healing, for during this service the faithful, one by one, speak words like these: "Please forgive me for any hurt or offense I have caused you in any way."

The response, "God forgives. Please forgive me for any hurt or offense I have caused you in any way," exemplifies the Church's teaching that we can only forgive others if we have Christ in us, for it is Christ who gives us the power to forgive. Since God forgives us, we too can forgive.

MARCH 14

The Lenten Journey and the Banishment of Hell

When I was a young man, one of my favorite authors was Thomas Merton, the Trappist monk. In the introduction to his work *New Seeds of Contemplation* he wrote, "Hell is where no one has anything in common with anyone else except the fact that they all hate one another and cannot get away from each other and from themselves."[6]

This very much fits the Orthodox view of hell as being in the presence of God for all eternity—and hating it. For the one who has never loved and who is consumed in his own ego and his own passions, being with God for all eternity will be hell to him. Without love, we cannot experience the fire of God without being burned.

The Lenten journey is the perfect time to reconnect with God's love by strengthening love within our own hearts. By reaching out with an ever-expanding love and charity for everyone around us—be they family members, fellow believers in our parish, or strangers on the street—loving others becomes our Lenten goal. As love increases, hate and anger decrease. As Christ increases in our own heart, the power of hate and sin decreases around us, and hell is banished.

How to Become Humble

We have a fairly clear idea of what humility is, for we've all met people who are truly humble. Metropolitan Laurus of blessed memory, the saintly man who led the Russian Orthodox Church Outside Russia as her chief hierarch, was such a man.

Our brotherhood's beloved Father Spiridon (a Scotsman whose humility inspired us, and who died a few years ago) told us a wonderful story of humility in action. It concerned the ever-memorable Metropolitan Laurus.

Rimmon Stuart (the future Monk Spiridon) came from England to be baptized into the Orthodox Church at Holy Trinity Monastery in Jordanville, New York. Upon arrival at the monastery, he settled into his guest cell and proceeded to take a walk around the grounds of the monastery. He saw an old man in bib overalls crouched down in a large vegetable garden, pulling weeds. Being an avid gardener himself, Rimmon asked the old man if he'd mind having some help with the weeding. The man replied with a smile and welcomed this Scotsman to join him.

Sometime later, the bells of the monastery began tolling, and the old man stood up, announcing it was time to head to the cathedral for the service. Rimmon headed to his guest cell to change into clean clothes and then walked to Holy Trinity Cathedral, where he found the assembled monks awaiting the arrival of their abbot, then Archbishop Laurus.

As the church banners flickered in the wind, the assembled vested priest-monks, together with the whole of the monastic brotherhood, awaited the arrival of their archbishop. You can imagine the shock awaiting Rimmon when he saw that Archbishop Laurus was the very man he'd been toiling away with, weeding in the garden.

St. Seraphim of Sarov said it is easy to be humble before God, but real humility is formed in our hearts when we humble ourselves before men.

Joyful Sorrow in the Expectation of the Resurrection

The main reason Christianity spread so rapidly after the Resurrection of Christ was the power behind the Resurrection. The truth of His Resurrection empowered believers to embrace martyrdom joyfully, knowing they would be joined in eternal bliss with their resurrected Savior. Although their martyrdom would involve both mental and physical anguish, they were almost joyful in their willingness to go to their deaths rather than betray their faith.

That's not the kind of thing one would do just to be part of some "religion." Many contemporaries observed that these Christians faced their martyr's death as though they were about to be married. They were not grim, but had a certain light in their countenance as they embraced their crown of martyrdom. When St. Polycarp was sentenced, he responded by asking why they were delaying his death by burning.

These believers rejoiced as they faced their imminent death, for their knowledge of the bodily resurrection of Christ was proof enough to give them an invincible courage. Grand Duchess Elizabeth and Nun Barbara were said to have been singing hymns after having been thrown into a well by Bolsheviks, as they prepared for eternal life with Christ.

Early Christian apologists cited hundreds of eyewitnesses of those who willingly and resolutely endured prolonged torture and death rather than repudiate their testimony. Their willingness to suffer death ruled out deception on their part. According to the historical record, most Christians could have ended their suffering simply by renouncing the faith. Instead, most opted to endure the suffering and proclaim Christ's Resurrection unto their death.

What makes the earliest Christian martyrs remarkable is that they knew what they were professing was true. Some saw Jesus Christ alive and well after His death; some did not. If it was all just a lie, why would so many Christians perpetuate a myth, given their circumstances? Why would they all knowingly cling to such an unprofitable lie in the face of persecution, imprisonment, torture, and death?

The Holy of Holies, Past and Present

Orthodox temples have kept to the same form and function since ancient times. Using the Old Testament temple model, Orthodox churches are divided into several courts or spaces peculiar to their function. The Holy Table, upon which the Eucharist is celebrated, is at the east end of the building behind the iconostasis (icon screen). This is a continuation of and corresponds to the holy of holies in the ancient Israelite temple in Jerusalem.

The whole area behind the iconostasis is called the altar and is considered the most sacred part of the temple. While great respect must be shown throughout the Church, the altar is very special. It is there that the Holy Spirit descends, making the offering of bread and wine into the Body and Blood of Christ.

Only those who receive the specific blessing of the bishop or the priest or who have a particular task or function may enter behind the iconostasis. A blessing must be received each and every time, even if a person serves there regularly. No one should ever simply wander into the altar without a blessing.

The Holy Table, the proskomedia table (table of preparation), the discos, and the chalice should never be touched by anyone other than a bishop, priest, or deacon. These items are sacred because the Church has blessed them all for the worship of God.

We approach our God with fear and awe, bowing down in worship before His throne in wonder. We worship the Holy Trinity with the same reverence as did the ancients. The very God who created us and who condescended to join His divinity with our humanity is worshiped in temples just as beautiful as the one He commanded to be built in the Holy City, because He has invited us into communion with Him. The worship we offer on this earth is an image of what is taking place before the throne in heaven.

The Simple Message of the Way of Christ

I received an email from a man from India, asking why there is evil in the world and how he could come to know the true God, overcome sin, and live a life in transformation. This is my response to him:

We live in a fallen world, one that was created in perfection, beauty, and goodness. Evil entered into this world when humans turned from God, made themselves gods, and fell into pride and arrogance. The result is our alienation from God as well as the finality of death.

As followers of the Way of Christ, we believe God humbled Himself and pitched His tent in our world as one of us. This God, who is worshiped in Holy Trinity, came down as the second member of this Trinity and became man. Jesus Christ, we believe, is the Logos, the very Word by which everything that came into being was created.

As the Word made flesh, Jesus dwelt among us and taught us how to live the commandments of God and how to love God above everything else. He taught us that we must, if we are to be saved, keep the two Great Commandments: that we love God with our whole heart, mind, and soul, and love our neighbor as being our self.

Jesus, the Name above every other name, suffered, was crucified, died, and was buried, and on the third day conquered the power of death by His Holy Resurrection. When we accept the invitation to commune with this God, who has offered forgiveness for our sins and offers us the possibility to commune with Him, His Resurrection becomes our resurrection. We, although sinners, are forgiven, and we become the sons and daughters of the Most High.

This message is a simple one. All who open their hearts, repent of their sins, and ask God to come into their hearts will be made whole.

MARCH 19

Why We Forget the Things of God

The passions that create a state of unrest in our hearts cause us to forget the real purpose of our lives, which is union with God. St. Basil the Great tells us we cannot approach the knowledge of the truth with a disturbed heart. Conflict, downheartedness, lust, worry, and judging others are all things that cannot be allowed to distract us from the goal. Letting ourselves become troubled or full of anxiety does nothing to further our journey into the heart. Giving ourselves over to the passions depletes us and leaves us waylaid along the side of the narrow path into the Kingdom of God.

We must not be so self-consumed as to have no compassion for others. St. Basil the Great tells us that a person who has two coats or two pairs of shoes when her neighbor has none is a thief. In the Holy Scriptures we read, "The earth *is* the LORD's, and all its fullness, / The world and those who dwell therein" (Psalm 24:1).

No one can be saved, according to St. John Chrysostom, without giving alms and without caring for the poor. We are but stewards of what belongs to God, and Great Lent is the perfect time to share the gifts of God's creation with one another as much as we can. Storing up earthly possessions, according to Christ, is the epitome of foolishness, and a rich man will hardly be saved (Luke 12:15–21).

When we turn our attention toward the needs of others, our focus changes, and we are no longer consumed with self. In this turning of the heart toward those in need, we are turning our hearts to God. Jesus said, "Assuredly, I say to you, inasmuch as you did it to one of the least of these My brethren, you did it to Me" (Matt. 25:40). In our fasting, increased time spent in prayer, and acts of almsgiving, we are energized in our battle against the passions, and our hearts come to rest in Christ.

Beware of False Idols

I dolatry is a pejorative term for the worship of an idol, a physical object worshiped as though it were a god. Idolatry can also involve objects, persons, entertainment, and even self. Anything that replaces the centrality of God in our life can be a form of idolatry. A job, music, money, sex, popularity, success—all can become forms of idolatry. Even nationalism can be idolatrous.

Ours is a troubling time, when so many have given themselves over to the worship of celebrities, financial success, new cars, clothes, trends, and even political parties. How many ministers have the American flag placed centrally in their "worship centers," as though God were an American and salvation were linked to patriotism? How many ministers spend more time preaching a nationalistic form of Christianity while forgetting that Christ transcends cultures and nations?

At the very time we need Christ the most, we allow ourselves as a nation to be distracted by entertainment, jobs, money, and politics. We as a people are bowing down before false idols.

The centrality of Christ and our personal relationship with Him must be guarded against any intrusion of idols. We must examine our lives, making sure nothing has become an idol for us. Like the people of Israel in ancient times, who turned back to God, repenting of their worship of a false idol, so we too must put down our golden calves.

The Saints: Our Friends in High Places

We Orthodox are known for our veneration of the saints, recognizing as we do the truth that there is no separation between the Church Militant here on earth and the Church Triumphant in heaven. In the Church's services, we are not gathered together alone as mortals, but we are joined in our worship before the throne of God by the cloud of witnesses, who are joined with us in Christ.

This truth is exemplified by our use of icons depicting the saints. Their images surround us, reminding us that heaven awaits us. When we enter our temples, we venerate the icons with a kiss, not because we believe the saints reside within these icons, but because, by our veneration, we pass on our love to the archetypes. This is not really any different from kissing a photo of a beloved relative. In our veneration of the icons, we are not worshiping the saints, but showing honor and love to our friends. They stand before us as witnesses to the truth that eternal life is a reality because of the sacrifice of Jesus Christ. Because of His redemptive act upon the Cross, the saints are not dead, but alive.

The saints gaze upon the glory of Christ in the Kingdom of heaven. The great grace that resides within the saints allows them to embrace the whole world with their love; they see how we languish in affliction, and they never cease to intercede for us with God.

The saints, having won the good fight, encourage us by their example and pray for us to be victorious. Their lives give witness to the importance of living in repentance and of placing Jesus above all else, for it is in Jesus Christ that they have gained eternal life. It is in Him that we, like the saints who have gone on before us, have the promise of life eternal. As our friends, the saints await the day when we will join them, and they offer their prayers for that end.

Human Justice or Divine Justice?

In an age when so many seek justice, it is good to remember that true justice comes only when our communion with God has been restored. When we humble ourselves before the Lord and do not seek justice or honor from others, we become like Christ, who was at the very bottom of the social ladder. Seeking the approval of others only furthers our alienation from God, and our spiritual progress is arrested. When we humble ourselves, we find we only need the approval of God, and communion with Him is restored.

If we seek the approval of others, we drive God from our hearts, preferring, as we do, an honor that is transitory. We must flee from the praise of others as though fleeing from fire, for their praise burns us and destroys the humble heart. If we truly desire to acquire a humble and contrite heart, we must embrace what God sends us and not seek human justice, but welcome what humbles us. Medicine is not always pleasant, but it is necessary for the healing of the heart and the restoration of communion with God.

The Church: Unity in Faith

The Lord Jesus Christ desires that we all be joined together in unity within the confines of His Church. This union of all who confess Christ as true God and true man, and who are united as one Body in Him, has as its goal the spiritual perfection that can come only through Him. The life of holiness is about adherence not to a religion, but to a way of life that brings about healing of body and soul.

Being a Christian is not about rules and formulas of conduct, nor is it about ritual. Being a Christian is about putting on Christ daily. It is about committing to a relationship with the very God who created us. Being a Christian means we are committed to acquiring a humble and contrite heart, which is made possible by the grace that is found in abundance within the confines of the Church.

It is important to note that the Church is not some invisible, mystical body, as Protestants teach. The Church is the very visible institution founded by Christ Himself, the Orthodox Church, from which we receive the medicine needed to bring about the transformation that comes from our encounter with the God of mercy, who has invited us into the unity of this Body, where grace abounds.

The Eucharist: Sharing in the Divine Nature

At the Mystical Supper in the Upper Room, Jesus gave a dramatically new meaning to the food and drink of the sacred meal. He identified Himself with the bread and wine: "Take, eat; this is my Body. Drink of it, all of you; for this is my Blood of the New Covenant" (see Matt. 26:26–28).

Food has always sustained the earthly existence of every person, but in the Eucharist, the Lord gave us a unique human food: bread and wine that, by the power of the Holy Spirit, has become the gift of life. Consecrated and sanctified, the bread and wine become the Body and Blood of Christ. This change is not physical but mystical and sacramental. While the qualities of the bread and wine remain, we partake of the true Body and Blood of Christ.

In the eucharistic meal, God enters into such a communion of life that He feeds humanity with His own being while still remaining distinct. In the words of St. Maximos the Confessor, Christ "transmits to us divine life, making Himself eatable." The Author of life shatters the limitations of our createdness. Christ acts so that we "may be partakers of the divine nature" (2 Pet. 1:4).

The Eucharist is the preeminent sacrament, as it completes all the others and recapitulates the entire economy of salvation. Through the Eucharist our new life in Christ is renewed and increased. The Eucharist imparts life, and the life it gives is the life of God.

The Divine Liturgy: Uniting Heaven and Earth

From the moment Christ instituted the Eucharist, it became the center of the Church's life and her most profound prayer. The Eucharist is both the source and the summit of our life in Christ. In the Eucharist the Church is changed from a mere human community into the Body of Christ, the temple of the Holy Spirit, and the people of God.

The Church is the place where heaven and earth are united and where we can live as we were meant to, as before the Fall. The Church's Divine Liturgy is the place where the disunity that came with the Fall is put aside, and communion with God is restored. Our participation in the Divine Liturgy is the moment when we are restored to the Garden of Eden, and God and humans walk together. The Divine Liturgy unites us to the heavenly banquet that is taking place before the throne of God.

The Divine Liturgy transcends time and space, uniting believers in the worship in the Kingdom of God along with all the heavenly hosts, the saints, and the celestial angels. To this end, everything in the Liturgy is seen as symbolic—yet not merely symbolic, but making the unseen reality manifest in our midst.

We do not attend the Divine Liturgy; we participate in it. For in communing with God, we receive the Bread of Life. The Liturgy lifts us up above the disordered and dysfunctional world, and we are placed on the path to restoration and wholeness, healed by the self-emptying love of Christ. Our communion with God is restored.

MARCH 26

Holy Tradition: The Memory of the Church

The fact that Protestants, by and large, have traveled far from the faith
and traditions of the apostolic Church is testament to what happens
when one departs from the "memory" of the Church. This memory is
kept alive through Holy Tradition, from which came the very canon of the
New Testament. Deciding what the early Church believed and how they
worshiped, without Holy Tradition as the guide, has resulted in more than
forty-one thousand denominations, all of which have departed, in various
degrees, from the Church founded by Christ Himself.

"Rituals" are not important to Orthodox, for they are simply external forms of religion. What is important is that we follow the grace-filled
services and practices preserved from the time of the ancient Church. We
do not need to reinvent worship every few years in a sad attempt to remain
relevant to the culture around us. Rather, we attempt to resist the fallen
culture around us while infusing modern culture, devoid of Christian values and beliefs, with a culture steeped in Orthodoxy.

We don't try to understand a particular scripture passage outside the
mind of the Church, for we know that the Church has always made
decisions about teachings, worship practices, and the canon of Scripture
according to what was taught always, everywhere, and at all times. We
believe Christ's promise that the gates of hell will not prevail against the
Church and that the Church is protected, as long as she sticks with her
conciliar nature, which has guided her for over two thousand years.

The Orthodox Church one hundred years from now—provided the
Lord has not returned before then—will be the same as she is today in
worship, doctrine, and faith. In the end, it doesn't matter what I think or
how I might interpret a passage in the Bible. What matters is that I cultivate the mind of the Church within myself.

Bullying: Kindness Must Be Taught Early

More and more frequently we read about children taking their own lives, having reached a place where they would rather be dead than suffer another hour from bullying. Too often parents and teachers have ignored the problem of bullying, dismissing it as nothing more than "kids will be kids" or "kids can be cruel."

The truth is that children, from the earliest age, can be taught to treat other children with kindness and encouraged to be sensitive to the plight of other children. The youngest can be taught the importance of sharing their toys and of including other children in their neighborhood games. Even the smallest child can be taught to treat others as she wishes to be treated.

My own youthful struggle with depression and suicidal thoughts, revolving around my perceived failures and my sense of hopelessness, was offset by one high school teacher who took me under her wing and helped me become a champion debater. She believed in me when no one else would. All it takes is that one person willing to reach out to a child who is suffering, or one child who learns from his parents the importance of treating a bullied child with kindness and of stepping up to defend and befriend that child.

Children are all wonderful gifts from God who are pliable and open, ready to learn from the adults who are their parents, teachers, pastors, and neighbors. They depend on us for comfort, support, and protection. They are in our care, and God expects us to take this responsibility very seriously. Children are the future of our country, our Church, and our world, and they must be taught the importance of being kind and generous toward others.

Children who are raised in the ways of the Lord will raise their own children in the ways of God. Let us not pass on the sins and failures of one generation to the generations to come. Let peace, love, justice, and charity be the hallmark of what we pass on to the next generation. And most importantly, let us instill in our children the love of Christ.

Neither Self-Esteem nor Self-Loathing

Humility does not require that we think poorly of ourselves or that we be given over to self-loathing. Just as we must not exalt ourselves, we must not sink to a state of self-loathing, for both states have their basis in the ego. I would be the last person to suggest that anyone be trapped in a state of self-hatred or wallow in the mire of low self-esteem. I am rather concerned for those who are drawn into the sin of pride, which is often the result of a false attempt at self-esteem. Feeling good about yourself is not the same as being puffed up with pride.

C. S. Lewis wrote that it is not wrong or sinful for a pretty woman to look in a mirror and notice her beauty, but it is better that she walk away and forget about it. In the same way, it is not pride that leads us to notice we have a special gift as a musician, a writer, an orator, or a caretaker of children. What is important for the Christian is to give thanks to God for our gifts while turning our faces toward Christ with gratitude, thankful for the opportunity to use our gifts in service to God and to our neighbor.

When we possess a healthy humility, we can immerse ourselves in service to the God who created us—as we are. We do not stand like the Pharisee, giving thanks that we are not like other people, but, like the publican, we stand before God in all our nakedness, asking to be made whole. We confess before the Lord our unworthiness yet give thanks for the status we have as His children. We are a royal people, delivered from our sin and death by the Savior who came down as a servant.

I was a practicing therapist for many years before becoming a monk. It is sometimes good for people to see a psychologist, but the problem with psychology is its humanistic base. Orthodoxy psychotherapy, as expounded so beautifully by Metropolitan Hierotheos in his book by that name, is far superior for bringing about healing and, with it, humility.

Loving Others Selflessly

Many years ago, I worked with a fellow teacher who was arrogant and condescending. In the same school was a wonderful woman of wisdom who served as the head cook in the school's cafeteria. I'd often sit with her and enjoy a cup of coffee along with her wonderful homemade cookies. One day the other teacher walked into the cafeteria and asked me about one of the students. He totally ignored the cook.

As he walked away, I found myself apologizing for his behavior, only to have the cook tell me that she loved him regardless of his treatment of her, for she knew Jesus loved him. "He doesn't have to love me for me to love him," she told me.

I don't always succeed in loving everyone, and there are certain people I sometimes find myself wishing I could avoid. But the cook's words linger in my heart, and I try to love everyone and return good for evil.

The Apostle Paul tells us, "I can do all things through Christ who strengthens me" (Phil. 4:13), for he said of himself, "For what I am doing, I do not understand. For what I will to do, that I do not practice; but what I hate, that I do" (Rom. 7:15). He also said, "I have been crucified with Christ; it is no longer I who live, but Christ lives in me; and the life which I now live in the flesh I live by faith in the Son of God, who loved me and gave Himself for me" (Gal. 2:20).

The Struggle toward Holiness

We may attempt to change bad habits that dominate our lives, but we cannot do battle with the passions unless we surrender ourselves in humility to God, for such change can come about only by God's grace. Struggle as we may, our flesh will resist until the moment we seek help from the Lord of mercy, who is quick to hear our plea for help.

When we invite Christ into our hearts, it is important that we keep His commandments and follow His example. To expect Christ to change our behavior without us making an effort of our own is to invite failure. The Christian life is one of ascetic struggle—and not just in regard to keeping the fasts and standing in prayerful vigil. If we are to be transformed by the power of the Holy Spirit, we must put the message of the Gospels into practice.

If there is someone we don't like, we must put on Christ, interacting with that person as though we did love him, for by being obedient to Christ, we will find that we can, indeed, love him. If we find ourselves being jealous of another person, say a coworker who has received a promotion, we must congratulate her and offer our support. Even if others are telling us we should have been the one who received the promotion, we embrace the decision of office management as though it came from God and as an opportunity to grow in humility.

It is easy to compartmentalize our Christian faith, reserving the "spiritual" for times spent in church. However, it is in the day-to-day, mundane moments that we can find opportunities to grow in Christ. These are the moments when we must put into action what we've received during the services, knowing that Christ is providing us the means by which we can attain the sanctification that makes us one with Him.

If we think our journey into the heart should be easy, we are fooling ourselves.

The Gift of Life

This earthly life we have been given has no meaning unless we see it as a workshop for the future life. We must not neglect what is of an eternal nature, for the Creator has bestowed this life upon us as a time of preparation for eternity with Him. This is the time when we should be progressing from God's image to God's likeness. This life takes a tragic turn if we do not look beyond the confines of this earthly existence, for the gift of love that is Christ helps us escape the nightmare of an all-consuming death.

The Apostle Paul gives an account of the Christian understanding of death, saying, "When this corruptible has put on incorruption, and this mortal has put on immortality, then shall be brought to pass the saying that is written: 'Death is swallowed up in victory'" (1 Cor. 15:54). It is in this life that we "put on Christ," for in doing so we attain the holiness that is necessary for us to stand in the presence of God for all eternity and not be burned. To focus on this life as anything but a time of preparation for eternity is to ignore the reality that God has given us life for that purpose.

The Importance of Cemeteries

Cemeteries can play a role in our spiritual lives, for they are clear reminders of our mortality. I have already picked the plot on the grounds of our monastery where my remains will be placed. Seeing where I will eventually be laid to rest is a good way to remember my eventual death, reminding me of my mortality and that I need to use my remaining days wisely.

In ancient times, pagans either burned the bodies of their dead or left them for birds to consume, whereas Jews and Christians placed their dead in tombs or in the earth to await the bodily resurrection. The belief that the body was the temple of the Holy Spirit and therefore sacred made the burning of bodies unacceptable. Bodies of the dead were always to be treated with great reverence. Today the Orthodox Church forbids bringing cremated remains into the temple for services or for any other reason, and holding funeral services over cremated remains is forbidden.

My parents converted to Orthodoxy in their mid-seventies and are buried in the churchyard next to St. John the Baptist Church in Post Falls, Idaho. Having them in an Orthodox cemetery, side by side, means a lot to me, and I visit their graves whenever I am in Northern Idaho visiting my family.

Having a plot to visit continues that connection and allows me a chance to show my love for them by placing flowers on their graves as I offer prayers for their souls. It saddens me that so many people have deprived themselves of such moments, having spread their loved one's ashes over a golf course or on a beach. I am convinced the loss of family cemeteries has contributed to the breakdown of the all-important extended families that were at one time so important to the cohesiveness of family values.

Are These the End Times?

The cultural and spiritual warfare taking place between the "Christian" West and the Islamic Middle East, together with the extreme climate changes taking place around the world, have become a source of concern for many. These issues, coupled with the polarization of the people within the United States and the mass apostasy from Christianity in the West, have many Christians thinking we must be entering the period of the end times.

Yet when we consider the words of the Our Father, "Thy will be done, on earth as it is in heaven," we must know that our prayers do make a difference. The faithful of the early Church looked at events taking place in their world as possible signs of the imminent Second Coming of Christ, yet they kept their focus on the possibility that there could be a "first resurrection," as described in the twentieth chapter of the Book of Revelation, where the Church would experience a triumph in this world.

It is this hope that must be the ground of our daily living, for as Christians we are not to be giving ourselves over to fate but to the hope that comes from Christ. God is in charge, and He is not bound by anything. When we pray, "Thy will be done," we must mean it!

APRIL 3

Our Homegrown Philanthropic Selves

As any history buff knows, these times we are living in can seem like reruns. News reports are filled with stories of wars, disasters, dictators, attacks on the innocent, increased crime, and the ever-present persecution of Christians in various parts of the world. With the Arab Spring, we've witnessed increased attacks against Coptic Christians in Egypt as well as the expulsion of the entire Christian population from parts of Syria. Political unrest is happening in many parts of the world, and genocide is being perpetrated upon ethnic groups in parts of Africa. The American economy is in shambles, not unlike what was seen in Germany prior to World War II, and the percentage of homeless families is nearing the percentage during the Great Depression.

Times like ours call for us to become spiritually fit so we can be beacons of light among those who have lost all hope. The challenges we all face are not for the faint of heart. The spiritually fit can triumph over anything, and we must continue to encourage this new generation of young people to be prepared for whatever may be coming. Those who have developed a strong faith must be willing to share their faith-based strength with those who are on the edge.

What is missing, it seems to me, is a sense of community, of a people who are united to find solutions and who are not at war with each other. During times like these, we must refocus our attention on the things that build community. Rather than giving ourselves over to entertainment or online friendships (which are not always bad), we can involve ourselves in philanthropic activities.

APRIL 4

The Power and Influence of Good Deeds

For this is the will of God, that by doing good you may put to silence the ignorance of foolish men.

1 Peter 2:15

Bishop Nikolai Velimirovic tells us in *The Prologue from Ochrid* that we are better off if we do not engage others in lengthy debates and fruitless discussions; we can better change their hearts by our love and good deeds. Arguing with others, even over matters of faith, is usually a fruitless venture that rarely leads the other to ponder the truth of your words. Better to demonstrate truth by holiness of life, patience, and kindness in our responses. Exchanging heated words most often leads to a standoff, where only the demons win in the end. Bishop Nikolai writes:

> *It is difficult, my brethren, to dispute with an atheist; it is difficult to converse with a stupid man; it is difficult to change an embittered man. It is only with the greatest difficulty that you will convince an atheist, a stupid man, or an embittered man, with words.*
>
> *If you argue with an atheist on his own diabolical terms, you simply strengthen the demon of atheism. If you converse with a stupid man in a spirit of derision, the darkness of stupidity will be made the greater. If you think to change a bitter man by anger, you will merely add more fuel to the fire of bitterness.*[7]

Responding to the embittered person, the angry person, or the stupid person, while hoping to win him over, does nothing for him and eventually gives power to the demon who would devour the man's soul—and your own. Thinking you have to prove the correctness of your point of view does nothing for truth but only gives power to the demons of pride, anger, and stupidity. The power and influence of good deeds always wins out in the end.

APRIL 5

God in Art and Music

Some time ago I wrote, "Some secular music sounds like it had its birth in the depths of hell." Certainly music itself cannot come from Satan, for it is given birth in the creative minds of people. Some people, however, are influenced by evil powers, and their music and their art can appear as though it had come from the depths of hell.

We are created in God's image and share in a lesser way our Creator's ability to create. However, not all art and music is good, for some is influenced by our fallen nature. Overcoming the impact of the Fall is humankind's true vocation, and when we act in concert with God's will, our creative and artistic abilities reflect the beauty of God. The most beautiful music and the most sublime art reflect God's creation in a pure way.

Music with foul language and harsh tones does not reflect the sublime nature found at the core of the human heart. The connection between the human artist and the Creator God, the ultimate Artist, can be found only in beauty. True art and music are a reflection of the soul that is journeying into the heart of God and is a mirror of God's beauty and light.

APRIL 6

The Inverted Pyramid and the Way of Humility

The recently glorified St. Sophrony of Essex, England, himself the spiritual son and biographer of St. Silouan of the Holy Mountain, wrote that empirical existence is like a pyramid: at the top sit the powerful of the earth, who exercise dominion over others, and at the bottom stand the common people, who demand equality and justice and who are not satisfied with this "pyramid of being."

Christ, however, took this pyramid and inverted it, putting Himself at the bottom, becoming its Head. In taking upon Himself the weight of our sin, He showed us that we must go downward to be united with Him, the Head of the inverted pyramid, because it is there that the fragrance of the Holy Spirit is found. At the bottom of this inverted pyramid, the power of divine life is to be found. It is therefore essential for us to find the way to go down, which is the way of humility, the way of the Lord.

Being Sensitive to Other People's Crosses

We humans are capable of great sensitivity and compassion, yet we are also capable of much cruelty. The outpouring of aid and support received by Japanese citizens following the terrible earthquake and tsunami is an example of human hearts being opened wide. The international organizations that bring children born with deformities to Western countries for treatment demonstrate the capacity for charity that resides within the human spirit.

Yet we are also capable of terrible cruelty. Staring at people with facial deformities or who may have peculiar, physically malformed bodies may satisfy our innate curiosity, but the cruelty inflicted upon the sufferer is great. As a child, I learned the importance of being sensitive to other people's differences, for I was raised in a family that had a number of members with inherited deformities, from a goiter to dwarfism to an enlarged head.

When I was in grade school, a time when children can be cruel, I befriended classmates who were rejected by other children. One girl came from a Gypsy family and had pierced ears at a time when even adult American women rarely had them. I also befriended a classmate with a deformed leg who had transferred from another school in the middle of the year.

I was not an exceptional child, just a little boy who was blessed to grow up in a family with wonderful, loving relatives who were, in a few cases, different. All my relatives demonstrated the importance of accepting others just as God had created them. As all children do, I watched the adults in our extended family and learned the importance of charity, love, and acceptance.

These are lessons I always shared with my high school students, for I learned that young people are open, if only someone is willing to demonstrate to them the importance of cultivating a sympathetic and loving heart.

APRIL 8

Take the First Step: Draw Nigh to God

While I was pumping gas in Seattle recently, a man on the opposite side of the pumps asked me how one could begin a relationship with God. He said he'd really like to know God but didn't know how to begin.

Wishing I had more time to speak with him, I gave him my card and invited him to call me when he had the opportunity. I also told him I would be happy to have him come to Vashon Island for a sit-down conversation in my office, anytime he felt the need.

As we were parting ways, I quoted James 4:8: "Draw near to God and He will draw near to you." The simplest prayer can begin a lifelong relationship with God, because our God desires that we commune with Him. Letting God know we'd like a relationship is the basic first step. God will do the rest.

I hope the man calls me.

APRIL 9

When You Fall, Get Up Again

We often fail to keep God's commandments and find ourselves despondent—unable, it seems, to make progress in the battle over our sins. When the same sins constantly plague us, despondency is our enemy. It is the tool demons use to distract us from the goal, making us feel we will never attain holiness. The demons want us to give up the battle, and despondency is their chief ally.

Holiness requires struggle, and the despondent person is unable to see the possibility of victory, so she surrenders to despair. The first step toward victory is simple. We just get up again. If you fall a second time, get up a second time. However many times we have to get up, we do so keeping our gaze on Christ, through whom we are given the grace to conquer the repetitive sins that plague us.

By keeping our eyes on Jesus Christ, we are empowered to move toward holiness of life, for the good that rises up in our hearts comes from Him. As we struggle for transformation of heart, even if we fall a dozen times, we do make progress, and each step we take brings us closer to the Kingdom of God.

Asceticism: Living in Total Commitment

Christianity is a religion of asceticism; it instructs us to store up our treasures in heaven, where the benefits have eternal value. Throughout the New Testament, we read of the importance of struggle, where focus on the acquisition of a humble and contrite heart is paramount to what it means to be a Christian. The Lord Jesus Christ tells us that if we are to be worthy of Him, we must be willing to take up our cross and follow Him. He calls us to holiness, and this change of heart can be brought about only through struggle.

Our world places a great deal of emphasis on being comfortable, and we tend to avoid anything that does not bring pleasure. If being open about our Christian faith invites ridicule, we remain silent. If keeping the fasting rules of the Church prevents us from enjoying evenings out with our friends, we ignore the fast. Is it any wonder we are therefore unprepared to stand firm when facing real trials that come our way, having avoided the very things that would transform us into strong, committed Christians?

If we embrace Christianity with dedication of heart and mind, we receive the power to live in this world—filled as it is with temptations and disappointments. This helps us remain true to our vocation as a holy people. Committing ourselves to being full-time Christians empowers us to live in such a way that we give glory and witness to the very Christ whom we worship.

If, however, we avoid ascetic struggle and choose to keep our Christian faith sidelined, rejecting real commitment, we will ultimately become Christian in name only. Those who choose to relegate fasting, private prayer, and even church attendance to something done only when they are "in the mood" will stand before the throne of God in the end with a darkened heart that cannot withstand the power of God, and eternity will be a lake of fire.

APRIL 11

Created with Free Will

One of the primary differences between Islam and Christianity has to do with their understanding of the nature of God. Islam teaches total surrender to Allah, who demands submission. There is no invitation to enter into a relationship freely, nor is there room for an individual to choose or not choose to love the Creator, for Allah is far above his creation.

By contrast, the God of Christianity is one who invites us into a relationship that is personal. As in all relationships based on love, we are free to choose to commune—or not—with a God who is, by His very nature, relational. There is no force behind this invitation, for we are free to choose—or not—just as any relationship based on love requires both parties to be free to choose—or not. Our obedience is a religious act that must be free, and it must be based on love.

Our Lord Jesus Christ used parables to teach, precisely because He was inviting us to freely choose to follow Him and to keep His commandments. He showed us the way to eternal life, not by giving commands as the Son of God, but as a loving teacher whose wisdom was imparted in a way that left the choice up to us.

Muhammad, by contrast, gave his followers specific laws that must be followed, including total submission to Allah. And should they ever renounce Islam, they would face a penalty of death. This lack of freedom in the teachings of Muhammad has its roots in his failure to teach about the notion of personhood.

In Christ we have the image of the Pantocrator, a fresco that is traditionally the primary focus in the dome of an Orthodox temple. The Pantocrator is He who holds all things in His hands, through His love and forbearance. This God of Christianity does not punish; He educates, just as Christ educated His disciples through the use of parables.

God Is Heard in the Silence of the Heart

The very heart of Orthodox monasticism is found in *hesychia*—that is, keeping stillness. The hesychast denies in order to affirm. Based on Christ's injunction in the Gospel of St. Matthew to "go into your room" to pray (6:6), hesychasm has traditionally been the process of retiring inward by ceasing to register the input of the senses, in order to achieve an experiential knowledge of God.

St. Isaac the Syrian said it is better to acquire inner purity than to convert the whole world of heathens from error. Venerable Isaac was not discounting missionary work but simply saying that unless we acquire a peaceful heart, we cannot accomplish anything else.

In this world filled with noise, we must make time for silence, for God speaks to us in the silence of our heart. This seeking after silence is not world-denying but world-embracing.

APRIL 13

The Temple: Where Heaven and Earth Are Joined

Whenever we have non–Orthodox visitors, I am touched by the looks on their faces as they gaze for the first time on the sublime, otherworldly beauty of the interior of our little temple. This first glimpse leaves them silent as they attempt to process something that seems foreign, yet so familiar. It is as though they have taken a peek into heaven itself, which is really what they are experiencing.

Orthodox temples and churches bespeak the truth of the Orthodox teaching that there is no separation between the Church Militant here on earth and the Church Triumphant in heaven, for they are places where heaven and earth come together. Within them, the divine services gather mortals and link us in worship before the throne of God, joining us to the cloud of witnesses spoken of in the Scriptures.

The Orthodox depictions of the saints are reminders that they stand before us as witnesses, by their lives, to the truth that eternal life is a reality. Because of Christ's redemptive act on the Cross, the saints are not dead, but alive, and together we all gaze upon the glory of Christ in the Kingdom of heaven. The great grace that resides within these depicted saints allows them to embrace the whole world with their love, for they see how we languish in affliction, and they never cease to intercede for us before the throne of God.

The saints depicted in icons, having won the good fight, witness to the importance of living in repentance and of placing Jesus above all else, for it is in Him that they have gained eternal life. It is in Him that we, like the saints who have gone before us, have the same promise of immortality. As our friends, they await the day when we will join them, and they offer their prayers for that end. In gratitude and love, we kiss their holy icons, knowing they are our true friends and family and that we are united with them as one, in Christ Jesus our Lord.

Thinking about Our Own Death

St. Sisoes, the great ascetic, stood before the tomb of Alexander the Great and beheld the skeletal remains of one who had once been covered in magnificent garments. Astonished, the saint mourned for the vicissitudes of time and the transience of glory, and he tearfully proclaimed, "The mere sight of you, tomb, dismays me and causes my heart to shed tears as I contemplate the debt we, all men, owe. How can I possibly stand it? Oh, death! Who can evade you?"

As a police and fire chaplain, I have attended more funerals during the past few years than in all my previous years combined. Many of these officers were killed in the line of duty, often by criminals whose lives were being thoughtlessly lived out and whose own end will likely be tragic, given the eternal consequences of their actions. During these past few years, I have also lost a number of old friends, and given my age, I expect to lose more friends as the years progress.

Death will come for us all, and it is to our benefit not to avoid the thought, for we never know when we will be required to account for our lives. Our days of fasting should be filled with thoughts of our own eventual death and how we should use whatever time God has given to us in repentance for our own sins and in service to others.

For the Christian, death itself is not to be feared, for Christ's Holy Resurrection will be ours as well. Yet we also know that in order to be joined to His Kingdom, we must have been transformed, that the fire of God will not be a lake of fire for us.

APRIL 15

"Are You Saved?"

Most of us have been asked the question "Are you saved?" at least once. Having its origin in Protestant soteriology (doctrine of salvation), this question has clearly become part of our American cultural lexicon. It is often asked by evangelical Christians as a way of establishing whether we are fellow "born-again" Christians and therefore fellow believers.

Believing that a declaration of Jesus Christ as one's Savior guarantees eternal life is comforting. Yet for the Orthodox Christian, the question can be disconcerting, even awkward, for we would never presume to think of ourselves as saved. We could say we are being saved, and hope to be saved, but we would never be so presumptuous as to declare we are saved.

Like our evangelical friends, we Orthodox Christians understand that Christ's death on the Cross was accomplished for our salvation and that salvation is a gift. We know that we are not saved by our works and that we, "having been justified by faith" (Rom. 5:1), are totally dependent on God's mercy for our salvation. Yet we have a parting of the ways when it comes to the theology of redemption.

Like the ancient Church, we believe that an intellectual acceptance of Christ as our Savior is only the beginning of a life journey into the heart of God. At the moment we declare Christ as our Savior, the therapy begins, and we are drawn into the hospital of the soul (the Church). There we begin the transformation that leads to deification, which is completed only with our cooperation with God's grace.

In the Parable of the Good Samaritan, we see the image of Christ, who cures the wounded man by leading him to the inn, which is the Church. Christ is the physician who cures, and the cure takes place within the hospital, which is the Church. We cannot say that we are saved, for we have been given this life wherein we are to cooperate with God's grace and be transformed into His likeness, that we might be capable of spending eternity in His divine presence without being burned.

Can a Christian Be Racist?

It is important to understand that, genetically, all humans are of one race. Indians, Arabs, Jews, Caucasians, Africans, and Asians are not different races, but different ethnicities of the human race. God created all humans with the same physical characteristics, with only minor variations. Furthermore, He created all humans in His image and likeness (Gen. 1:26–27) and has invited all of us to enter into communion with Him. A black man is just as much my brother as a fellow Norwegian with blue eyes like mine.

In the Book of Acts we read that with the coming of the Holy Spirit, diverse languages were being spoken. And in Revelation we see a glimpse of eternity with men and women from every tongue, tribe, and nation making up the choir of eternal praise (Rev. 7:9). That the writers of Scripture took notice of ethnicity and saw diversity as good makes it impossible for a Christian to hold to thoughts of racial superiority or separation of the races.

The Apostle John acknowledged prejudice concerning Jesus when he recorded that Nathanael exclaimed, "Can anything good come out of Nazareth?" (John 1:46). How can we dare hold to racist opinions when the Lord Jesus Christ presented parables that even offended the religious leaders of His time? The Parable of the Good Samaritan (Luke 10) and the story of the Samaritan woman at the well (John 4) make it impossible for us to hold to ideas of ethnic superiority. Even our Orthodox iconography intentionally reflects the full range of skin hues.

All forms of racism, prejudice, and discrimination are affronts to the work of Christ on the Cross. Jesus Christ died that all might be saved. Ethnicity should mean nothing for the Christian, and our parishes should demonstrate the truth of the ethnic diversity of the Kingdom of God. If we hold to racist beliefs, we only demonstrate how far we have distanced ourselves from the teachings of our Lord.

Can a Christian be a racist? The answer is an emphatic no!

APRIL 17

Holding on to Guilt and Shame

Many people cling to memories of past sins, reliving things long ago confessed as though they happened yesterday. They struggle with regrets, often revisiting shame as though they were archeologists, digging for historical artifacts that must be preserved.

Such is not the case with God, for His interest is not in our past but in our future. Confessed sins are counted as nothing, for God looks with interest on the transformed heart that has been made anew through contrition. God looks to our future, for His loving mercy is upon those who have confessed their sins, and those sins are counted as nothing. God is interested in what we are doing with our future, and as a loving Father, He takes pleasure in the steps we take in our journey toward Him.

For us to look back is to reject the role of confession, for if we cling to regrets, we are rejecting the meaning of repentance—a change of heart. To repent is to take a direction that is all about the future.

Transformation does not happen in an instant but is a journey toward holiness. And as long as we look to the future with hope, transformation of the heart continues, and our past becomes but a fading memory.

APRIL 18

Being the Leaven in a Post-Christian Era

As Christians in this post-Christian era, we must live with the knowledge that God still reigns, even though the evidence is to the contrary. In this era, we are like exiles, but like the Jews who were in bondage under the Babylonians, we cannot live in the past, remembering only the time when society was Christian. Nor can we focus on critiquing the present secular age. Rather, we must become the leaven for restoring the faith of our neighbors.

We must energize the nation by being agents of love, mercy, beauty, and peace. We must become the reconciling force between the secular world and God. Even if our churches are closed for lack of membership, we must be living repositories of the wisdom and grace of faith, bringing about, by our lives, the restoration of Christianity in this age of unbelief. We must show our neighbors what love looks like and be that shining light of Christ in this age of darkness. We must not let this era change us; we must change this era.

APRIL 19

Embracing Absolute Truth

In an age when many people think truth is relative, the knowledge that there is such a thing as absolute truth can be comforting. The knowledge that we are able to embrace teachings that are a continuation of an unbroken line dating back to apostolic times is liberating. As Orthodox Christians, we do not face the troubling task of interpreting the Scriptures anew, or deciding moral and dogmatic teachings for ourselves, or trying to make our faith relevant for this age. Rather, we can immerse ourselves in the knowledge that we have embraced the mind of the ancient universal Church.

We haven't had to reinvent the Faith, because we have aligned ourselves with the Church that is both ancient and relevant for the modern seeker. We know the Church's teachings are not based on the finite mind or the imagination of our own fallen nature, but on the eternal truths that have endured from ancient times.

It is comforting to know that the Church has remained true to her inheritance for some two thousand years. It is liberating to know ancient Christian dogmas, ways of worship, and moral teachings are guiding our lives, just as they have for two thousand years.

Truth is not relative, but absolute. There is no greater freedom than to be able to receive as our own the transcending truth that has made saints from ancient times. There is no greater freedom than being able to embrace the absolute truth that has transcended time, space, culture, and race. There is no greater joy than to be counted as belonging to Christ and being joined to the very Church He founded.

Human Reason and the Knowledge of God

There is the seen and there is the unseen, the material and the immaterial. The material can be scientifically examined and experienced; the immaterial can only be seen and experienced spiritually. These two worlds are only seemingly at odds with one another. If you attempt to examine things of a spiritual nature using a science that is by its very nature meant to explore the material realm, you will fail.

The things that are of God are far beyond the capabilities of our finite mind to comprehend. The divine can be known only through the nous, that place in the heart that is our true center. The nous is capable of knowledge that is beyond the brain's comprehension.

When we try to apply words to what is apprehended by the nous, we fail. We can no more explain God than we can explain quantum physics, since both are unseen. God is outside the realm of human intellectual understanding. The Eastern Church approaches things of God as mysteries, since God can be known only in His divine energies, not in His essence. If scientists can believe in quantum physics, the unseen, why can't they believe in God, whom they have not seen? If we can believe in the concept of infinity, something that goes on and on without end, why can't we believe in God?

The soul can be examined and experienced only through the activation of the nous. The nous in Orthodox Christian theology is the eye of the heart or soul, or the mind of the heart. God created us with the nous because the human intellect is not capable of knowing Him without it; human reasoning is limited to things of a material nature. God is unknowable without His divine revelation, and only the nous can perceive this knowledge. Science has its place, but only the heart can know God.

APRIL 21

Collaborating with God

I f we are to be healthy spiritually, we must cooperate with God's divine grace. The nous, the center of our being, is the noetic energy that functions in the heart of every spiritually healthy person. Only the Holy Spirit can bring about the healing of the nous, but such healing requires our cooperation. We must collaborate with God's grace if we are to be healed and made whole. Healing takes place when our nous is made "free of conceit and evil," according to St. Gregory Palamas.

When we immerse ourselves in the life of the Church, we become collaborators with the action of the Holy Spirit, and the road to healing is opened to us. Our life in Christ changes us, and we become the children of the Most High. This is a gift of God because of His great mercy; but because He has created us with free will, our cooperation is necessary.

Our Thoughts Determine Our Lives

*Our life depends on the kind of thoughts we nurture. If our
thoughts are peaceful, calm, meek, and kind, then that is what
our life is like. If our attention is turned to the circumstances in
which we live, we are drawn into a whirlpool of thoughts and can
have neither peace nor tranquility.*

Elder Thaddeus of Vitovnica

Having been created in the image of God, we are part of the divine
thought that was made material in time and space. We not only influence those around us with our thoughts, but we even influence the cosmos.
If we focus on the negative, those negative thoughts affect everyone around
us, and even the whole world. Elder Thaddeus tells us we can be either very
good or very bad, depending on the thoughts and desires we breed.

A lot is wrong with the world, but it begins with us. If there is to be
peace in our world, it must begin with us. If hatred, anger, envy, lust, and
spite are to end, it must end with us. When we allow destructive thoughts
to destroy our peace, the peace around us is destroyed. We cannot blame
the world or even those around us, for what happens around us radiates
from us. Blame for all that is wrong with the world cannot be placed
beyond our own hearts.

The Dark Night of the Soul

Sometimes we enter a dark night of the soul, where God seems distant from us. This is only an illusion, for God is closer to us than our own breath. These times are allowed by God to bring us closer to Him, much as a loving mother stands her child on his feet, walks a few feet away holding out her arms, and waits for the child to take his first steps. She is ever ready to reach out and lift the child up should he start to fall, but she knows she must distance herself for a few moments if the child is going to learn to stand on his own two feet. We are like that.

When you find it difficult to pray, light your lamp before your icons and sit silently before them. Say to God, "I am unable to speak to You, so I need You to speak to my heart." Sometimes the most profitable spiritual growth can take place in such periods of brokenness because we see in those moments how very much we need God and depend upon Him.

Be not fearful, dear ones, for God is near and will not leave you. The Lord is allowing dry moments in which you fear He has left you as the way of making you reach out to Him. When we are struggling, or even suffering, we grow stronger in our faith. Prayer will return as long as you give God moments in your life when you avail yourself of silence and listen for His voice.

The parent who constantly does a child's homework does her no favor, for the child never learns to stand on her own and will forever remain dependent on her parent. The Lord wants us to grow strong in our faith while entering into a mature relationship with Him. If we do not learn to stand on our own, we will forever be like a dependent child, never having the skills to reach high places and forever remaining weak and fearful.

Arming Our Children with Spiritual Weapons

It is essential that we expose our youths to the teachings of the Church and offer them serious facts about traditional Christianity, while letting them see that faith is not simply a religious expression of the ethnic heritage of their parents, not simply a family tradition. If our youths don't know the faith and are not helped in making faith their own and internalizing it into their hearts, how do we expect to break the decline in church attendance that is happening across the nation? If we insist on being aloof in our priestly bearing, how will the youths feel free to come to us with their doubts and struggles with belief in God?

How will these wonderful young people resist the secularism, humanism, and atheism that are pounded into their young minds, if we do not arm them with a faith that can withstand the challenges of professors and classmates who set out to destroy what they would call "the provincial and ethnic beliefs taught by backward parents, uneducated grandparents, and self-serving clergy"?

We are at war! If we don't arm our children with spiritual weapons, they will be lost to the enemy, and we will have only ourselves to blame. If our faith is to them a backward religion they don't understand, and if they do not sense the love of Christ in the hearts of their parents, priests, and bishops, they will depart to the greener pastures of a society that has had it with religious pomposity, hypocrisy, and scandal. If the youths don't feel loved and respected by their bishops and priests, they will turn against all we stand for, and we will see them only at our ethnic church bazaars and the occasional wedding or funeral.

If these youths are not taught the True Faith and helped to make it their own by our example of holiness of life and by our love for them, they will not have the armor and ammunition to withstand the atheism of our age. And they will be lost.

Suffer Criticism as Profitable for Your Salvation

If we stop rejecting the criticism of others, be it justified or unjustified, and see such criticism as profitable for our salvation, we will gain a great spiritual treasure. When we gain the ability to see our own sinfulness, we see that even the good deeds we do are saturated with sin. When we have gained the humility that comes from embracing the criticism of others, we will see that we are unable to heal ourselves, but are entirely dependent upon God as our only source of healing.

When we take notice of our own sinfulness, we stop judging others, seeing in them the same pitiful state and realizing that they are our kinfolk and that we are all journeying together toward God. They can no longer hurt or offend us with their criticism, for we pity them, just as we pity ourselves for our own sinfulness, and we see them as our friends in this common struggle for sanctification and holiness.

The famous Russian abbot of the 1950s and '60s, Father Nikon, was said to have told a spiritual child that when he sees his own sin, he stops exalting some and belittling others, seeing everyone as his brother or sister. He begins to love everyone as his co-struggler.

APRIL 26

Being Transparent before God

Transparency of the heart must rule if we are to have an honest relationship with God. Nothing can be hidden from the Lord, yet we often live as though we could hide what we know is not pleasing to Him. Putting on a face may work with relatives, but trying to fake piety and goodness does not work with God. If we are truly desirous of a relationship with God, we must begin by being honest with ourselves, confronting that part of us that needs to be changed.

Honesty with self begins with confession, revealing our sins openly and without reservation to our confessor. Because it is easy to hide the truth from ourselves, the role of the confessor becomes all the more important, for the priest acts as a witness before Christ, helping us dig deeper, exposing the sin that needs to be rooted out. It is impossible to continue a charade when we have revealed our faults before a witness, and the spiritual direction we receive from our confessor helps us in our struggle for conversion of life.

Transformation begins with the grace that is received from God when we have made a good confession, which helps us set the course for change. Being honest with our confessor is like washing a very dirty window. We can see through the window for the first time; the nous is opened, making way for the Lord to take up residence in our heart. This cleansing of the nous is a cleaning up of the pollution that has kept us trapped in bad behavior and unable, or perhaps unwilling, to look closely at our darkened, corrupted self. With this transparency comes compunction, and with compunction comes the gift of tears, washing away the grit and grime that has darkened the nous and kept God at bay.

Hollow Orthodoxy

We must guard against noticing when another parishioner seems careless in making the sign of the cross, while we go about demonstrating the proper way for all around us. When we make sweeping signs of the cross in such a way as to be almost a caricature, followed by profound bows, we can end up distracting fellow worshipers. If we make a public display of our fasting, making sure our non-Orthodox family and friends know how strict we are, we miss the point of fasting. If we struggle to make our icon corner the largest and most complete of any in the parish, but never stand before it in prayer, we treat it as nothing more than art.

If we allow ourselves to become spiritual gluttons and turn the traditions of Orthodoxy into occasions for sensual and prideful displays, we will not embrace the grace that can be ours through quiet and penitential struggle. If our public displays of piety become distractions for fellow worshipers, we can be diverting our attention from the all-important confrontation of our personal sin. Externals, while important to Orthodox piety and the deepening of our faith, must not be allowed to replace the mystery of faith that comes only with the acquisition of a humble and contrite heart.

We must remember that these traditions and pious practices were designed to serve as aids for deepening our faith by connecting our bodies and souls on this journey to God. Without giving our full attention to the struggle for holiness and deepening our prayer time, we will end with a weak form of Orthodoxy that is beautiful on the outside but hollow on the inside. Taking simple little steps under the guidance and direction of one's priest or spiritual father or the pious old woman whose face radiates the light of Christ, we will be able to enter into the Kingdom of God, having gained the humility and joy that do not necessitate being extravagant with the externals.

APRIL 28

The Necessity of Christian Friendships

In this age, when secularism is on the rise and materialism has become a major distraction from spiritual pursuits, Christian friendship has never been more important.

The pursuit of personal fulfillment, entertainment, worldly pleasure, and material goods is the dominant theme of our age. Families that once placed the life of the Church as the center of their week have drifted away from God. Having made idols of worldly pleasures and pursuits, their family life is focused on transitory goals, leaving them in a state of spiritual bankruptcy.

Our spiritual illness has infected our youths like a virus, leaving them with little to sustain them when times get tough. The economic, political, and social instability of our age demands that we be spiritually fit, yet we give our youths virtually nothing that will help them through the hardships ahead.

The life of a Christian has never been easy, but in an age that is proving to be hostile toward the things of God, Christian friendship is all the more important. We need each other. As we face a world that has rejected Christ, we need the encouragement that Christian friendship can give us. The unity we have when we receive the Body and Blood of the Savior during each and every celebration of the Divine Liturgy gives us strength to withstand whatever may be coming. When our culture, economy, and material world has fallen into ruin, only faith will have the power to sustain us.

It is only our faith, supported and strengthened by our fellowship in Christ, that will have the lasting power to keep us from falling into despair as our world enters into a darkness that will seem unconquerable. Lifting each other up as we share our faith in Christ, who came to make all things new, is the only hope we have. Let us not waste this life God has given us, but let us move forward in faith together, knowing that ultimately the gates of hell will not prevail against those who love God.

APRIL 29

Destructive and Addictive Behaviors

Twittering mindlessly for hours on end and spending whole evenings sitting before a computer, communicating with people whom we do not know personally and who may not even be who they claim to be, are examples of squandering time that would be spent better in spiritual pursuits. Forgoing time with family and friends in the room by texting someone is counterproductive to solid, healthy relationships. Allowing ourselves to be consumed with messaging, texting, or endlessly talking on cell phones is a form of self-destruction, for it ultimately leads to separation and alienation from profitable relationships.

Communal relationships, where we grow spiritually and socially, are all-important for anyone who desires to have a deeper relationship with God, for such relationships become the foundation stone for learning true love. It is not possible to become a loving person if we turn ourselves over to a life immersed in technology. Students who sit in lecture halls texting their friends are not participating in the learning process that is the hallmark of the classroom. People who leave their cell phones in vibrate mode while attending the divine services may be demonstrating that their friends are more important to them than the worship of God.

If we are going to mature in the faith, we have to take the steps that lead to a deepening of our relationship with God, just as we must do if we are to have successful marriages or lasting friendships. The age of technological advancement has its advantages, but it also has a dark side. When we spend the majority of our waking hours messaging, talking on mobile phones, and being lost in cyberspace, we've become self-destructive, having succumbed to an addictive behavior that blocks true spiritual, social, and mental growth. Living within the life of the Church—giving ourselves over to spiritual reading, personal prayer, frequent confession, and properly preparing to receive the Holy Mysteries—must be the priority of every Christian's week. Technology has its place, but it must not be allowed to become a god unto itself.

APRIL 30

Passing on the Gift of Love

My father was a golf pro during my grade-school and early mid-dle-school years, and the country club was the center of our fam-ily's social life. Our whole family golfed together. Those early years were wonderful, and I often think of how lucky I was to have been blessed with such wonderful, loving parents.

I was also fortunate to have a close relationship with both my father and my mother during the last years of their lives. As an adult, I had enough time to let both of them know how much I loved them and how I was a product of both their lives. I was able to tell my dad that I saw much of him in myself. I inherited his humor, comfortableness with all kinds of people, joy in life, love of history, and even his size. My mother's love of music, architecture, and interior design are also a part of me. They pro-vided me with the skills to work with an architect on the design of our monastery and to design all the interiors of our monastic buildings. I am clearly the inheritor of the best that my parents displayed in their lives, and I will forever be grateful to them.

Yet the most important gift I received from my parents was the gift of love. They demonstrated their love for me throughout their lives. They also showed me how to love others, and their willingness to be open to love and to demonstrate love eventually allowed me to love God. From my parents I discovered that God is not simply there as a cosmic prob-lem-solver or gift-giver but as One who loves me, just as they did. God, like my parents, first loved me, and the lessons of love I learned from my parents enabled me to be open to the love of God. In turn, the gift of love that came from my parents allowed me to see God not as my own private possession, but as One I wanted to share with others.

MAY 1

Political Ideologies and the Church

I was recently asked which political party I thought was the best fit for an Orthodox Christian. My response was that, as a servant of Christ's Church, I did not think I should answer. Within the Orthodox Church internationally, we Orthodox are politically aligned across the map. Yet, as Orthodox Christians, it is important that we remember our true allegiance should be to the Church herself and to Christ, her Founder and Head.

Political ideologues, political parties, and earthly rulers are a part of this world. In Christ, our true national identity should be Orthodoxy. Galatians 3:28 tells us that in Christ, we are "neither Jew nor Greek . . . neither male nor female." We could easily add, "Neither American nor Russian nor Norwegian." Our true identity is in Christ. For me, as an Orthodox priest, to push my own political opinions could potentially undermine the teaching authority of the Church regarding what is eternal and salvific.

Many years ago, a Greek politician ran for the presidency of our great nation. Although this man was a baptized Orthodox Christian, he did not hold to basic teachings of our Church, such as the sanctity of the life of the unborn. Additionally, his wife was not a Christian. Thus he was not an Orthodox Christian in good standing with the Church. Yet many Greek clergy (and bishops) rallied around him simply because he was a Greek.

It is important that the Church stand in witness to the moral and spiritual truths that are of eternal importance and not to things that are transitory. History is rife with stories of the Church being discredited in the minds of the common people because she failed to stand apart from the political powers of the day. The most important role of a priest—or a bishop, for that matter—is the proclamation of Christ's gospel and the eternal truth that we must love one another. All else is of this world.

MAY 2

Ask for Repentance

In our struggle on the path to God, repentance must be the central theme. Only in repentance do we find the true meaning of life, for only in repentance can we enter into communion with God. This life has been given to us for one purpose: that we might be deified and united with God, as was His purpose from the very beginning. In our fallen state, our brokenness keeps us separated from God, for our darkened nous cannot see clearly. Repentance changes our nous, clearing the way for complete union with Christ and making us whole.

Elder Paisios of Mount Athos said,

> *Ask for repentance in your prayer and nothing else, neither for divine lights, nor miracles, nor prophecies, nor spiritual gifts— nothing but repentance. Repentance will bring you humility, humility will bring you the grace of God, and God will have in His grace everything you need for your salvation, or anything you might need to help another soul.*[8]

Doubt: The Ultimate Sickness

On St. Thomas Sunday, the Church commemorates doubting Thomas. The Apostle Thomas, though he had been a disciple of Christ and had witnessed the Lord's many miracles, still insisted he would not believe in the Resurrection unless he could place his hands in the wounds of his Lord. In his doubt, the apostle revealed our ultimate sickness: unbelief.

This world is a great hospital wherein we are prepared for the Kingdom that is to come. In this hospital, we find our medicine for the cure of our sickness within the life of the Church, which is the hospital of the soul.

In this world, there is no medicine for this sickness, for the only medicine that can heal us is Christ Himself. If we are unwilling to receive this medicine, we will never be healed, and we will never know the joys of the eternal Kingdom that is to come. Our doubt is usually based on our failure to avail ourselves of the medicine that is abundantly available within the life of the Church.

The Lord said that those who have not seen yet believe are blessed. This faith comes as a free gift from a God who so loves us that He gave His only begotten Son that whoever believes in Him will have eternal life. All we need to do is cooperate with God's grace, and doubt will be gone. When we receive the Word of God into our hearts, we have touched His wounds. When we confess our sins and receive the Holy Mysteries of His Body and Blood, we have thrust our hand into His side. Doubt has, at that moment, no place to reside in our heart. And like the Apostle Thomas, we believe.

MAY 4

Asking for Miracles in Our Smugness

Asking for miracles in order to believe betrays a sort of smugness on our part; it's like asking for an expensive gift from a potential friend before considering his overture of friendship.

God could easily create miracles that would make all people believers, but He does not wish to interfere with our freedom. As God awaits our decision, will we respond to His love or not? He desires that we choose to commune with Him, not because of His power, but because of His love for us.

The person who demands a miracle is asking God to prove Himself worthy of being worshiped. This is no different from saying, "Give me a car for my birthday, Dad, and I'll consider loving you as my father." We must approach God in all humbleness of mind and heart, leaving the rest up to Him.

It is also quite possible that when a miracle does come our way, our smugness and pride prevent us from seeing it. I once asked a young Egyptian Christian why the Holy Virgin had appeared to crowds of people in Cairo, on the dome of St. Mary's Coptic Church, where many people, even Muslims, Jews, and atheists, were able to see her. He responded that Christians in the Middle East live in expectation of miracles, so when they come, they are not surprised, but receive them with joy. He went on to say that Westerners, in their collective pride, are skeptics who ignore miracles sent by God each and every day.

If we are awaiting the day when God will prove Himself to us, we fail to notice that He has been doing just that from the very beginning; our smugness and pride have blinded us to what has always been there.

MAY 5

Suffering with a Co-suffering Savior

When faced with tragedies, we must trust in God and not react, resent, or lose our peace. These things can happen for our purification and to prepare us for the world to come. Since we live in a fallen world, there is death and suffering, but all things are being made new in Christ. All things work together for good for those who love God, as the Scriptures say.

As Orthodox Christians, we don't believe in the gospel of prosperity—that is, if you believe, everything will go well. God allows things that will make us grow because He loves us. One elder who suffered greatly with an illness said, "I don't pray that I be healed but pray that I don't lose my faith." It is the work of the devil to try to get us to lose our faith.

God does not send us suffering and sorrow; our collective sin brings it on. God sends things that heal us. We are powerless against a world that is dark and full of hatred, ugliness, and death, but we must refuse to give ourselves over to that darkness. We must pray, immerse ourselves in the Liturgy, and continue to live for God. We live in witness to the eternal truth that Jesus Christ is alive and reigns in our heart. We have reason to be joyful, even when faced with suffering. We are comforted in our suffering, knowing that our Lord wept when hearing Lazarus had died. And He gives us the ability to be joyful, even as we weep with those who weep.

God allows us to suffer under heavy crosses during different times in our lives, but He does not leave us to suffer alone, for He is our co-suffering Savior, who lifts us up—if we let Him.

MAY 6

Avoiding Hypocrisy in Our Journey to God

It is very easy to live in hypocrisy if we are not mindful of the pitfalls of the spiritual life. We can become Pharisees without even noticing, if we let our Christianity be artificially lived. Putting on the mask of Christianity is not living in Christ. If we live as though a stage director had rehearsed us, we will accomplish nothing and will remain no more than actors. An honest, daily examination of our conscience, together with regular guidance from our confessor, is the only way we can live a Christian life that will lead to transformation of the heart.

If we simply put on a show of being a Christian without true repentance, we will remain mired in false religiosity, and our hearts will grow dark. Christ must be invited into the heart on a daily basis, through prayer and an honest examination of our conscience, without which there can be no spiritual growth. We cannot play at being Christians, for doing so leads to spiritual death.

We must "put on Christ" daily and make sure our public expression of our faith is not being acted out for others but that we are ever entering into a deeper relationship with this very Christ. Playing at spirituality only leads to spiritual death. If our life does not give witness to Christ in us, and if our attention is given over to self-promotion or a desire to please others but avoids an honest examination of our sins, we will be like fruit that dies on the vine.

MAY 7

The Economic Quagmire and Imagined Security

Our world is going through economic difficulties, with many families suffering great losses. Mortgage foreclosures have displaced many from their homes, and increasing numbers of children attending school are counted among the homeless. They live in motels or in family vans, feeling shame and despair. Husbands and fathers feel like losers as they are unable to find jobs to support their families.

At the same time, many others are doing very well. High-end restaurants in many cities have no shortage of customers. Two young engineers from Russia, who work part of the year in Seattle for the Boeing Company, told me that the restaurants in Moscow are frequented only by the very rich; the average person is unable to afford them. Due to high rental rates in many places, single city-dwellers are forced to live with roommates, something that was not necessary when I was a young man.

We are fast becoming a society of the haves and the have-nots. Many people who have abundance ignore the plight of those unfortunate enough to have lost everything, perhaps fearing they may be next. They've given themselves over to the pursuit of pleasure and enjoyment, like the grasshopper of storybook fame, fiddling away instead of preparing for winter.

Having a job and money often leads to a false sense of security, and we can get distracted from the real meaning of life. We dare not allow ourselves to ignore the spiritual, especially if we are feeling comfortable with our job security and abundance. All this could be taken away in an instant, and we would have squandered valuable time.

As a desert father said:

> *The eyes of pigs have a natural conformation which makes them*
> *turn towards the ground and they can never look up to Heaven.*
> *So is the soul of one who lets himself be carried away by pleasure.*
> *Once the soul is allowed to slip into the slough of enjoyment, she*
> *can no longer get out again.*[9]

The Church Shows Charity to Her Neighbors

Great and Holy Lent is the perfect time for us to support and enter into collaboration with charitable organizations such as RACS (Russian American Community Services), the Orthodox charity based in San Francisco that feeds hundreds of the poor. International Orthodox Christian Charities (IOCC), another worthy organization, is also deserving of our support. Almost every community has a food bank that is in desperate need of donated food, as the number of the poor and homeless grows at an astounding rate.

This is a time when the Church and her people face a need that offers us the chance to reflect on the cultural and spiritual issues related to charity. In the face of a "contemporary culture that promotes the marginalization of those who are weak, it is increasingly necessary to restore the centrality in the lives of Christians, of the encounter with the poor and their questions, especially in the context of uncertainty produced by the complexity and uncertainty of the globalized world" (from a statement by the Moscow Patriarchate).

St. Jerome said, "Our church walls sparkle with gold, which also glitters upon our ceilings—while the capitals of our pillars are lavishly decorated. The holy vessels are beaten out of costly elements and precious stones. Yet Christ is dying at our doors in the person of His poor, naked and hungry."

And St. Maria of Paris wrote, "At the Last Judgment I will not be asked whether I satisfactorily practiced asceticism, nor how many bows I have made before the divine altar. I will be asked whether I fed the hungry, clothed the naked, visited the sick, and the prisoner in his jail. That is all I will be asked."

MAY 9

A Mass of Sinners Living as the Presence of Christ

According to St. Ephraim the Syrian (306–373), "The Church is not the assembly of saints; it is the mass of sinners who repent, who, sinners though they are, have turned towards God and are oriented towards Him." As a people whose focus is on God, we are sinners who are committed to living as the presence of Christ in the world, and our holiness cannot be separated from the holiness of God at work in this world.

Our sin is a pervading sickness or a failure to achieve the goal of being truly human. We are called to fulfill our divine design and function as the created image of God. Our sin, therefore, does not merely imply guilt for violating God's commandments, but must also be the impetus for becoming something other than what we are in our fallen state. Because each of us has a unique experience, conquering our sinful habits requires all our attention and correction.

The ultimate goal of this salvific process is to become deified, which is simply to reflect the divine likeness. By becoming Christlike in our behavior and in our thinking, we cooperate with God in this healing process and are returned to God's likeness.

From this perspective we recognize our vocation as being Christ in the midst of this fallen world. For this world is called into the process of divinization. As we acquire a humble and contrite heart, we reveal Christ to the world and promote the transformation of the whole of the cosmos into the image and likeness of our Creator God.

MAY IO

The ER for the Soul

Orthodoxy offers a very precise way to enter into communion with God. It is a way that must be learned, for simply "becoming Orthodox" will not lead the seeker into an inner life that transforms and enlightens. Membership in the Church is not enough, for the Church is not just about beautiful services, icons, and mystical theology. As a hospital for the soul, it is a place where we can receive healing for what ails us.

Yet patients can't simply walk into an emergency room and expect to be healed. They have to submit themselves to examination by the ER staff, who ask them to describe what is going on and where they are hurting, who run tests, and who prescribe the necessary medication or treatment that will bring about healing.

Within the hospital of the soul—that is, the Church—priests act in the same capacity as ER personnel. They interview the patient (parishioner), examine the heart to find the sickness, and recommend the cure. The priest becomes the therapeutic guide, recommending what the parishioner can do in order to be made whole.

A prayer rule, the daily reading of the Holy Scriptures, and frequent confession and reception of the Holy Mysteries are all part of the Church's medicine that will bring about the cure. Just as the doctor prescribes the proper dosage after getting to know her patient, so the priest prescribes what will help his spiritual son or daughter.

The spiritual life needs to be learned, perhaps more so now than at any time in history. As godlessness increases, so do obstacles to spiritual progress. The degradation of the whole of our society and the depths of depravity that have become a normal part of our age have made this a dangerous time. Going it alone spirituality can leave one vulnerable to spiritual delusion. We all need a trusted and experienced guide who can help us avoid the pitfalls of the pride and self-will that would lead us down to perdition.

Render to God What Is God's

"Render to Caesar the things that are Caesar's, and to God the things that are God's" (Mark 12:17). These words, spoken by Christ to His disciples, are a good reminder to all of us to walk in all humbleness, love, and compassion. We must be quick to forgive others and to overlook, and even hide, the sins of our neighbor. We must speak out against injustice and work for peace and equality for everyone. We must become living icons of the Lord of mercy, letting the light of Christ shine through us.

Imposing moral suppositions on people is bound to fail, for only when we render unto God the things that are His do our hearts change. In our own transformation, the society around us will be changed, and that which is Caesar's will be transformed and made holy.

Force of arms changes nothing, for until people's hearts become the dwelling place of the Holy Spirit, our world will remain a place of injustice, wickedness, and all kinds of lawlessness, depravity, and evil. Infanticide and abortion, hatred, discrimination, lawlessness, and exploitation will continue unbridled until society itself is transformed by her people. Only when the population of a nation has entered into repentance can that nation, as a whole, become a holy people.

The Repentance of Egotism Trumps Alienation

The collective human condition is one of alienation from God, due to the sinful tendency of us all. Every problem in the world has its roots in this state of alienation. This includes divisions within families, nations, religions, social classes—all that keeps us apart. Only when we acquire peace, which is a gift from God, can this alienation be dispelled.

The root cause of alienation can be found in the ego, which sees itself as the center of everything and sees self as all-important; it caused the Fall of humankind. The cure of this spiritual illness is the acquisition of a humble and contrite heart.

When we struggle against the ego, with the desire to be transformed by the Holy Spirit, we see that all our neighbors, including those who are of other faiths, nations, and races, are our brothers and sisters (our relatives). We see that money, the acquisition of things, our social status, and our "tribe" are all but part of our collective human condition of alienation from God. Even our polluting of the environment and our cruelty to animals are related to that alienation.

Our world is on the brink of disaster, and we refuse to notice because we are so centered on ourselves. If we wonder why there are divisions among the peoples of the world, we need look no further than ourselves. When war breaks out with another country, we assume it is their fault, because, after all, "God is on our side." We are like families, always wanting to put the blame on one relative, yet refusing to believe that it might be we who are in need of change.

The only way to end this alienation is in true repentance. When we start to speak like the Apostle Paul, saying with true conviction, "I am the chief of sinners," grace abounds, and God changes our hearts. Without the acquisition of a humble and contrite heart, it will always be about "them."

Lay Monasticism: Your Commute Can Be a Monastic Cell

Over the past thirty years, I have lost count of the number of lay-people who have told me of their interest in monasticism. They find themselves drawn to the rhythms of silence, liturgy, study, prayer, and work. Many pious Christians feel a romantic tug toward a lifestyle that seems peaceful and worry-free. Many yearn for an elusive silence and spiritual depth, and they think it impossible for the ordinary layperson to cultivate regular times of deep, undistracted prayer. With the commute and jobs and bills and dinner and children, there seems to be no room for an inner life like those found in monasteries.

But a car, train, bus, or bike used to commute can actually serve as a monastic cell, a place cut off from the demands and noise of the world. Turn your commute into your sacred space and your car or train into a monastery. Instead of zoning out to music or news broadcasts, listen to podcasts from Ancient Faith Radio, pray the Morning and Evening Prayers, or listen to the Holy Scriptures or sacred Orthodox music. The Jesus Prayer is the perfect prayer for a commute, for it allows you to enter into a deep form of prayer, one that ushers in peace and joy and opens your heart wide to Jesus.

There will be days when the best approach for turning your commute into your monastic cell will be to simply turn off all outside stimulation and enter into the silence. Silence allows for that moment when we can begin to listen for the voice of God. It can initially be scary, for we've become so used to noise, music, and talk that silence makes us nervous. Yet it is in silence that we can begin to enter into the heart of God and usher in the peace of Christ, which will transform our hearts and give us the peace that has eluded us.

The Devil Cannot Violate Our Freedom

The devil does not have power over us—unless we give it to him. His power to tempt us or to fight against us is never beyond our ability to resist, for his power can never violate our freedom. We alone give him power over us, without which he can do nothing. It depends totally on us whether we succumb to his attacks against us. Any exercise of his evil authority is directly related to our decisions and whether we allow him to distort our freedom.

St. Symeon the New Theologian said that if the members of a person are not driven by Christ as chariots, they are driven by the devil with the consent and cooperation of that person.

We are never alone and vulnerable to the attacks of the evil one; the Fathers of the Church stress that God is with us. The Lord's grace is sufficient for us to resist the attacks of Satan.

MAY 15

Confession Leads to Conversion of Heart

The importance of having a regular confessor cannot be underestimated. Most of us find it uncomfortable to think about our faults, failures, and sins, because we like to feel good about ourselves. We puff up our image around others, brag about our accomplishments, and feign humility. We try to keep a good public image with our friends and coworkers while refusing to closely examine our behaviors that are in need of change.

Having a regular confessor is the very best way to orchestrate conversion of heart, for if we meet regularly with a priest who knows us, we have an ally who can help us see those sins we'd like to ignore. A regular confessor can help us work through the sins that have become habitual and help us attain true conversion of heart. He can direct us into a deeper prayer life, one that is based in repentance, and help bring about the transformation of our heart by God's grace.

Living a life of repentance allows us to have a relationship with Christ that enables conversion of heart, for only in the remembrance of God can conversion of heart take place. St. Diadochos of Photiki said, "Very few men can accurately recognize all their own faults; indeed, only those can do this whose intellect is never torn away from the remembrance of God."

MAY 16

The Danger of Prideful Self-Assurance

There is a minefield many do not notice, one that masquerades as the spiritual life. Academic theology, although it can be used in service to the Church, has been the spiritual destruction of many. True theology comes from the mastery of prayer and is not associated with academic pursuits. When theology becomes our philosophy, we are no different from the pagans. We give birth to pride, and self-assurance can become the minefield that brings about the destruction of our soul.

The true theologian is one who, through the mastery of prayer and the cultivation of humility, finds God noetically—that is, in the heart. Elder Paisios of Mount Athos said, "The devil does not hunt after those who are lost; he hunts after those who are aware, those who are close to God. He takes from them trust in God and begins to afflict them with self-assurance, logic, thinking, criticism. Therefore we should not trust our logical minds. Never believe your thoughts."[10]

Like the academic theologian, a monk who thinks himself an authority on the monastic life, but who has not lived in obedience to an elder, knows nothing of monasticism. For it cannot be studied from afar, but must be lived out in community, under obedience.

The acquisition of both a humble and a contrite heart is at the heart of Orthodox monasticism and theology, without which one can know nothing. St. John Chrysostom said in warning to those who would seek out the things of God without humility, "The path to hell is paved with the skulls of priests." None of us, perhaps especially the clergy, is immune to the temptation to think we know the things of God, when in fact we might know only the pride that has taken root in our academic pursuit of God. We must all guard our hearts, ripping away all traces of pride, for only then will we become true theologians. Theology without God is but philosophy. Monasticism without ascetic struggle and obedience is nothing but an alternative lifestyle.

Judging Others Instead of Myself

Every aspect of my life should be a reflection of my faith in Christ, yet I utterly fall short in living this out. I find it difficult to look closely at myself and at my relationships with others. How easily I fall into the trap of judging others, finding fault with them while allowing myself to avoid what needs to change in me.

In focusing on the failures of others, I postpone the day of my own repentance. I walk backward. Step by step, I retreat from the way of the Lord. I avoid true spiritual progress, clinging to self-will and to my ego. Trying desperately to preserve my honor, I sacrifice my inheritance.

As long as we concentrate on the failings of others, inner transformation will elude us, and the world will remain in darkness. If we remain stuck in the quagmire of sin and focused on the failings of others, we will fail in the work of conforming ourselves to the will of God.

It is much more personally comfortable to notice the failings and the sins of others, of course, but if we do not take stock of ourselves, we will do great harm to our soul. Judging others opens wide the gates for evil spirits to enter, laying waste the grace of baptism that resides within our hearts. We are in a battle against evil forces, and we had better be on guard. Our eternal life depends on it.

Start Out Your Day with God

Each and every day should begin with our thoughts turned toward God. At the very moment we open our eyes, we should be thanking the Lord for having slept through the night safely and giving thanks for a new day.

Every day before we leave for our job or make breakfast for the children or begin whatever our main task is, we should light our lamp, stand before our icons, and observe Morning Prayer. Before we walk out the door or start our work, we should offer ourselves in service to God, asking Him to keep us safe from all harm. And we should ask for help in living out another day according to the Gospels.

When we begin our day in prayer, we are empowered with a peaceful heart and enabled to bear witness to Christ. And our life shines forth in holiness and love.

The Obediences of Monasticism and Marriage

*He who wishes to tear up the account of his sins and to be
inscribed in the divine book of the saved, can find for this purpose
no better means than obedience.*

Ss. Callistus and Ignatius

One of the beautiful teachings of the Orthodox Church is about the role obedience plays in our journey to salvation. The Church teaches that there are two paths to salvation, both of which involve obedience. It is in obedience that we find the means of destroying the ego, which separates us from Christ.

These two paths involving obedience are monasticism and marriage. Both have obedience as their salvific role. The monk gives himself over to obedience to the monastery's rule and to the abbot. In marriage, the husband and wife give themselves over to each other in obedience. Thus, both monasticism and marriage teach us to put aside our own wants and desires, and to give ourselves over to the common good. This obedience is our way of surrendering to the will of Christ.

We Are Crucified with Christ

Central to living in all holiness of life is the acquisition of a humble and contrite heart. Humility does not come without contrition, and both are obtained with much suffering and trial. Spiritual reading, together with prayer, are necessary components of this journey to God, but they must be accompanied by spiritual direction, confession, and the acceptance of correction.

If we are so proud and puffed up that we swiftly take on the role of defense attorney when confronted with correction or the critique of another, we will simply fall further under the control of the ego, and humility will not be a part of our makeup. Often the critical observations of others, which we'd like to fend off, can become a tool for regeneration; for such corrections, even if offered by someone with ill intent, can be occasions for tremendous spiritual progress.

I am reminded of my late spiritual father, Archimandrite Dimitry of Santa Rosa. He was slandered by a local priest in a very public setting. When told of this, Elder Dimitry stood up from his desk, walked across the room, and began winding a wall clock. Asked why he seemingly cared little that he'd been so falsely and viciously slandered, his only response was to say, "Many sins have been forgiven because of this."

Making spiritual progress is never easy; it requires much effort on our part. It can come only through humility, which means we can expect to be humiliated. If we do not flee from suffering and humiliation, but learn to accept it for our salvation, holiness can be ours, and our lives will truly reflect this scripture: "I have been crucified with Christ; it is no longer I who live, but Christ lives in me; and the life which I now live in the flesh I live by faith in the Son of God, who loved me and gave Himself for me" (Gal. 2:20).

Taking Sunday Off

*Let no one out of laziness or continuous worldly occupations miss
these holy Sunday gatherings, which God Himself handed down
to us, lest he be justly abandoned by God. . . . If you are detained
and do not attend on one occasion, make up for it the next time,
bringing yourself to Christ's Church. Otherwise you may remain
uncured, suffering from unbelief in your soul because of deeds or
words, and failing to approach Christ's surgery to receive . . . holy
healing.*

St. Gregory Palamas

It seems we all go through periods when our church attendance drops off.
Our work and home life seem hectic, and we fall into the trap of letting
ourselves feel overwhelmed. Given the fast pace of our lives, in which we
feel we just don't have enough time in the day, it is easy to let the Sunday
Divine Liturgy fall by the wayside and to convince ourselves that we need
to take a Sunday off.

St. Gregory Palamas begs to differ with us! He calls our failure to
keep our Sunday obligation what it is: laziness. This great hierarch of the
Church even went so far as to remind us that our very belief in God is in
jeopardy, for we are not availing ourselves of "Christ's surgery to receive
. . . holy healing."

MAY 22

Come Against a Critical Spirit

When we fear a loss of control, we are likely to construct a wall of defense around ourselves, keeping authenticity at bay. Fearing rejection, we see ourselves as unlovable, and we blame others. Knowing we are inauthentic, we flee from the truth by becoming critical of others. We lie to ourselves and to others, hiding our insecurity and unworthiness and walling ourselves off from love. We feel we are unworthy of love, so we reject the love of others—and ultimately the love of God.

When confronted with our own critical spirit, we must ask the Holy Spirit to reveal to us the source of it. Why do we choose to be critical of others, when in truth we are wounded souls, suffering within a cloak of deception? We find fault in others only because we dare not face our own inauthentic self.

The fullness of life is knowing ourselves and giving back to others. When we don't forgive ourselves for falling short, we blame others. Insecure, we reject the love and friendship of others, thinking ourselves unworthy. We are fraudulent. We lie to ourselves and to others. We tell lies big and small, and ultimately we lie to God. We live in fear that we will be found out, and we mask the truth by being critical of others. We seek authority over others because we are not authentic, and we have no integrity.

And Romans 14:10–13 says, "But why do you judge your brother? Or why do you show contempt for your brother? For we shall all stand before the judgment seat of Christ. For it is written: 'As I live, says the LORD, / Every knee shall bow to Me, / And every tongue shall confess to God.' So then each of us shall give account of himself to God. Therefore let us not judge one another anymore, but rather resolve this, not to put a stumbling block or a cause to fall in our brother's way."

MAY 23

Practicing Love in Our Parish

As Christians, we are always finding ourselves struggling against the passions and trying, with Christ's help, to live according to the commandments. St. John the Evangelist told us we must love our neighbor, whom we've seen, if we are to love God, whom we've not seen (1 John 4:20). Yet the struggle to really love others is often the most trying and difficult when it comes to loving fellow church members.

Most of us have experienced the strife and anger that can arise on a parish level. Some of us have even contributed to that strife, such as by gossiping against our priest, making his job even more difficult. Not even the demons are as destructive in their collective attacks against the Body of Christ as we often are. Unlike the demons, who would never attack another demon, we attack other humans on a regular basis. We sometimes even criticize our bishops, whom Christ has called to be as fathers to us, treating them with disrespect.

Under the influence of Satan, we give in to the pressure of Satan's malice, and we turn against our brothers, Christian against Christian. Unless we truly seek out God's redemptive grace, we have no hope of winning the battle against the passions. Only with the acquisition of the Holy Spirit and the gaining of a humble and contrite heart will our lives on this earth have been successful. Christ stands before us with arms outstretched. Let us not turn away.

Chief of Sinners

As Orthodox Christians, what is our responsibility regarding those who do not live according to biblical morality? We first remember that we have fallen short of the glory of God and say, like St. Paul, "This is a faithful saying and worthy of all acceptance, that Christ Jesus came into the world to save sinners, of whom I am chief" (1 Tim. 1:15).

When we say the words "of whom I am chief" before receiving the Holy Mysteries, we must mean it! To focus on the evilness of another person's lifestyle only takes the focus off our own sin. And we fail to remove the log from our own eye.

When we look only upon our own fallen nature, upon our own sin, we find the mercy of God for ourselves. And we become far more merciful toward others as a result. We are given the grace to love even the worst of sinners, because Christ is in us. We know that the Lord does not love us because we are good or because we keep the commandments. He loves us because His very nature is love. When His love dwells in us, we are empowered to love.

It is our love, as Christians, together with our prayers for those who seem lost, that will change hearts and lead others to repentance. This I believe with my whole heart.

We Must Strive to Restrain Anger

*Anger is by nature designed for waging war with the demons and
for struggling with every kind of sinful pleasure. Therefore angels,
arousing spiritual pleasure in us and giving us to taste its blessedness, incline us to direct our anger against the demons. But the
demons, enticing us towards worldly lusts, make us use anger to
fight with men, which is against nature, so that the mind, thus
stupefied and darkened, should become a traitor to virtues.*

Abba Evagrius the Monk

The Fathers tell us that whenever anyone takes God's name in vain, the
ramifications reverberate throughout the cosmos. However insignificant we may think our angry words are, they impact the whole of God's
universe. Redemption is not just about us, but about the whole of the universe. My salvation and your salvation are interconnected. When a Christian falls into such sin, it is especially tragic, for there are many nonbelievers
who guard their words better than many who profess Christ.

We must strive by every means to preserve peace of soul and not allow
ourselves to be disturbed by offenses from others. In every way we must
strive to restrain anger and remain attentive to our mind and heart. We
must make every effort to bear the offenses and insults of others and to
accustom ourselves to such a disposition of spirit that their offenses do not
concern us. By guarding our thoughts, we can give quietness to our hearts
and make them dwellings for God Himself.

Abba Nilus said, "Prayer is the seed of gentleness and the absence of
anger." If we truly are of Christ, we have the means to change, for it is
because we have Christ in us that victory over the passions can be ours.
There is simply no excuse for Christians to lose their temper.

So "do not let the sun go down on your wrath," and "let no corrupt
word proceed out of your mouth, but what is good for necessary edifica-
tion, that it may impart grace to the hearers" (Eph. 4:26, 29).

Do We Tell God We Love Him?

We hear it might rain on the weekend, and we've been planning a hike in the mountains, so we ask God to provide the coveted sunshine. We're taxiing down the runway, so we ask God to give us a safe journey. Our boss seemed irritated with us, so we pray that we still have a job on Monday morning.

Prayer, for most people, is all about me—about my wants, my needs, my fears. Yet the biblical God who has invited us to have a relationship with Him is not Santa Claus. Our prayer life should not be like a little child's visit to ask Santa to give him what he desires.

Many years ago, I was counseling a couple that was having marital problems. The wife had decided she wanted a divorce, feeling the marriage lacked love. The husband was dumbfounded; after all, he came home every night, spent the whole of the evening with her, and was there on week-ends. When I asked if he'd regularly told his wife he loved her, he said he didn't need to because she knew it already. She sat glaring at him.

When was the last time we told God that we love Him? When did we simply sit, praying before our holy icons, and invite the Lord to fill us with Himself?

When Christ said, "He who has seen Me has seen the Father," He was telling us that we can have a relationship with the God who created us (John 14:9). Christ revealed God to us as a loving Father who wants His children to return that love. It is not about demanding love, for that would not be genuine love. A child does not love his mother because she'll beat him if he doesn't, but because she's loved him all along, even when he wasn't good.

Are we going to wait until the end of our life—when it is too late—or are we going to tell God now that we love Him and want a relationship with Him? A one-sided relationship is no relationship at all.

God Never Abandons Us to Temptation

Even when we seem overpowered by temptations, God never abandons us. He knows our weakness makes us vulnerable, and He never allows us to be tempted beyond our ability to resist.

We sometimes feel as though we were beasts of burden, carrying loads that weigh us down. St. Paul tells us, "For what I am doing, I do not understand. For what I will to do, that I do not practice; but what I hate, that I do" (Rom. 7:15).

We feel like a potter's clay bowl, being fired in a kiln, burning with temptations. Yet the potter is Christ Himself, who will not allow the clay to stay in the fire long enough to crack. He tempers the flame that we might be formed in His image, made whole by His grace. Remembering Christ's promise not to leave us alone, we grow in faith and holiness because God's grace sustains and strengthens us. We are never abandoned or left alone.

When We Conceal Our Sins from Our Confessor

Some people are hesitant to confess certain sins for fear of being embarrassed before their priest. One woman told me she couldn't handle the idea that a man would hear the details of her sinful actions, and she wondered what the priest would think of her after hearing her confession. (It should be noted that a spiritual mother can also hear the confessions of her daughters, with the priest simply pronouncing the absolution with the spiritual mother's blessing, as is often done in women's monasteries.)

I have been a priest-monk for over thirty years, and I must say I cannot think of a sin I have not heard before. Not one person has shared anything that shocked me, for the human condition is shared by all. What I have experienced is the joy of hearing a good confession. Seeing both the burden of guilt and shame lifted and the tears of true repentance is a joyful thing. The fear of shame before a priest has kept many from receiving the lifting of the burden of sin and the banishment of guilt.

No priest thinks less of a penitent, for all priests rejoice when beholding the lifting of the burden of sin and shame in the Mystery of Confession. Like the penitent, the priest witnesses the mercy of Christ, and the priest, as a sinner himself, is lifted up; for he too is in need of Christ's mercy and forgiveness.

Our lives become full of passions and sinful habits because we fail to do battle against the very sins that need to be confessed. Our wounds and sores are inflamed because we refuse to apply any remedy to them. The woman at the well beheld the mercy of Christ, and we too stand at the well before the Lord when we stand with the priest, as the witness before Christ, who is quick to forgive.

MAY 29

Discipline Removes the Paralysis of Fear

The soul suffers from a certain blindness when it comes to itself. In our desire to relax, indolence, insensitivity, and deceit rule our souls. And in our refusal to master the work of salvation, complacency sets in. Since no one can enter into your inner life but you, you are the only one who can persuade yourself to bring discipline into your spiritual life. You are the one who must reason with yourself before depravity and sin extinguish the light of the knowledge of the truth.

If we are complacent in our spiritual life, we become fearful. In truth, change can come about only when it begins in the soul of one person. Throwing off your own blindness can in itself bring light to countless others.

This task is not just for monks or professional religious people; it is for you. You are the one that must overcome your disinclination to do anything that has salvation at the forefront; otherwise you will be the person who drags down those around you.

The Goal of the Church

Our human nature will take what is good and spoil it, because our nature is to be in control. This perpetuates a neurotic way of dealing with our feelings and emotions, and even our spiritual life. We are living in an age when everything is in a constant state of flux and when people are in constant pursuit of pleasure. Given the state of our world, it is easy to approach our life in the Church in a state of neurosis.

What is the goal of the Church, and what do we do that moves us toward this goal? Is our experience of the Orthodox Church simply one of culture, perhaps Greek, Russian, or Serbian? Is our experience one of focusing on the form rather than on the essence of Orthodoxy?

The good news is found in the very nature of the Church herself. The Church is not a religious institution. The Church is a living organism and a hospital of the soul, where one finds wholeness and healing. When we give ourselves over to the life-changing and life-giving grace that abounds in the Church, we can find true happiness and lasting peace. It is only when we treat the Church as though it were a religious institution that we remain sick, neurotic, self-centered cripples.

The goal of the Church is to bring healing to the human heart. Her priests are those who sought out healing for themselves and, in the process, became the Church's therapists. When we give ourselves over to the Holy Mysteries (the Sacraments), the Holy Scriptures, and the reading of the sayings of the Church Fathers and the lives of the saints, we avail ourselves of the transformational power of the Church. Each time we confess our sins, receive Communion, and otherwise attend to our spiritual selves, we allow the Holy Spirit to work in our hearts, and a transformation takes place. But if we use the Church simply as a cultural fix, we become Pharisees and bring spiritual stagnation, or even spiritual death, upon ourselves.

MAY 31

What to Do When We're Broken

It is only human to become despondent when we fail in keeping to our moral, ethical, and spiritual standards. Our Orthodox Faith teaches that we must be compassionate toward others, loving, quick to forgive, and always demonstrating to the world that we belong to Christ. Yet we also know we fail, most of the time, in living up to the standards of the Gospels; we appear to be no different from the pagans.

Over and over, we sink in the muck and mire of sin, becoming broken, downtrodden, and sick. In our brokenness we betray the Gospels, our own standards of behavior, and the expectations of others. We know the truth of the words, "No one is good but One, that is, God" (Matt. 19:17) because we fail over and over in our seeming inability to live as we believe.

Nevertheless, even as we struggle with our sins, we must remember that God specifically created us for participation in His Divinity. We have been called by Him and have become a royal people, specifically created to share fully in the life of God. The key to this life in God is repentance. Even in our brokenness, we must not give in to despondency, for our Savior is quick to forgive. When we find ourselves falling short of the glory of God, we must turn toward this very God in repentance.

During those times when we fail in our Christian vocation, we must embrace the hope that comes with a repentant heart and see in our brokenness the reminder that we must always keep our hearts and minds in the knowledge that we have a God who is quick to forgive. Despair is the enemy of our salvation, because in despair, the evil one would have us believe there is no hope—and therefore no salvation. We must turn our gaze toward our co-suffering Savior, the One who lifts us out of our brokenness, making us whole and granting us forgiveness and life.

An Angel Unawares

Almost thirty years ago, during my first year as a monk, I was walking down a street in San Francisco with an elderly bishop. Walking in our direction about half a block away was a man whose clothes were filthy and tattered. As we got closer to him, I could see the bottoms of his feet; his shoes had no soles.

I instinctively took the bishop's arm and tried to direct him to the other side of the street. When he said we should continue as we were, I commented that we needed to cross the street to avoid the crazed-looking man who was approaching us. The bishop ignored my protests, and we continued toward the filthy street person.

Just as we met up with the man, the bishop stopped, reached out to him, took his filthy hands into his own, and gave him a twenty-dollar bill, telling him to buy himself something to eat. The man, who'd been looking toward the ground the whole time, looked directly at us, and with the clearest blue eyes I'd ever seen, he smiled and took the money.

I was stunned, and as we continued to walk, I commented that those eyes were not the eyes of a crazy man or even of a down-and-out street person, but those of a very intelligent person. The bishop responded that we'd just met "an angel unawares."

The memory of this man, whose eyes seemed full of wisdom and divine love, has never left me and has served as a reminder to this day that we must greet everyone we meet as though he or she were Christ Himself.

Turning to Christ As Our Refuge from the Storm

These difficult times are causing more and more people to lose hope. The struggle just to stay the course has become increasingly stressful for ever-increasing numbers of people, and Christians are no exception. When we are down, it is good for us to turn our faces toward Christ, remembering these words from the Gospel of Matthew: "Truly You are the Son of God" (14:33). This world promises us nothing, but in Christ we have everything, for He is our only refuge in times of trial.

Elder Thaddeus of Vitovnica said, "Here on earth there is nothing that can give us inner peace. For neither riches, nor glory, nor honor, nor position, nor family, nor neighbors can give us unshakable inner peace. There is only one giver of life, peace and joy—God."[11]

As Christians we must not allow anything to disturb our peace of heart, for we know that this life is transitory. Abbess Thaisia of Leushino said, "If you think to find paradise on earth, even in a monastery, then you are very mistaken. Paradise—full blessedness—does not exist on earth, and cannot, because man was not created for earth, but for heaven."[12]

JUNE 3

Finding Rest in the Forest

When I was a sophomore in high school, we lived in a hundred-year-old house on the beach of one of the largest freshwater lakes in the country. The close proximity to the lake afforded me the opportunity to spend a lot of time walking on the beach. About a half-mile from our home was a trailhead that led up from the beach and into a small forest. Not far from that trail, I created a special place no one else knew about. I cleared a secret path on the other side of a row of bushes by pushing aside one of the shrubs. Anyone walking by would have had no way of knowing there was a path behind those bushes.

I walked a short distance further and made a small clearing. Then I constructed a small table out of driftwood that served as my altar. I made a cross for the top, again out of driftwood, and placed two small candles on either side of the cross. This private outdoor chapel was my favorite place to pray.

Each of us needs such a place of refuge, a place where we can be alone with God. Over the years, I've always found myself drawn to forests and the solitude that only a forest seems to offer me. The southern view from the study of my little cabin looks directly into our forest. But even after all these years, I still find the greatest peace within the depths of a forest, where I am alone with the sounds of the wind through the trees, the chirping of birds, and the stirring of chipmunks and squirrels. It is there that my heart is the most open to the voice of God speaking to me.

JUNE 4

Proclaiming the Good News

We cannot give Christ to others unless we have welcomed Him into the central place in our own hearts. We must know and love Christ personally before others can see Him in us. When we are willing to sacrifice self for the sake of Christ and to live according to the Gospels, we will become living temples of the Most High, and the whole world will be changed.

The Gospel of Christ is imparted by word and example, and the love of Christ shines forth by our witness. We love and please God by following the commandments and proclaiming the Good News. That is our vocation.

We are not called to minimal holiness, but to a full expression of holiness. We are empowered for this transformed life by the action of the Holy Spirit. God's sanctifying grace is not merely the absence of evil or sin, but the presence of divine love in the soul.

We are called to holiness, for the Scriptures say, "Be perfect, just as your Father in heaven is perfect" (Matt. 5:48). We were created by God to share in His divinity, and we will never be completely happy until we have died to self and been made alive in Christ.

JUNE 5

Medicine for the Heart

One medicine for the heart is the use of a prayer rule. This rule is of the utmost importance, for it helps us develop the discipline we all need to progress spiritually. It is one of the great tools the Orthodox Way has to offer, handed down from the earliest of times, through the Fathers of the Church. The art of prayer comes from the experience of the early Church.

Along with keeping the fasting rules of the Church, including the Wednesday and Friday fasts, a prayer rule given to you by your spiritual father, spiritual mother, or confessor is the medicine that will help you progress spiritually on your journey to God.

The Morning and Evening Prayers should be said as though one's life depends on it, for, in a profound way, our spiritual life does depend on it. The precommunion prayers as well as the post-communion prayers, together with abstinence from all food and drink from midnight on prior to receiving the Holy Mysteries, are also disciplines that not only are commanded by the Church, but properly prepare us for the reception of our Lord's Body and Blood. It is in the reception of His very Body and Blood that we receive healing of both body and soul.

Finally, the use of the Jesus Prayer—"Lord Jesus Christ, Son of God, have mercy on me, a sinner"—throughout the day aids us in a most powerful way to live out our life focused on Christ. There is power in the Holy Name of Jesus, and this prayer fulfills St. Paul's injunction that we "pray always." The Jesus Prayer, also known as the prayer of the heart, gives us the strength to walk with Jesus throughout the day, even when driving through heavy traffic, weeding the garden, waiting for the bus, or sitting in a long board meeting.

Correcting Others Is Like Hitting Them

When focusing on the sins of others, we often set for ourselves the mission of correcting them. We see ourselves as called to help the poor unfortunate ones by pointing out their sins and telling them how they can be better people. We are not being critical but helpful, we tell ourselves. "Don't take offense," we say. "I am only trying to help you see your flaws, so you can become a better person. As a caring person, I want what is best for you."

In truth, the spirit of judgment is likely to be counterproductive, as our corrections can be like hitting a person, and our critical analysis of his behavior or personality or even his sins can cause more damage than good. If we truly wish to help someone, we offer good and kind thoughts, speak with words of love and encouragement, and pray for her. We are not doing her a favor by serving as her self-appointed therapist. Words of encouragement are far more likely to help the person than negative and critical feedback.

Only Christ can change the heart, lead the sinner to repentance, and bring about healing. We can be agents of this transformation by allowing Christ's love to shine through us and by demonstrating His transformational grace by the way we live, love, and do not judge.

That said, there are certainly times when people need to be corrected for their own good. When these occasions arise, we must make sure the correction is given in the spirit of love, so the delivery does not get in the way of the message. Priests, parents, bosses, and sometimes even friends may be called upon to offer such counsel, but the spirit of love must always remain central to the message.

The Holy Spirit gives us the power to live in Christ and to love others. Only the grace of God can change hearts, and we must not allow our own critical spirit to hinder the work of the Holy Spirit in others.

JUNE 7

Beware the Egoism That Can Come with Education

One of the great saints of our age, Elder Paisios of Mount Athos, said in one of his letters that people who are filled with egoism and pride because of their education "resemble satellites that orbit in the sky, giving one the impression that they are stars. If, however, you observe them carefully you will see their crooked steps and see that it is all a human sham."

The holy elder went on to say, "Internally oriented people, on account of their humility, are the true stars that move at dizzying speeds, but noiselessly and humbly, without anyone understanding how they move even though they are immense planets. They hide in the depths of heaven and give men the impression that they are little oil lamps aflame with a humble light."[13]

These words of wisdom from Elder Paisios should be taken into our hearts and become the central theme of our journey to God. It is easy to get puffed up about ourselves when those around us recognize our accomplishments, but this life is not about careers, education, or success; it is about our relationship with God. Only one who has acquired a humble and contrite heart will move at "dizzying speeds."

Education in itself is not to be avoided, nor are we expected to avoid success in our chosen field. We must, however, avoid self-promotion if we are to gain humility.

JUNE 8

God Is with Us in the Intimacy of Grief

One of the most tremendously rewarding and challenging aspects of the priesthood is comforting people in their darkest moments of sorrow. Do not be mistaken and think priests are exempt from the pain of those whom they try to comfort or that we have magical words that somehow ease the pain or bring order to the chaos of grief. Platitudes are useless in dark days of mourning.

We need to honor the bereavement process. Grief is confirmation that the one lost was a person of value. It is the way we honor a well-lived life. In grieving, we follow the example of Jesus, who wept at the grave of his friend Lazarus.

As a priest and monk of the Russian Orthodox Church, I am comfortable with this mystery, as all Christians should be. Death can be a mystery precisely because the triumph over death is not a mystery. As the Russian Orthodox theologian Alexander Schmemann wrote, "In essence, Christianity is not concerned with coming to terms with death, but rather with the victory over it." In the light of everlasting life, in the name of Jesus Christ, the dreadful threat and dark mystery that is death is transformed into a happy and victorious event for the believer, and "death is swallowed up in victory" (1 Cor. 15:54).

Yet there is no saying, no claim, no scripture that will give us peace in our loss or even calm our troubled souls. But we can find comfort and peace in God, who is present with us and in us and through us in the intimacy of grief.

Christian Mourning Affirms Life

Mourning is an ancient ritual, one in which Jesus participated, as did those of His faith before Him. Death is a common element of humanity—the common trait we share and the common enemy of our loved ones. And like grief, victory over death binds people together in a larger, more powerful community: the community that is found in the Christian faith.

However, people sometimes accuse Christians of being members of a "death cult," obsessed with a dying Savior and focused on the afterlife to the exclusion of the present. But they are wrong. Christianity does not deny life. It affirms life even in death, because for Christians, death does not remove the relationship that exists between people. Death has taken its victim, but it has also provided those left behind with the opportunity to live with the hope of one day joining her. And a life with hope is a good life.

For us, death is the beginning of the true life that awaits us beyond the grave, if indeed we have begun to live it here. Christ, "the resurrection and the life" (John 11:25), transformed death. He assumed human flesh; He was crucified, resurrected, ascended to heaven, and waits for us there; and He ushers us into new life both now and after our death.

Therefore, even as death exposes our frailty and our grief, it does not reveal our finiteness; instead it reveals our infiniteness, our eternity. To this end, the Christian does not ponder the mystery of death in a way that is paralyzing, negative, and apathetic, but in a way that is productive, positive, and dynamic.

The Importance of Our Saint's Name

There is great power in a name, and when we are named after a saint, we have a spiritual connection with that saint that lasts a lifetime. When we finally stand before the throne of God, we will know the name God has given us from the beginning. Meanwhile we must honor our saint by using that name.

Our Orthodox name, given to us at baptism (if we are converts, or at the naming ceremony, if we are infants), is the sacred name by which we should travel through our whole journey to God. To use another name is to show dishonor toward our saint and to break the connection we have with that saint.

Thus, the naming service of a newborn child is spiritually very important and should be honored by all. St. John the Wonderworker would not commune anyone who did not use his saint's name when approaching the Holy Mysteries. Many adult converts even have their names changed legally to take on their Christian name, just as St. Paul gave up his given name, Saul.

JUNE 11

Counsel to a Young Atheist

At the age of sixty-five, I find myself spending an ever-increasing amount of time on college campuses and hosting a growing number of young people who visit the monastery. I've discovered that grandparents are often more sympathetic to the burdens and challenges young people face than their parents are. Age seems to make us more understanding of these challenges. We become less judgmental because we've been down the same road and know that, in the end, these young people will come out just fine.

Some time ago, a mother arrived at the monastery with her thirteen-year-old son in tow. He had declared himself an atheist, and she was afraid he was in danger of eternal damnation. I sat down with him and told him that each one of us has to come to a personal awareness of the reality of God for ourselves. Doubting the existence of God is part of building a personal relationship with Him. If we simply go through the motions without seeking a real relationship, we might as well be atheists. My own youth was filled with great spiritual struggle as I sought to fill the void I felt within my heart. I was filled with anxiety for the future and fearful of making the wrong decisions.

I told the mother to let her son explore for himself the reality of God. It was better for him to question the existence of God than to feign belief. At the same time I told the boy he needed to attend church with his family because it was important to be obedient to his parents and supportive of his younger brother. After all, one does not tell his parents he's not going to attend school just because he doesn't see his studies as important.

Reject the False God

The God many people reject is the false image of God that I have long rejected. The God I have come to know personally is not the same god I rejected in my youth. The God revealed in Jesus Christ is the One whom I've personally experienced and who first sought me out.

If we are to have a personal relationship with God, we must be open and honest and unafraid to question. The Lord wants us to be real with Him. Like the sound relationship one sees in a long and successful marriage, a relationship with God must first and foremost be based in honesty and truth. Love and trust come with time and experience. Our relationship with God is something that builds over time, like all relationships.

These sixty-five years have led to a great deal of peace in my heart and an ever-growing love for the God who first loved me. I know God exists because I've experienced His great love in a personal way. It is now my heartfelt desire to share my love for God with the youths of today who reject the false god. They, like me, need to discover God for themselves and build upon a relationship that began with their conception.

JUNE 13

Joy Despite Destruction

The economy, high unemployment, and record-setting hurricanes, tornadoes, tsunamis, earthquakes, fires, floods, and droughts in recent years have given us all pause. A week ago a woman came up to me in a Seattle bookstore and asked me why God was allowing all this to happen to us. She pointed out that America's Bible Belt had suffered much of our nation's destructive storms. She began to shed a few tears as she shared her growing anxiety and despondency.

I shared with this dear woman that I too was concerned about all these things. My heart goes out to all those who've lost everything, and I pray daily for the suffering peoples all over the world. Yet I remain peaceful in my heart because I place myself in the presence of God every day and stay focused on all that I am thankful for.

The Scriptures tell us that we should give thanks for all things and that peace passes all understanding. If we connect with the Lord in our heart, wherein lies the Kingdom of God, we can live in a state of joy; our hearts can rejoice even when destruction reigns all around us. We can learn to let go of our worry and give it over to God.

We must get out of our heads and into our hearts. When we come into the presence of God, the world cannot disturb our peace. Our true home is not of this world, and we do not have to wait for the next world to find the peace that comes from God.

Change is happening all around us, and things are not going to get better until we humans turn back to God in repentance. We must focus, not on all that is wrong, but on what we can do to change what is happening in our hearts. We must be proactive rather than reactive.

JUNE 14

Without God, We Can Do Nothing

If we are to be true to our calling as the children of God, we must live in imitation of Christ. We must imitate His meekness and humility. We must love others just as He did. We must be willing to be transformed and made whole, that others can see in us the light of Christ. To do this, we must pray and fast, seeking the help only Christ can give us. That which is impossible with us is possible with the help of Christ. Only Christ can ignite our soul with the love of God, but we must cooperate by making our hearts open to Him.

We must not allow ourselves to be complacent in our journey into the heart of God. Our Christian faith demands that we take heaven violently, storming heaven as it were. Only when we are ruthless toward ourselves and quick to condemn ourselves as the worst of sinners will we truly be flooded with the grace we need to be transformed and made whole. Like the Holy Apostle Paul, we must see ourselves as the worst of sinners and any good we do as Christ working in us.

Just as we light lamps and candles before holy icons, symbolizing the light of Christ, so too must we struggle each and every day to let the light of Christ shine forth in us. If we live our Christian faith with little effort, the light will be dim, and neither the angels in heaven nor those who come in contact with us will notice in us anything different from an unbeliever. We are, as Christians, called to be a holy people, living "not of this world" but ever in the Kingdom that is to come.

Birth Control and the Orthodox Christian

Marriage, for the Orthodox Christian, is to have its foundation in Jesus Christ and a commitment to live in full communion with the Church. When a couple is joined together in this mystical (sacramental) union with one another, they become one flesh and begin their relationship as one. The crowning ceremony symbolizes martyrdom of self and a commitment to sacrifice self-will.

Marriage is not about sexual gratification, although sexual intimacy is an important component of any healthy marriage. But the intimacy of the marriage bed should be open to the possibility of having children. The Church allows no form of contraception that is abortifacient, and the Fathers of the Church, such as Ss. Athanasius the Great, John Chrysostom, Epiphanios, Jerome, Ambrose, Augustine of Hippo, Caesarius, Gregory the Great, Augustine of Canterbury, and Maximos the Confessor, explicitly condemned abortion as well as the use of abortifacients.

The bottom line is that a Christian couple must be open to having children. A couple who would choose to have no children or to limit the number of children based on a desire for financial and lifestyle security forgoes the joy that only children can bring to a Christian marriage. The use of birth control should never be based on selfish motives, such as the desire to live a more comfortable lifestyle. This life is not meant for personal gratification or personal gain, but that we might give glory and worship to God in all we do.

JUNE 16

Substance and Shadow

A shadow is an area where direct light from a source, such as the sun, cannot reach due to obstruction by an object. It occupies all the space behind an object with light in front of it. Substance, on the other hand, is that which is solid and practical in character, quality, or importance.

In icons used in worship by the Orthodox Church, the images cast no shadows. The light comes not from the sun, but from our Lord, who is the Sun of Righteousness. The light comes from within and represents the light of Christ, who dwells in His saints and whose sanctity and love do not obscure this light.

As Christians we must live in such a way that the light of Christ shines through us and does not cast a shadow. If we live our lives in humility and repentance, the Lord's love and light are not obscured but shine forth with substance: Christ is in us. This very Christ Jesus is therefore seen by others and spreads the love of God throughout the very cosmos.

JUNE 17

Authenticity and the Authority of the Church

If she is true to herself, the Church acts with an authority grounded in love. She holds the authority to make her people the children of God. She has the authority to forgive and the capacity to love. And just like her Head, Jesus Christ, she exists to serve and not to be served. She guides her people with love, recognizing that each person is unique and is to be ministered to with an authority based on serving, not being served.

Christianity itself is in crisis as many people are embracing the materialist approach of self-help rather than ascetic struggle and self-denial. Increased numbers of young people are turning to atheism or wandering in a wasteland of spiritual confusion, having witnessed the betrayal of Christian morality and faith by many religious leaders.

Metropolitan Hierotheos of Nafpaktos said,

> The incarnation of Christ was considered and was celebrated by the Fathers of the Church and the worshiping ecclesiastical community as the abolishing of religion and its transformation into a Church. In fact, the memorable Father John Romanides has said in the most categorical way that Christ became human, in order to free us of the illness of religion.[14]

Until we put off religion and put on Christ, we will continue to fail in our vocation as servants. Unless the Church demonstrates, with holiness and humility, an imitation of the image of our Savior as servant, she will have become nothing but a religion that has lost its way. And the authentic witness of Christ will have been lost.

The youths of today are drawn to authenticity, and until they see Christ in the lives of parishioners who are living icons of Christ and who are loving, humble servants of this very Christ, they will continue looking for truth in a wasteland of spiritual confusion. The Church must proclaim the Good News in all humility and love, for "the Son of Man did not come to be served, but to serve" (Mark 10:45).

JUNE 18

Establishing Communities of Love, Not Fear

There are a lot of fear-based communities in our world. Some are religious and some are political. All are guilty of missing the mark. For the Christian, the true self is created in the image and likeness of God. As children of the Most High, we are meant to live, not in fear, but in a joyful state, knowing and experiencing the love of God. Our God is not a god of anger and vengeance, but one who invites us into a relationship based in loving communion. God is not waiting to send down fire upon our heads, but rather is a loving Father who desires that we connect with our true self and put off our false self.

When we live as problem-centered people, we miss the mark. If we focus on negative things in our lives, such as struggles with a particular sin, we fail to live up to our true self. Many therapists keep their patients in a codependent state by giving them labels that speak of mental illness. Political parties keep themselves in power by playing to the negative labels they've created for the opposition. Religions often do the same thing with their own adherents, keeping them hooked in a negative pattern that disallows spiritual growth that leads to healing and spiritual well-being.

Fear-based communities abuse their people to keep them in line, leaving them in a state of perpetual infancy, unable to reach their full potential, and preventing them from realizing their true self. Such institutions, political or religious, prevent people from flourishing.

God invites us to integrate our lives as His children and utilize all the gifts He has given us, which lead to fulfilled lives. Fear is vanquished for Christians precisely because we are His children. In Orthodoxy, the priests and bishops are called upon to encourage the faithful to live in faithfulness to God's commandments, not because there will be grave consequences if we don't, but because of the great joy that is ours when we have communion with Him.

Little by Little, We Make Progress in Holiness

In our struggle to cooperate with God's grace, the transformation of our souls that leads to holiness can seem daunting. We feel discouraged when we struggle to change our bad behaviors or to overcome sins that seem to follow us like bad debt. We feel overwhelmed and wonder if we will ever have victory. During times like these, it is good to remember the words of St. Peter of Damaskos: "It is through victories in small things that the Fathers won their great battles."

Holiness is not just about the saints, whose icons we venerate and whose lives we read. Holiness is better understood as wholeness, being made whole, or healed. We seek healing from the darkness and estrangement we've inherited as a result of the Fall. We seek out the God of righteousness, who alone can heal us of our infirmity. As Christ increases in us, our fallen nature decreases. We replace our fallen self by keeping God's commandments and loving God before all else. When we do so, the ego is trampled down and we become children of the Most High.

Our goal is to acquire the Holy Spirit, from whom comes true repentance and a humble and contrite heart. This relationship that brings healing also brings healing for the world. St. Seraphim of Sarov said that if you acquire inner peace, a thousand around you will be saved. As Christians we must focus on cooperating with God's grace, that transformation by the Holy Spirit will make us worthy of eternity with God.

JUNE 20

What I've Learned from Evangelicals

Many evangelical Christians visit our monastery. Many are seeking something they sense is older and more stable than the present-day expression of evangelical Christianity. Some are finding that the entertainment approach to worship leaves them hungering for something more meaningful. These people often share their frustration with a form of Christianity that is constantly trying to reinvent worship in an attempt to bring in crowds. They sense in Orthodox Christianity an eternal and unchanging connection with the early Church.

Orthodox worship, with its otherworldly and mystical approach, makes many feel as though they've worshiped for the very first time. They recognize that Orthodox worship of the Holy Trinity is profound in ways they've never experienced before. I've even had visitors to the Sunday Divine Liturgy express the feeling that they'd entered into a service where there was neither time nor space, and where they experienced God in a heavenly way. One evangelical pastor even made the profound observation that he'd better love Orthodox worship, since heavenly worship is liturgical, as is shown in the Book of Revelation.

I have a special place in my heart for evangelicals and admire their missionary efforts to bring others to Christ. We Orthodox would do well to imitate their evangelical zeal and share with others the eternal truth that is found within the Orthodox Faith. It seems sad to me that we Orthodox rest in the assurance that we have the fullness of absolute truth and are members of the very Church Christ founded, yet we seem uninterested in reaching out to others and sharing the pearl of great price. We've lost touch with the profound missionary history of our Church, one that brought Orthodoxy to all corners of the earth. In our attempts to preserve our ethnic traditions, we've lost the vision of sharing Orthodox Tradition.

JUNE 21

True Fasting

Fasting has always been an important element in the lives of Christians. The Lord Himself fasted in the desert for forty days before beginning His ministry, and both the Old Testament synagogues and the New Testament churches regarded fasting as an essential element of the spiritual life.

In today's society, we often hear of fasting in relation to a weight-loss program, with the spiritual aspects not even considered. However valuable fasting may be for weight loss, the essential purpose of fasting is to clear the way for spiritual growth. Depriving ourselves of the consumption of dairy products, eggs, meat, and even dessert is a way of bringing ourselves into a spiritual awareness that is otherwise not possible. These periods of fasting also call for increased effort in our prayer life and spiritual reading.

Yet, given all this, St. Basil the Great said, "True fasting lies in rejecting evil, holding one's tongue, suppressing one's hatred, and banishing one's lust, evil words, lying, and betrayal of vows."

JUNE 22

When Prayer Becomes Dry

When we find ourselves struggling with prayer, feeling it has become dry and lifeless, we are sometimes tempted to stop praying. When our prayer has become a struggle, it is good to remember that God knows our needs and even knows what we want to say when we don't seem to know. This is the time we need to just pray without worrying about it. When we find we can't keep our minds focused on the formal morning and evening prayers, as found in our prayer book, it is perfectly acceptable simply to light our *lampada* (hanging oil lamp), sit quietly before our icons, and let silence be our voice.

God wants to enter into our heart, and He requires only our permission and cooperation. This relationship does not require an emotional response, for, as with all relationships, we are not always open to an emotional response. Being real with God is far more important than being emotional, since emotions can be contrived and fleshly. As in all relationships, there are times when we do feel moved by emotions, but the lack of such feelings in no way represents a lack of love for God, because God cares for us, and He knows we love Him, even when we suffer in those dry times.

The Blight of Addiction

We of the twenty-first century have given ourselves over to self-consuming addictions more than any people in history. Even a casual look at how we live makes it abundantly clear that we are so caught up in our addictions, we can't even begin to notice that our world is on the brink of disaster.

Because of our addiction to having it all, we've put our collective head in the sand, pretending that all is going to be just fine. We are a technologically advanced race that can take care of any eventuality, we tell ourselves. We live in denial, much like the alcoholic who's been confronted by his family.

As a race we have turned our backs on God. We've adopted abundance and prosperity theologies that have led us to believe that God wants us to exploit the planet. We've put our priorities in the wrong place. Simple living has been relegated to those losers who can't afford the good life. Meanwhile, we fiddle like the grasshopper of the childhood story, all the while running out of time.

In our pride and arrogance, we ignore a clear message. God is calling us to repentance. He is calling on us to turn back to the things that are eternal. Our planet is spewing us up like so much vomit because our sins of overconsumption, greed, and acquisition have led us to forget God. We've been worshiping the false gods of prosperity, gluttony, and consumption while ignoring the invitation of our Creator to place our hearts and minds at His disposal.

St. Basil the Great said, "It is the sign of an infantile mind not to care for oneself with the resources that are available, but rather to partake of something clearly and undeniably harmful while trusting in unseen hopes" (*Against Those Who Lend at Interest*).

The Reformation of My Nation Begins with Me

The wife of a priest friend, a schoolteacher, told me how horrified a number of her fellow teachers were when they found out her husband was a priest. One teacher avoided talking to her for the next three months, and another commented that she must feel very limited by the restrictions placed upon her because she was married to a priest.

In this age of political and religious polarization, I am afraid we are going to see such overt hostility toward Christianity become ever more common. People are becoming hostile toward the values and teachings of Christianity, yet ever more accommodating to the rising presence and popularity of Islam and other religions.

The Christian response to such changing attitudes within American society should be met not with hostility and anger, but with a renewed commitment on our part to return Christ to a place of prominence in our nation through a spiritual revival within our own hearts. Our fellow Americans must see in us the love of Christ, and the joy of our life in Christ must translate into a life lived in harmony with our environment, in peaceful coexistence with those of different religious and social persuasions, and in a nonjudgmental embrace of others.

Christianity should not be reduced to political activism or the enforcement of morality, for societal reformation can take place only when Christ is allowed to change the heart of every citizen. All men and women who enter into a personal relationship with Christ are confronted with the knowledge that they have fallen far short of the glory of God and are in need of forgiveness.

The negative attitudes seen in growing numbers of Americans toward Christianity is the result, I am convinced, of our failure as Christians to truly live the gospel. I must ask Christ to change this nation by beginning with me. The reformation of the nation must begin with my own reformation.

JUNE 25

A Fast That Is Pleasing to God

O ur fasting is pleasing to the Lord when it is accompanied by mercy
and kindness and done without hypocrisy or pride. Fasting brings
the passions under control by not only taming the body, but also bringing
victory over the demons. Fasting gives us power over the demons because
it has a powerful impact on our own spirit. The body is brought under
submission by fasting and gains freedom, sobriety, purity, and strength.
"But I put on sackcloth when they [the demons] troubled me, / And I
humbled my soul with fasting; And my prayer will return into my bosom"
(Ps. 35:13 OSB).

Another benefit of fasting is what it does for our health. What we put
into our bodies does matter, and the periods of fasting given to us by the
Church afford us the opportunity to cleanse our bodies of toxins and
extra weight. An important part of keeping the fast is the reduction of the
amount of food we eat, not just the types of food. Some make the mistake
of simply eating foods that are devoid of eggs, dairy, fish, and meat. Rather
than replacing these foods with beans, vegetables, soups, salads, and whole
grains, they replace them with soy products and other prepared foods.

Fasting is a good time to bring all the passions under control, including
our compulsive food intake. Eating only whole organic foods during these
fasting periods makes us feel lighter. It clears the mind and makes us more
open to the things of God.

Finally, periods of fasting should be approached with joy. This is not
about deprivation but about the renewal of body and soul.

JUNE 26

Squandering Our God-Given Resources

A ccording to St. Gregory Palamas, God has given us lordship over all the earth because of our capacity for sovereignty. With this sovereignty comes the responsibility to be good stewards of what God has given us. He said, "There is within our soul's nature a governing and ruling faculty, and there is also that which is naturally subservient and obedient, namely, will, appetite, sense-perception, and in general everything that is sequent to the intellect and that was created by God together with the intellect."

Our fallen nature has also given us the capacity to reject the will of God and to misuse our sovereignty, refusing to use our freedom in a God-pleasing way. We overindulge ourselves with food and drink, overgraze our lands, destroy our rain forests, saturate our oceans and atmosphere with pollution, pave over our food-producing farmlands, and pump chemicals and other pollutants into our rivers and streams.

As though that were not enough, we squander our mental faculties with endless hours before our computers, TVs, and iPads. As creatures who were created to commune with God, we waste our time in mindless pursuits, giving little thought to things that are spiritual and of eternal value. We battle not only against the all-ruling God but also against the ruling power inherent in our nature.

Laziness Delays Our Transformation

St. John Chrysostom tells us that when we fail in our spiritual journey toward transformation, it is not due to "the nature of the trial, but by your own laziness." Since God created us with free will, He does not force salvation on us, but offers it freely to us as a gift. The only thing required of us is that we cooperate with His offer of communion with Him.

When our sins block the pathway to God, it is not because He does not open the way, but because our laziness keeps us off the path. Daily we must face up to our part in this journey and force ourselves to make an effort at becoming like Christ. We must imitate the Lord in every aspect of our life, for it is in how we love, in how we are quick to forgive, in how we reach out to others in charity, and in how we become peacemakers that progress is made.

Christianity has a bad name in our world today, because many professing Christians live the same way as the world—and sometimes worse than the world. If we have been joined to the Lord, then we are one spirit (1 Cor. 6:15–17), and others see Christ in us. If I take the Lord's name in vain, it reflects on Christ. If I lose my temper, it affects the Body of Christ. Our behavior is important because we represent Christ to a lost and dying world. What we do and what we say are seen by the world as representing Christ.

God has opened the gates of paradise to us, but our movement toward the gates requires the navigation of a straight and narrow path. This journey requires commitment on our part, and this commitment begins with repentance, for it is only in repentance that we are given the grace needed to navigate the dangerous road that is before us. Through love of God and love of neighbor, we will enter into the Kingdom of God and live forever.

JUNE 28

The Garden of the Heart

Both my Norwegian grandfather and my mother were avid gardeners, so I grew up surrounded by the beauty of plants and flowers. The cottage garden is a distinct style of garden that is certainly my favorite. The use of traditional materials in an informal design, together with dense plantings and a mixture of ornamental and edible plants, is identified the world over as English in origin. The grandeur and formal structure found in classical English estate gardens has surrendered to homey and functional gardens that are filled with grace and charm.

The massive plantings of perennials, annuals, and vegetables of every size and color display, like nothing else, the variety of beauty that characterizes God's creation. These gardens remind me of how people come in every size and color, all beautiful in our own special way. Some are like climbing roses, reaching to the heavens and God's glory. Others are like creepers, hugging the ground and covering large areas like a carpet of green. Some are like cactus, needing little water, while able to live in the ascetic splendor of an Egyptian desert. Others, like water lilies, display beautiful blooms, even while floating in squalid water.

Like plants, we need watering and tending. For Christians, the water of life is found in baptism, where we are immersed in the living waters that bring us into life. We stand before the Creator, who, like the gardener, tends to our needs, that we may grow and bloom to our full potential.

As we tend to our own heart, we must make sure we have guarded ourselves against the weeds that would strangle us and smother our potential as children of God. We must make sure we avail ourselves of the life-sustaining food and water that comes from God as His uncreated grace. And as the Body of Christ, the Church ("neither Jew nor Greek . . . neither male nor female," Gal. 3:28), we will flower together, making up a garden of beautiful souls, basking in the light of the Sun of Righteousness.

Transmitting Orthodoxy to Our Children's Hearts

If we expect our children and grandchildren to grow into adulthood as practicing Orthodox Christians, we must give daily witness to the importance of our faith. If we are lax in our fasting, church attendance, and piety, our children will see by our lack of seriousness a compartmentalized religion that is of no value to them.

If they do not see us seriously practicing our faith, they will ultimately reject Orthodoxy as something that is of no personal value. If they do not see us praying, they will not have prayer as a part of their lives. If they do not see us putting the divine services before entertainment, they will abandon Orthodoxy as irrelevant to them. If they do not see Christ in us, they will reject Christ themselves.

If they do not see in their parents a Christian who is quick to forgive, quick to show mercy, and quick to give to the poor, they will not see Christ. If they do not see in a parent one who loves his neighbor, as Christ commanded, they will not see the Christ who changes and transforms lives.

Just as a child has to be educated in the arts of poetry, reading, and painting and in the sciences, a child is taught the importance of faith by the example of his parents. St. Isaac the Syrian said, "Faith is the door to mysteries. What the bodily eyes are to sensory objects, the same is faith to the eyes of the intellect that gaze at hidden treasures." To educate a child in the humanities and the sciences, but to fail to implant faith by our example, is to cheat the child of the most important gift of all: the gift of faith.

Practicing Hospitality with Church Visitors

U nlocking the temple doors is worthless if a visitor is greeted with
a frown upon entering. I've lost count of how many people have
shared their experience of being ignored by worshipers upon entering an
Orthodox parish for the first time. Numerous people have told me about
being confronted with the question, "Are you Greek?" When they said
no, they were asked, "Then why are you here?" Others have shared their
sadness at having been ignored in the parish hall because they did not speak
Russian.

A Roman Catholic friar once told me he went to a Russian cathedral to
attend his first Divine Liturgy. The service had concluded, and as the clergy
walked down the steps of the cathedral, they looked right through him
as though he were invisible, even though he was wearing his Franciscan
habit. He felt so unwelcome, he left.

What kind of witness was this? Have we reduced Orthodoxy to a private club? Do we see the Church only in ethnic terms? What if Ss. Cyril
and Methodius had treated the Slavs in such a manner? What if the Jewish
Christians of the first century had treated the Gentiles in such a manner?

We are all called to be evangelists for the Orthodox faith. Not one of us
is deserving of this pearl of great price, yet we wish to preserve it only for
ourselves. How can we say we love Christ if we do not wish that all know
Him? Can we be saved, in the end, if we wish salvation only for "our
people"?

We must invite our friends and neighbors to "taste and see" the great
treasure that is Orthodoxy. And it is our responsibility, as Christians, to
reach out in kindness and with a welcoming smile when we see strangers
enter our temples.

Orthodox clergy must remember that they are the first line of witness
for the Faith. If we hold ourselves aloof while wearing our cassocks and
crosses in public, we cannot call ourselves disciples of the Lord, for in
keeping ourselves aloof, we bring shame upon the Cross of Christ.

The Church Must Encourage Her Children

It deeply saddens me when I see some in the Church taking the stand that the Church must be the enforcer of God's law. I remember a fellow high school teacher who had a good list and a bad list. The good list included students he liked, the ones whose grades were above average. On the bad list were those who were academically challenged and who more often than not already had a very low self-image.

Many of these students would walk into my classroom the following period, and I could tell their grades from the looks on their faces. It took considerable effort on my part to lift the spirits of those "bad" students. I followed the grading approach of an older, more experienced teacher. If there were twenty questions on a test, and the student got only four correct answers, I wrote 4+, with a little smiling star next to the number. I'd tell the student that four correct answers was a good start, and his or her grades always went up from there.

As the hospital for the soul, the Church should view everyone who walks through the narthex in the same light. Some people are always early for services, make good confessions, receive the Holy Mysteries frequently, and volunteer for whatever task is set before them. Others struggle with the Christian life and are barely identifiable as belonging to Christ. Yet both sets of people are in need of the healing that comes in an encounter with the living God.

If the Church loves only those who are in the first list, we have failed, for those in the second list are in need of more attention and love than those on the first. A mother once told me she loved her youngest son the most, not because he was smart or polite or obedient or handsome, like her other two sons, but because he was troubled, homely, disobedient, and angry. That son needed her encouragement and love more than the others.

This is why I have always loved the image of the Church as our mother.

How We Dress Matters

The Old Testament is filled with images of God's people being a holy people, set apart. The ancient Israelites were not like their neighbors. Their values and their faith affected everything about them. They dressed differently from many of the neighboring pagan tribes. Their worship was centered on the God who had revealed Himself to them and made them His chosen people. Their spiritual and moral views reflected this relationship with the one God who had entered into communion with them and who had revealed divine truth through the prophets.

The Church is the continuation of the Church of the Old Testament, and as such we are the chosen people of God. Our lives should reflect this truth in everything we do and in the moral standards that guide our daily living.

These standards of faith should even govern the way we dress. It is not only Orthodox monks and priests who should hold themselves to dress codes that reflect modesty and purity. We are all called to be a people set apart from this world. Christ's Kingdom is not of this world, and we need to dress in a way that does not bring temptation to others. For the Orthodox Christian, tight and revealing clothing are not appropriate. We should not reserve modest clothing for church services or when making pilgrimages to our monasteries.

What happens in the heart assists us in the battle against the passions. The center of our being is in the heart, and the attention of the mind must be fixed in the heart, not outwardly. Modest attire for the layperson is just as important as the robes of a monk in the quest for living a life given over to being, in every way, God's chosen people.

Suffering Is for Our Salvation

The Lord does not allow anything beyond our power of endurance to afflict us. Whenever difficulties come our way, we sin only if we are unwilling to endure. Suffering is meant to be salvific, for the Apostle Paul tells us, "God is faithful, who will not allow you to be tempted beyond what you are able" (1 Cor. 10:13).

We must humbly and with patience labor under the trials and temptations God allows, lest we squander the opportunity put before us and fall back into our fallen nature. When we joyfully receive every trial and temptation, knowing the Lord is with us, we become victorious in the battle. And we are ever drawn closer to the Lord, whom we love and serve.

Without suffering and trials, there can be no victory. Without the Cross, there can be no resurrection. When we trust in Christ and do not give in to despair, we share in His victory, and His life becomes ours. If, however, we attempt to go it alone, struggling against temptations and difficulties without seeking God's help, we will ultimately fail, and victory will have been vanquished.

JULY 4

Freedom

It would seem to be a genetic trait of us humans to desire freedom. We want to live in a free society, to have freedom to make our own choices and freedom from the tyranny of others. Yet we fail to realize that the freedom we desire from the innermost part of our being is not really freedom in and of itself. The true desire for freedom is the desire for God.

God yielded to us a piece of His divine authority, which instilled in us this sense that freedom is something good. In this freedom we are given the power to voluntarily approach God, offering our freedom in sacrifice to Him. For at the moment we submit our freedom to God, we become truly free, for we have been freed from the bondage that has kept our true nature subjugated to sin and death.

St. Theophan the Recluse wrote, "Therefore, if you have mastered yourself, now give yourself to God. When you sinned, you not only lost yourself, but in losing yourself you took yourself away from God. Now, having returned from the captivity of sin, after you have mastered yourself, return yourself also to God."[15]

This then becomes the moment of true emancipation, for we will have found freedom from all that has separated us from our true selves, and we will have become one with God.

Putting Aside All Hypocrisy

How easy it is to worship with all piety and correctness while stand-ing in a service in an Orthodox temple, yet make no effort to live Orthodoxy during the rest of our week. If we are abusive toward our spouse, abrasive with a coworker, or short-tempered with a neighbor, all the piety and liturgical correctness of our Sunday morning is of no value.

If we cheat on our taxes, steal pens from the office, or refuse to point out an error to a clerk who has given us too much change, we will have reduced our life in Christ to no more than membership in a club. If we walk past a child who is being bullied and don't intervene, we have become the bully. If we smile at the racist joke of a coworker, we are just as guilty of racism as he.

Being a Christian is far more than adherence to a set of doctrines or the adaptation of liturgical forms of worship and piety. To be a follower of Christ is not like joining the Elks Club, where paying your dues and attending meetings makes you a member. Taking the name of the Savior for ourselves and calling ourselves Christian must mean that we imitate the Savior's life. It must mean that others see Christ in us, each and every hour of our day.

We must be the neighborhood peacemaker, the one who is quick to forgive when wronged, the person who is always looking for ways of being of service to others. If we truly wish to be called Christians, we must put aside hypocrisy in all its forms—and live Christ.

We must work toward changing the world. Justice and peace do not come with revolution, but when the Holy Spirit transforms the hearts of men and women. And this change can begin only when we put aside all hypocrisy and replace it with genuine, heartfelt commitment to Jesus Christ, living in imitation of the Savior.

Binding Our Anger

If we think we have to be slaves to anger, we deceive ourselves. Anger is not a normal part of anyone's personality, and as with any addictive pattern of behavior, it can be changed. As long as we continue to justify our anger, we remain trapped, and we avoid God-pleasing holiness. Christ awaits our decision to move forward with His help, to receive the grace we need to be made whole. We do not have to go it alone, for the Savior of our souls is quick to forgive and ready to bring healing.

No one consumed with anger can be happy, for the passion of anger destroys the soul and spreads unhappiness to those unfortunate enough to be in the proximity of the angry person. Transformation can begin only when we invite the Great Physician to enter into our hearts and change us.

Our Victory in Christ

As we struggle with anger, gluttony, judging others, sexual impurity, and any other of a myriad of passions, it is easy to feel overwhelmed and powerless. We find ourselves feeling defeated and tempted to give up the battle. Sometimes we even tell ourselves we have no choice, for we were born that way, or our temperament is the result of our upbringing.

There is certainly a kernel of truth in all this, for we were born into a fallen world and are therefore influenced by the results of our firstborn parents' rejection of God's love. Yet this struggle is not about our power or strength, but simply about surrendering to the Lord of mercy, who would save us.

This same merciful God knows how difficult a struggle we have and has given us the strength we need to progress toward purity and holiness. He also rewards us based on our willingness to commit to the struggle—a struggle that is empowered by the grace that abounds when we call upon His Holy Name.

What do we do when we seem to succumb to the same old sins over and over? Do we simply surrender in defeat? Or do we ask God to help us with our anger and confess before a priest when we have fallen, and then ask the person we have hurt to forgive us? Do we ask for God's forgiveness when we've given in to lust and promise to better guard our hearts and our eyes? Do we choose to remain silent when others around us are gossiping—and perhaps even avoid those social settings?

The good news is that we do not have to struggle alone. Our Lord Jesus Christ has promised to help us in our quest for purity and holiness. Like the Apostle Paul, we can say it is not by our own power, but by Christ in us, that we are able to do good. Transformation of the heart is the direct result of the indwelling of the Holy Spirit, from whom we are given the power to change. All we have to do is approach God with a humble and contrite heart, and victory will be ours.

Conspiracy Theories and Living the Christian Life

It is spiritually fruitless if we allow ourselves to be distracted by the delusions created by Satan that draw us away from the awareness of the presence of God. When we allow the thrall of conspiracy theories to fill us with fear, anxiety, and mental, emotional, and spiritual turmoil, we become distracted from the peace that should reign in our lives.

Living the Christian life is what will bring us into the Kingdom—that is, into communion with God, where we find true knowledge and understanding by divine illumination. Through this, God reveals to us what He knows we need to know for our spiritual advancement.

For pastors and archpastors, more awareness of the things of this world may be necessary in order to guide and protect the flock. But much of the fear, confusion, anxiety, distraction, and even desperation that can spring from delving into conspiracy theories is not spiritually healthy. It can become an addictive substitute for a healthy spiritual life and keep us from the task of the Christian, which is to "turn away from evil and do good . . . seek peace and pursue it" (1 Pet. 3:11).

JULY 9

The Church Calendar and Spiritual Maturation

One of the most spiritually profitable discoveries for me was when I started the observance of the liturgical calendar as a new Orthodox Christian. Each day of the year I was carried along with the cycle of commemorations that brought to life various events in the life of Christ. The calendar provided me with daily scripture readings that quenched my thirst. The historical memory of the Church, lived out in the various periods of fasts and feasts, allowed me to experience a Christianity that was vibrant and meaningful.

An important element in the calendar is the daily commemoration of Christian saints and martyrs. For me, these saints came alive with each day's offering, allowing me a chance to emulate the lives of those who'd already won the battle, acquiring holiness in the Lord. The daily commemoration of the saints allowed me to remember the mystical connection between the Church Militant here on earth and the Church Triumphant in heaven.

Just as a general of an army studies the military maneuvers of past generals in preparation for leading his soldiers into battle, so can we study the saints who've triumphed in spiritual warfare. If we want to struggle more faithfully in our own spiritual quest to deepen our love for God, we need look no further than the lives of the saints to find inspiration.

Monasticism in the World

M onasticism within the tradition of the Orthodox Church has many
expressions. Some are called to live in the wilderness as hermits,
living the solitary way of life. Others, such as St. Maria of Paris and St.
John of San Francisco, are called to live their monastic struggles within
cities, surrounded by people. Many live with varying degrees of contact
with others and the world, including friends and family, monastic brethren,
etc., and do so successfully. I also personally know of monastics, both nuns
and monks, who have become caretakers for members of their family out
of necessity.

We have all been instructed, both as laypeople and monastics, to love
God above all. The Lord went on to instruct us that we should also love
our neighbor as ourselves. There is therefore no benefit whatsoever if we
reach the highest perfection and precision in living by all the ascetic and
spiritual "rules" if we have only love for ourselves and pride in our accomplishments. We are called to do battle with the ego, to love both God and
our neighbor, and to make love the chief goal of our life. Everything else
ought to be subordinated and should contribute to this: that we love God
and that we love our neighbor.

A Contemporary Man in an Ancient Church

As an educated man, I have a broad interest in the arts, music, poetry, literature, and history. My father was a golf pro, and my mother was a professional church organist and piano teacher. I was trained in classical oil painting but prefer to paint in impressionistic freestyle. My photographic interests are directed toward traditionally expressed scenic photography. I love opera and country western music equally. I hold to liberal views when it comes to the environment, ecology, and universal health care. I'm conservative regarding moral and fiscal issues facing our country today.

My conservative religious views are tempered by a strong love of people that has afforded me a wide range of friendships spanning religious, political, cultural, and racial barriers. I'm comfortable enjoying a cup of coffee with a rabbi in the morning, listening to opera with an elderly shut-in in the afternoon, and spending time with college students in the evening.

These things about me are worthy of sharing because they demonstrate the great truth that, in Christ, there is room for everyone in the Orthodox Church. I attribute my ability to be comfortable with a wide variety of people to the universality of Orthodoxy. The Church is a living organism that brings healing to the world as a hospital of the soul, and as one of her therapists (priests), I am called to be all things to all men and women. The Christ I've invited to reign supreme in my life is Lord of all. He loves everyone equally and has called me, as His creature, to emulate this love for all those who cross my path.

In these days of great polarization, not seen in this country since the Civil War, it is imperative we Christians not allow political and religious differences to affect the way we interact with others. We must have hearts that are filled with love, not fear. In Christ there is only hope. Economics, politics, governments, and all earthly catastrophes are transitory. A life in Christ is eternal.

Orthodoxy and Beauty Are Inseparable

Orthodox Christianity attracted me from my very first encounter with the magnificence of her churches and the grandeur of her divine services. Having grown up amid the natural beauty of Northern Idaho, with mountains and lakes that could take my breath away, I'd previously found inspiration primarily in the world of nature.

Orthodoxy and beauty are inseparable because God and beauty are inseparable. The beauty of a sunset is a reflection of our Creator, just as the interior of a temple reflects our experience with the Creator God. We humans were formed as physical beings, placed in a material world, and invited to commune with our Creator. The majesty and beauty of the created world inspires us to an awareness of God's presence.

A bouquet of flowers placed in our icon corner has an internal effect on us. Created in God's image, we in turn become creators. The beauty that comes from the artist's brush or the poet's voice is an act of a creator. Taking our creative instincts into the realm of the spiritual unites us with God and connects us to the eternal. This is why an artist or a poet can experience the eternal when creating something of beauty.

God is the Creator of heaven and earth and is present through His creative energies. The material world, being good, is an important means through which God expresses Himself. It is through His created beauty that we are drawn into a relationship that is meant to be eternal and through which divine revelation can transform our nature. Then creation is completed, and the created is united to the Creator.

JULY 13

Tend to Your Own Business

When we hear of problems in the Church, many of us respond to our natural inclination to want to read all about it and root out all the details. Yet, if we want to benefit our souls, we should take this advice of Elder Paisios of Mount Athos:

> *If you wish to be calm do not read rebellious books or pamphlets that mention Church matters, since you are not responsible for such serious affairs. You have need of books that will assist you in your repentance. If you want to help the Church, correct yourself and immediately amendment is made to a small part of the Church. Naturally, if everyone did this, then the Church would be put in order.*

As long as we struggle against the passions and sins of this world, there will be problems in the Church. Just as nations and all human institutions suffer because of the passions of people, so does the Church. Although divinely instituted by Christ Himself, the Church is made up of sinful men and women who bring in the baggage of their sinful nature. This very place of healing, like all hospitals, houses both the healthy and the sick. If we desire to become numbered among the healthy, we must remain aloof from the din of Church politics and leave the governance of the Body to the hierarchs.

When we witness the fallen side of human nature within the walls of the Church, we must not respond like news reporters seeking out all the details. Nor should we think knowing the inner workings of the Church will make a difference. Better that we concentrate on the nurturing of our own soul and remain above the fray. Let those who have been called to service in the Church, the bishops, do their job. If we trust God and pray for our bishops, the Holy Spirit will guide them in their role as our shepherds, the Church will stay the course, and "the gates of Hades shall not prevail against it" (Matt. 16:18).

JULY 14

The Roots of Holiness: Good Soil

We all struggle with our passions, and like St. Paul, we can say that we do what we do not want to do, and we do not do what we want to do (see Rom. 7:15). The passions hold us down to the ground in our sin and fallen nature, and we are like dead plants. But God's grace is more than sufficient for holiness to take root.

When planting corn, you water twice a day so that the energy of the plant is expended upward, thus allowing the production of the cobs. Yet when planting flowers, you skip a daily watering to force the roots of the plant to go down deep, thus strengthening the plant so that it can bear lots of flowers and thrive for the whole of the summer months.

Salvation comes when we have acquired the Holy Spirit and the fruit of the Spirit: a humble and contrite heart. The word humility is related to humus, a very good type of soil with organic components formed by the decomposition of leaves and other plant material by soil microorganisms. The soil used for growing both vegetables and flowering plants must be healthy and fertile, for the best soil grows the best plants.

Plants grow out of rotting soil, just as we grow out of the rottenness of our sin and fallen nature. From the bad soil of our sinful nature, the acquisition of humility can transform what was rotten into good soil, out of which can grow the beautiful flower that God intended.

The gardener nurtures his plants, watering them and providing fertilizer, sunshine, and lots of loving care. The Church, much like the gardener, nurtures her children, providing the living waters of Baptism and the Holy Mysteries (Communion) that give us life, and helping us grow in the light of Christ, the Son of Righteousness.

JULY 15

Why Complaining Is a Failure

If we are always complaining about how unfairly we are treated, we will have failed in our imitation of Christ, who was abused by His enemies unto death. We should strive to reign with our Lord by loving our enemies and never complaining. Christ looked toward His heavenly Father, and when we are tempted to complain, we should gaze upon the Cross.

Complaining disturbs the heart and distracts us from the path. Complaining weakens our resolve and interferes with the acquisition of peace and holiness. When we complain, we are rejecting the role of suffering as a means toward union with God. Complaining keeps our hearts from soaring to the heavens and experiencing the joy we can find when we surrender ourselves into the protective arms of Jesus.

True Joy

How do we know we are living according to the will of God? We make sure we focus on Christ, and we do not let what is transitory rule us. For a life centered in Christ brings about true peace, wisdom, and knowledge, and we are given the grace to trust in God's divine providence for everything.

If we focus only on the things we haven't done and ignore the little things that bring us joy, we find ourselves in a rut, constantly thinking of where we'd rather be living or the job we'd rather have or the work that still needs to be completed. We'll wake up one day and realize all we've needed for happiness has been right in front of us all the time.

How do we know we're living according to the will of God? Elder Thaddeus of Vitovnica tells us, "He who lives according to God's will has no worries. When he needs something, he simply prays for it. If he does not receive that which he asked for, he is joyful as though he had received it. A soul that has given itself over to God has no fear of anything, not even robbers, sickness, or death. Whatever happens, such a soul always cries, 'It was the will of God.'"[16]

Loving Ourselves

Sometimes we've done things that cause us to wonder how we can ever forgive ourselves. Perhaps we've hurt someone we love or disappointed people we respect by behaving in a way we deeply regret. Maybe we've said some unkind thing to someone and caused them terrible hurt and embarrassment. We are so horrified by our behavior that we want to crawl under a rock. We've been able to ask their forgiveness, but forgiving ourselves is quite another matter.

When Christ gave us the Great Commandment, He told us we must love God above all things, and we must love our neighbor as ourselves. The ability to love others is in direct correlation to our love of God and self. If we hate ourselves, how can we begin to love God and neighbor?

Loving ourselves must begin with learning to forgive ourselves. The measure of love is to fulfill Christ's commandment to love others as yourself. Therefore you must love yourself (as well as others), in light of Jesus' words, "If you love Me, keep My commandments" (John 14:15).

JULY 18

The Jesus Prayer and the Acquisition of Inner Peace

The Jesus Prayer, also known as the prayer of the heart, is the central prayer for monastics. One of the early Desert Fathers, St. Macarius the Great, said, "There is no other perfect meditation than the saving and blessed Name of Our Lord Jesus Christ dwelling without interruption in you, as it is written 'I will cry out like the swallow and I will meditate like the turtledove!' This is what is done by the devout [person] who perseveres in invoking the saving Name of Our Lord Jesus Christ."

The profound simplicity of the Jesus Prayer—"Lord Jesus Christ, Son of God, have mercy on me, a sinner"—makes it the perfect prayer, allowing us to follow the injunction of our Lord that we should "pray always" (Luke 21:36). (The prayer can be said in various shortened versions, such as "Lord Jesus Christ, have mercy on me," or simply "Lord Jesus Christ.")

Over the years, many people have told me they have difficulty concentrating on their daily prayers. They've struggled with thoughts coming into their minds that distract them from prayer. For others, the same thing happens during the public services in the temple. The prayer of the heart can help, for it is a way to dispel outside thoughts and bring our attention back to the Holy Name of Jesus.

This prayer can be used throughout the day and in every situation. We can pray the Jesus Prayer while working, in heavy traffic (it is a splendid way to refrain from road rage), and even while sitting in boring meetings at the office. I use this prayer when hearing confessions and when counseling, since it is a way of seeking guidance from the Holy Spirit when giving spiritual direction.

I promise you, if you take up this prayer for yourself, it will contribute to peace of heart and stillness of the mind and will keep you centered in the things of God. It will also allow you to participate in a spiritual practice that is as old as the Church herself.

Situational Ethics Versus Biblical Morality

S ituational ethics have become the norm for our times, having replaced the biblical ethics held by past generations. In situational ethics, as long as no one (or at least no one recognized as a full-fledged person) is hurt in any obvious way, one can do as one pleases. Taking drugs, watching pornography, and aborting children all may be permitted under the flag of situational ethics.

Taking drugs is seen as morally neutral by increasing numbers of Americans. When we say we believe no one is hurt by our drug use, we are refusing to see the obvious connection between our drug purchases and the mass killings in Mexico by drug cartels that are in business because of the demand for drugs by American users. We also ignore the grief caused to our families and friends by seeing us become enslaved to addiction.

"There's nothing wrong with watching pornography," we tell ourselves, forgetting that the demand for pornography enslaves many people in prostitution. Pornography has become one of the major addictions of our times, keeping large numbers of people in bondage and preventing sound, healthy relationships.

Under situational ethics, parents believe that aborting their child is allowable if keeping that child would negatively affect their lifestyle. In situational ethics, the unborn have no voice whatsoever.

The Fathers knew that even the secret sins committed by people had an effect on the whole of the cosmos. The people who promote situational ethics would have us believe that nothing that is done in private hurts anyone. Biblical ethics tell us quite the opposite.

Remembering God by Helping Others

Today is the perfect day to start doing battle with the passions that create a state of unrest in our hearts. Tomorrow may be too late to begin this battle, for none of us knows the day we will face God and be called upon to account for our lives. In our forgetfulness, we allow the goal of union with God to become secondary to everything else. We must take control as though we were entering into a battle, for our eternal life is at stake.

St. Basil the Great tells us we cannot approach the knowledge of the truth with a disturbed heart. Conflict, downheartedness, lust, worry, and judging others are all things that cannot be allowed to distract us from the goal. Letting ourselves become troubled or full of anxiety does nothing to further our journey into the heart. Giving ourselves over to the passions depletes us and leaves us waylaid along the narrow path toward the Kingdom of God.

Perhaps the fastest way to realign the unrest in our hearts is to focus on the needs of others. No one can be saved, according to St. John Chrysostom, without giving alms and without caring for the poor. We are but stewards of what belongs to God, and now is the perfect time to share the gifts of God's creation with one another as much as we can. Storing up earthly possessions, according to Christ, is the epitome of foolishness (Luke 12:15–21).

When we turn our attention toward the needs of others, our focus changes, and we are no longer consumed with self. In this turning of the heart toward those in need, we are turning our hearts to God. Jesus said, "Assuredly, I say to you, inasmuch as you did it to one of the least of these My brethren, you did it to Me" (Matt. 25:40). In our fasting, increased time spent in prayer, and almsgiving (charity), we are energized in our battle against the passions, and our hearts come to rest in Christ.

When Your Priest's Homilies Are Hard to Hear

Every priest can tell you he's had his share of people who don't think he understands the difficulties they face with their jobs, families, and spouses. Many people think their priest expects too much of them, and they ignore the homilies that challenge them to go deeper into their faith.

Yet the Scriptures tell us we must seek first the Kingdom of heaven. Being successful in business and raising the perfect child are wonderful things, but they should not be on the top of our list. Making more money than your brother-in-law or having a better house than your neighbors should not be on your list at all. And working for a good retirement can be a good thing, but not at the expense of your eternal life.

If we are taking our faith seriously, we will be grateful for those hard-to-hear homilies that hit too close to home. If we don't want anyone telling us what to do or pointing out areas of our lives that need change, we can become off-kilter spiritually. A spiritual father, like a golf pro or a weight-lifting instructor, gives direction and sets standards based on experience. We seek out a golf pro in order to improve our swing, and we expect him to help us be a better golfer. The trainer in the gym is expected to help us be healthier and more fit.

If you don't already, start going to confession on a regular basis. And, whatever you do, don't allow yourself to be late for the services. Arrive from fifteen minutes to a half hour early to properly prepare yourself for the celebration of the Divine Liturgy. Get in the habit of attending Orthros, or Matins, if this service precedes the Sunday Liturgy, or attend the Vespers service or the Vigil on Saturday night. Make an effort to immerse yourself in the life of the Church.

Remember, if we let our ego be our spiritual guide, we will be following the direction of a fool.

Becoming a More Compassionate People

St. John Chrysostom taught, "The poor are not the spectacle of human misery and suffering that evokes compassion or disgust, but they are the icons of Christ, the presence of Christ in the broken world." The compassionate sharing of our resources with those in need is a primary teaching of our Church and a virtue that must be practiced if we are to be true to the teachings of our Lord.

In an age when so many rich are resisting the possibility of increased taxation, we must remember that we are all, rich or poor, required by the Gospels to share with those around us. Christian nations from the time of Byzantium have taxed the wealthy in order to provide for the least of their people.

The fact that almsgiving leads us to God is so pivotal to faith that it led St. Basil the Great to exhort even the poor to share their meager goods with others. The Christian culture of compassion requires all of us to find ways to lift up the least among us. We cannot remain secure in our own well-being while ignoring the needs of the poor and the elderly.

St. John of Kronstadt, in his "First Homily on the Beatitudes," said,

> Can wealthy people be poor in spirit? Of course they can, if they do not regard themselves as being great people only because they have perishable wealth and can do whatever they want with its help. How can they be poor in spirit? They can when they sincerely recognize that their wealth—and the wealth of the whole world, for that matter—means nothing in comparison with the immortal soul, and that wealth is a gift from God not only to us but to our neighbors as well, for material surpluses are given to us to help the poor.[17]

A compassionate heart leads to God as it places others above self. A wealthy Christian is a philanthropic person who cares for the poor and destitute and shares what God has given him, thus storing up in heaven the treasures that are eternal.

Push Aside Estrangement

When we feel estranged from God, it is a true sign we need to work more diligently on building up our faith. Faith is a gift from God that requires our cooperation. When we are feeling dry, we must quickly turn our eyes to Christ, asking Him to fill the void and quicken our belief. Our cooperative response begins when we commit to increasing our time in prayer, both corporate and in private. The corporate prayer of the Church brings us into contact with the Holy Mysteries, which in turn feed our souls.

The hearing of God's Word and the partaking of the Lord's Body and Blood, together with a repentant heart, push aside estrangement and open the door to a deepening faith. As a wife responds to the touch of her husband, so too does our soul respond to the love of God, and our faith comes alive by the power of the Holy Spirit.

A woman whose husband never says he loves her will feel her love diminish, whereas the husband who tenderly expresses his love for his wife will see the rebuilding of a relationship that began with love and passion. Our soul responds to our tenderly expressed love of God and sees our love for Christ increased and our faith restored to a state of blissful vigor, with all estrangement cast aside.

Putting Off the Old Self

As we struggle to make spiritual progress, we do battle with the old self. We work against old habits that have kept us stuck and prevented the change we so desire in our quest for communion with God. Our sins and passions have become familiar to us, almost like old friends, and laziness has set in. We may have become comfortable with the way we are, and change may seem like too much work.

We must confront spiritual laxity and sinful habits with a renewed commitment to live as children of God. But this struggle comes with a price tag; it requires real work on our part. The Kingdom of heaven must be taken by storm, but this struggle does not require us to battle on our own, for the Holy Spirit empowers us with the grace sufficient to win the battle over the old self. In Christ we become new creatures, and the old self is put aside.

JULY 25

How to Fit the Workplace into Your Spiritual Life

Balancing your spiritual life with the workplace can be quite challenging. Your day should begin with prayer. Some recite their prayer rule (something that should be worked out with a spiritual father, priest, or confessor) before leaving home. If you have children to tend to, you should get up an hour early so you have plenty of time before getting them breakfast and sending them off to school.

If you are a commuter who takes public transportation, get in the habit of reading spiritual books that are available in your parish bookstore or online. Again, your priest can suggest books that would be of benefit to you. I keep a book in our van so as to have spiritual reading while waiting on the dock or crossing on the ferry.

Use your coffee break to reread *The Morning Offering* or a few chapters in your commuter book. If you head out to lunch, why not take the book along as your companion?

You may also benefit from downloading programming from Ancient Faith Radio. And, of course, the Lord is our constant companion, and the continuous repetition of the Jesus Prayer can keep us grounded in our faith, even while working.

Using these simple methods can make a huge difference in your workday and add immensely to your spiritual growth.

The Importance of Preparing for the Divine Liturgy

It is a given that the Church requires us to prepare to receive the Holy Mysteries of the Body and Blood of Christ by saying the precommunion prayers prior to the celebration of the Divine Liturgy. The Church also requires us to fast from midnight on, abstaining from both food and drink until after we have received the Body and Blood of our Savior. The only exception is when we must, because of health issues, eat or drink something, but only with the blessing of our confessor or priest.

Although it's not required, if we read the appointed Epistle and Gospel readings prior to entering into the Liturgy, the Word can better enter our heart. When hearing God's Word for the second time, we are more receptive, and the Word penetrates deeply.

Perhaps the most important preparation we must make before attending the Divine Liturgy is to be sure we are at peace with all our brothers and sisters. We dare not approach the chalice with malice or hatred toward anyone, nor can we receive the holy gifts with a heart that refuses to forgive those who have hurt or offended us. An important part of forgiving others is for us to seek forgiveness. Thus, frequent confession is imperative.

Participating in the Divine Liturgy is a great privilege, for in this service we enter into a place where there is neither time nor space and where we are worshiping the Holy Trinity, together with the hosts of heaven.

In the Liturgy, we encounter God in a way that is beyond human comprehension, for we are invited to commune with our Creator in the most intimate way. To approach the Holy Mysteries (Communion) without thought, as though we were simply going to a movie, is beyond foolishness. To receive the "hot coals" (see Is. 6:6–7) that are meant to transform us and make us whole without proper preparation is a very dangerous thing to do.

Almsgiving: Keeping Our Lamps Lit

When our conscious relationship with God had its beginning, His grace was given in such free abundance that it brought us into the awareness of the redemptive love that had encompassed us. This grace manifested itself in the peace and joy that became our own and enabled us to live an exemplary life—as St. Paul said, it is not he himself, but Christ in him. This grace has given us the wisdom and desire to live "not of this world."

Now God expects us to fly like eagles, reaching the heavens by our good deeds, manifesting exemplary lives through our kindness toward others, being quick to forgive and generous in almsgiving. As we await the Bridegroom, we must not let our lamps become extinguished.

As St. John Chrysostom said,

> *Let us not extinguish our lamps, but keep them bright by almsgiving. It is by this means that the brightness of this fire is preserved. Let us, then, put oil in our vessels as long as we are here. It is not possible to buy it when we have taken our departure hence, or to receive it from any source other than the hands of the poor. Let us, therefore, collect it from there in great abundance, that is, if we wish to enter in with the bridegroom; if we do not do this, we must remain outside the bridal chamber. It is impossible, I repeat, even if we perform countless good works, to enter the portals of the kingdom without almsgiving.*

Kindness in Criticism

Criticism, like rain, should be gentle enough to nourish a man's growth without destroying his roots.

Frank A. Clark

When offering someone criticism, it is important that we do so with kindness. Studies have shown that ten positive comments are needed to counter one negative comment. When we receive criticism from another, positive wording can make all the difference in how we respond. Children are especially vulnerable to harsh criticism and should be corrected in a loving, gentle way.

When you are upset about a situation, if your tone of voice is calm, the other person can hear the criticism and respond to it rather than to the anger. Conversion rather than conformity, inner transformation rather than external compliance, must be the goal. Showing respect to the person being corrected helps bring about change. Angry words delivered in a harsh tone prevent the receiver from hearing the criticism.

Whenever we communicate with others, we must be grounded in God's love. The message of the Gospels is one of love and forgiveness, and conversion of life is possible, not because we are afraid, but because we are forgiven by our loving Savior. The employee who feels respected by his boss will respond to correction because he wants to please his boss by becoming the most productive employee. The child who feels loved wants to please her dad and be a good little girl. The wife who is told frequently by her husband that he loves her becomes his partner in the deepest sense and wants to please him because she loves him.

How we communicate with others makes all the difference in the world. If we allow ourselves to be loving, gentle communicators, we in turn receive the respect and love of those around us. We become happier; they become happier. What a wonderful world it would be if we all learned to communicate respect and love for others.

The Therapeutic Life of the Church

The Orthodox Church is a hospital for the soul and a living, therapeutic organism that can make us whole and bring healing of body and soul. It is not a legalistic or juridical institution wherein we are expected to plead our case before an angry judge, trying to convince him we are worthy of mercy. The Church is not about rules or ritual, but about participating in the spiritual therapy intended to cure us of the sickness of sin and to restore us to spiritual wholeness and health.

This spiritual therapy is to be found in the ascetic and mystical (sacramental) life of Orthodoxy. Just as a hospital treats physical health and sickness with the individual in mind in order to maximize the benefit, so does the Church offer her therapy in a way that meets individual needs. This therapy leads to the transformation of self and restoration to holiness.

It's all about becoming, not being; it's about transformation of ourselves and our restoration to holiness, not making God keep a bargain with us to give us what we want or expect. This is because each one of us has a different complex of illnesses, and we respond in different ways to the various spiritual, therapeutic regimens available to us in the Church.

The bottom line is that we avail ourselves of the healing, therapeutic life of the Church. Just as a hospital would be worthless to us if we failed to show up for a scheduled surgery, so too must we avail ourselves of the therapy the Church of Christ has to offer us.

How to Kill the Ego

Modern psychology has told us we must feel good about ourselves and has instructed us to reject the idea of guilt and sin. The idea of sin is seen as religion's instrument for keeping people in line, making them dependent on an institution that should be relegated to the Dark Ages. In an age where humans are elevated to being their own gods, religion is seen as a sort of enslavement. Up with self! Down with guilt!

Self as the new god is worshiped at the expense of community and enthroned in a position of the utmost importance. Worship of self has contributed to the downfall of families and societal stability, with careers, social and financial gain, and self-fulfillment reigning supreme.

Divine love does not tolerate this elevated status of self, for the ego is the enemy of our communion with God. In an age of financial collapse, mortgage foreclosures, and high unemployment, worship of self dooms us to a life of total loss.

We were created for communion with God, and the worship of the ego has led us into a state of spiritual bankruptcy. The meltdown of the economy and the destruction of the environment are direct results of our turning away from spiritual values. The foundation of economic and environmental collapse is to be found in our spiritual bankruptcy. We need to return to the worship of God and reject the worship of self.

The denial of guilt and sin is the ultimate example of our having accepted a lie perpetrated by the devil, the great deceiver. True happiness and true wealth come only through the fulfillment of our destinies and that for which we were created: communion with God. The destruction of the ego begins with repentance and the acquisition of a humble and contrite heart, that we might have this communion.

When Someone Is Irritated by Us

Because we are all brothers and sisters, we are responsible for the way we affect others. Often we are innocent, yet by our very existence we become a source of great irritation or anxiety for other people. The only way we can change that is by loving them and praying for them.

We don't offer prayers that they see their errors in not appreciating us and loving us, but that they may see that their hatred for us is bad for their soul. We pray that they be relieved of the burden of resenting us—or anyone.

If someone is awkward and socially blocked, his pain can be great, so we pray that he be relieved of his pain—not that he change his mind about us or love and accept us, but that he find the inner peace that dispels his resentment of anyone.

Avoiding people who dislike us does not prosper our souls, for avoiding people or ignoring them because they dislike us is not the way Christ would have us act. We love these people, and we pray for them—not to change their attitude about us, but that they find peace by seeing that their resentment is destroying their soul.

Repentance As a Step Toward Holiness

In all our busyness and with all the distractions that come our way on any given day, it is easy to forget that repentance is the only possible way we can embrace holiness. Since we sin daily and fall short of the glory of God, repentance is the necessary ingredient that allows us to grow spiritually. The holiness we seek is not unattainable, for a saint is not someone who never sins, but rather someone who is constantly cleansed of sin by repentance.

Repentance is not just about telling God we are sorry. To be truly repentant, we must push aside all our selfishness, cast aside all pride, and admit that we have done wrong. Since we know that no one can see the Lord without first becoming holy, the attainment of holiness must be our first priority.

A good step toward holiness is to practice being grateful for everything, demonstrating our gratitude to God for all that comes our way. Both the pleasant and the unpleasant things that come into our lives must be embraced with a joyful and contrite heart. We must never blame anyone for our misfortune, for to do so brings on spiritual death. We must never blame God, for that was Adam's sin ("The woman whom You gave *to be* with me, she gave me of the tree, and I ate" [Gen. 3:12]). We must, rather, "in everything give thanks" (1 Thess. 5:18) and take full responsibility for all the wrong we do.

Holiness is not an unattainable goal, but a necessary one that can be attained over a lifetime of struggle. The attainment of holiness must become the chief goal of each and every day, unto the end of our lives.

Impatience and Worry Versus Courage and Faith

If we are easily offended or lose our peace of mind when someone treats us badly, we cannot attain inner peace. The Christians who live with internal strife and worry neither edify other Christians nor reflect anything of Christianity that would be attractive to those who have no faith. Such people can even be serious stumbling blocks for others because their religiosity seems to be the cause of their weaknesses.

St. Paul said, "Love suffers long and is kind . . . bears all things, believes all things, hopes all things, endures all things" (1 Cor. 13:4, 7). If we are always complaining or worrying, we are not living according to the directive of the Apostle Paul. Worry is based on sentimentality regarding our Christian faith, creating a degenerate version of Orthodoxy that inspires no one and ultimately leads to the death of our own soul.

True Christians are patient with others, just as they are in need of the patience of their friends and family. As Christians we are called to be a faithful people, yet we often act in a way that betrays us as faithless. We ought to live by the power of God, yet we give in to a weakness that is subject to anxiety and fear. We are the children of the Most High, empowered by our God for a life of holiness and faith. Let us live with courage and faith, that we might acquire peace of heart and shine before all people the light of Christ.

AUGUST 3

The Value of Stability of Place

An elder said that just as a tree cannot bear fruit if it is often transplanted, so neither can a monk bear fruit if he frequently changes his abode. In an age when people change addresses as often as their socks, stability of place is almost unheard of. When I was a young man, I moved from city to city often. In one year alone, I lived in New York City, Berkeley, California, and Portland, Oregon. If I hated a job, I'd move. If my social life was on the rocks, I'd move. Reinventing myself in a new location became the norm.

As I grew older and wiser, I realized that with each move I was avoiding issues I needed to deal with. If I was ever to grow psychologically and spiritually, I needed to put down roots.

Stability is one of the four vows Orthodox monks take. From the very beginning of monasticism, monks realized that spiritual growth was not possible without struggle, and a good way to avoid struggle was to move from place to place. If you are living with others who know your weaknesses, it is hard to avoid change.

Many marriages end in divorce because the couples lack a stability of place that would allow them to confront issues. Moving from one church to another is just as destructive to the spiritual life as moving from city to city or relationship to relationship.

Stick with the priest or confessor who really knows you. Spiritual transformation takes time, and changing confessors inhibits growth, since it takes time for a new priest to get to know you. Would you change medical doctors every few years? How much more does our soul need the guidance of a priest who really knows us. We all need the guidance of one who doesn't allow us to avoid working on what inhibits growth in our relationship with God.

Stability can be the vehicle by which we are able to confront the habits, sins, and vices that inhibit God from transforming our lives and making us whole. Constant movement allows us to hide from ourselves.

Which Type of Christian Are You?

There are two types of Christians. There are those who can say with the Apostle Paul, "I have been crucified with Christ; it is no longer I who live, but Christ lives in me" (Gal. 2:20). And then there are those who believe Christ was crucified so that we do not have to crucify ourselves. The first are part of a Christianity of sacrifice, and the second are given over to the ego.

The Christian who believes she must be crucified with Christ will constantly call upon the Lord for help, and she will be willing to take up her own cross and follow Christ. She does not expect to have an easy road, nor is she easy on herself. This type of Christian is ever looking at her own sins, her own fallen nature, and seeing how far she has fallen short of the glory of God.

The second type of Christian expects the road to be easy. He sees himself as more spiritual than most and is constantly looking to see the error in his neighbor and offer correction. He rarely calls upon the Lord for help, for he expects an easy road and only prays for help when facing an unpleasant situation. He does not take up his cross, since he sees no value in suffering. This second type of Christian fails to notice that refusing to judge another brings down God's mercy on himself.

The Lord tells both types of Christians, "If anyone comes to Me and does not hate his father and mother, wife and children, brothers and sisters, yes, and his own life also, he cannot be My disciple" (Luke 14:26). Only the first type of Christian notices those words—and heeds them.

A Healthy Soul Seeks Silence

Our society is addicted to noise. We find it impossible to drive our vehicles without the radio on or a CD playing. Our televisions are running from the moment we return from work. We take our runs with earphones, filling our minds with music. We even walk with our friends while listening to our own music. We live as though we were afraid of silence, like little children who have to sleep with a night-light.

Our reasons for filling our hours with noise are varied. Some find silence disturbing and a reminder that they are alone. Others use noise as a way of keeping out the sounds of the city or the voices of their children. There are those who use noise as a way to keep from having to communicate with others. Some even use noise to avoid themselves.

Whatever the reason, noise keeps us from connecting with our inner self, wherein we have the opportunity for communion with God. Without silence, we are unable to hear the voice of God speaking in the stillness of our heart.

It is not just monks who should be seeking out moments throughout the day when solitude and silence allow us to enter into communion with God, for a humble soul and a penitent heart are fed by solitude and silence. The human heart is open to the voice of God when in silence and solitude.

AUGUST 6

Confession: Humbling Ourselves before Another Person

We are delusional if we believe we do not need others to see, understand, and treat our spiritual sickness. Anyone who believes that she alone can cure her spiritual diseases has isolated herself from the Mysteries of the Church and will come to ruin. Only with the help of others are we saved, for within the Christian faith, salvation comes not in a self-focused void, but in the collective nature that is the Church. The Mystery of Confession, established by our Lord, is a clear sign of the biblical truth that we need the Church.

In confession we do not simply regret past evil but recognize the darkened vision of our own condition, in which sin, by separating us from God, has reduced us to a divided, autonomous existence, depriving us of both our natural glory and our true freedom. "If we confess our sins, He is faithful and just to forgive us our sins and to cleanse us from all unrighteousness" (1 John 1:9).

The Sacrament of Confession is important because it constitutes the cure of spiritual illness. Since the goal of the Christian life is transformation in Christ, ridding ourselves of the corrupt and diseased fallen self must begin with the death of the ego. We humble ourselves before the priest when we confess our sins, for it is not just that Christ hears us; Christ hears us because of our act of humility in baring our souls in front of another person. Thus, Scripture establishes confession, recounting Christ's gift of authority to the Apostles and their successors to bestow forgiveness on penitents and exhorting us to confess even to one another (James 5:16). Through one another we achieve humility, and mystically this joins us to Christ.

AUGUST 7

The Key to a Good Prayer Life

It seems to be part of our human condition that we always want something. As children, we asked for candy or cookies and even sneaked food when our moms told us we had to wait till after dinner. As young people, we prayed only when we were facing an exam we weren't prepared for, asking God to help us pass the test. As adults, we pray for a better job, a nicer boss, or a bigger house. We pray that our children will be good, even if we have spent little time raising them up in the ways of God.

Our prayers reflect our self-centered nature. We see God as a sort of eternal parent who dispenses everything we think we need. A great deal of spiritual energy is spent asking for the things we just know we need for happiness; this demonstrates little trust that God will give us what we really need.

The beginning of a good prayer life can be found only in the truth of these divinely inspired words: "But seek first the kingdom of God and His righteousness, and all these things shall be added to you" (Matt. 6:33). Seek the Kingdom of God, and you will learn the true meaning of trust, the true meaning of love, and the true meaning of life.

The Kindly Priest and the American Tourist

A Protestant woman from Tacoma, Washington, was on vacation with her husband in the Greek city of Athens. Each day she walked to a small sidewalk cafe near the hotel for her coffee and watched the locals pass by. One of these locals was an Orthodox priest who'd pass by the cafe on his way to his parish church. The woman would smile, and the priest would nod, smile back, and continue on his way.

One day this Greek priest, who spoke English, noticed that the American woman looked sad, so he walked over to her table and asked if something was troubling her. She burst into tears and told the priest about her husband's medical problems and that she feared the worst. The priest sat with her and prayed for her and her husband. Each day he'd stop to sit at her table, praying for her husband's recovery. A few weeks passed, and the husband recovered from his illness and returned to the United States with his wife.

The memory of this priest's compassion for a foreign woman has remained with her all these many years. She shared her memories with her doctor, who is a friend of mine, and I now share them with you.

What a true disciple and servant of the Lord was this kindly priest. May we, like this priest, be attuned to those who are in need and to those the Lord places before us. May we reach out with open hearts and bring healing to those who are suffering, letting them know that we care and that they have a friend during their time of sorrow, need, or despair.

AUGUST 9

Bargaining with God

When we approach the Lord with our needs, we should take care that our prayer not be a form of bargaining. God knows our needs before we ask, and it is from our fallen nature that we approach God and try to bargain with Him. If we want to be healed of an illness that has befallen us or to ask for financial help, we should first ask God for strength and patience to endure whatever He has allowed to come our way.

The Lord knows what we need, and if we do not receive what we've asked for, we should cease to ask. It is more important that we gain peace of heart and spiritual strength. The more we learn patience and trust, the more we gain in the long run. Rather than persist in hounding God for what we think we need, we should seek first the Kingdom of God.

The best prayer of all is simply to say, "Lord Jesus Christ, have mercy on me, a sinner," knowing that union with Him is the ultimate goal. Having good health, money, things, or even earthly happiness must not be the focus of our prayer life.

It is far more beneficial in the long run if we seek inner peace first and learn to trust God for the rest. He loves us and desires that we come to the knowledge of the truth and inherit His Kingdom. When we've acquired a peaceful and contrite heart, we will seek to keep God's commandments and to love Him with all our hearts. Then we will have a true relationship with Him that is based on love rather than infantile bargaining.

AUGUST 10

The Transitory Nature of This Life

Ultimately, all is transitory, and there is no real security in this life. A number of years ago a fire in our forest came within one foot of destroying St. John Chapel. I haven't taken anything for granted ever since. Natural disasters and the economy have deprived countless American families of their homes, and the future does not look bright.

Most of us do not even own our homes, since taxes and mortgages are like a form of rent and make us vulnerable to banks and the Dow Jones average. Everything in this life is transitory and can disappear in a moment. Even our own life can end abruptly and without warning. Yet as Christians we keep moving forward, embracing whatever God has placed before us. Worrying about the future keeps us from focusing on the horizon and trusting that God is there with us every step of the way.

This life has been given to us as a time of preparation for the eternal life that is our inheritance as God's children. The transitory nature of this world will end when God's Kingdom is ushered in and we all stand before the Great Judgment Throne of God. Loss, pain, and suffering in this world will have not been in vain if we embrace everything as an occasion for transformation of self. To stand in the presence of God for eternity requires that we be deified, and all of life's suffering is meant to help prepare us for an eternity of communion with the Holy Trinity.

Educating the Mind while Ignoring the Heart

The importance of educating the mind is enormous. Without a solid education, we are told, our lives will amount to nothing.

One of my grandmothers grew up in Wisconsin as a simple, uneducated woman. She worked much of her life as a laundry woman, spoke in simple ways, and loved God and her family with all her heart and soul. By the world's standards, she was not a well-spoken woman, but when she spoke, her words went straight to the heart.

Whereas many rushed to become educated while ignoring the heart, my grandmother started with the heart. Her intellectual abilities were limited, but her amazing heart was what made her a great lady.

We endanger our souls if we educate ourselves without also developing our hearts, for the heart is life. The heart cannot grow if it is allowed to remain burdened by darkness and sin, and it must be purged by God, the source of life. We must kindle in our hearts the pure flame of life, letting it so burn that it will never go out.

AUGUST 12

Prayer: The Most Arduous of All Ascetic Practices

St. Gregory of Sinai said of the effort involved in prayer, "No bodily or spiritual activity without pain or toil ever brings fruit to him who practices it, because 'the kingdom of heaven suffers violence, and the violent take it by force' (Matt. 11:12)." Here, the word pain means remorse and contrition of spirit. For those who are weak physically, weeping and mourning for our sinfulness takes the place of physical effort.

It takes physical discipline for the heart to acquire the peace needed for prayer: "to the weak I became as weak, that I might win the weak" (1 Cor. 9:22). Those who are experienced in prayer must concentrate on the heart, and this should be done with great fear of God, because the union of the mind and heart (which precedes our union with God) is granted by divine grace.

"The great gift of prayer is usually preceded by some special sufferings and upheavals of the soul, which lead our spirit to realize the extent of our poverty and nothingness," according to St. Isaac the Syrian. In order to be worthy of this gift of grace, we need to be faithful in our humility and purity, and we must reject every sinful thought at its first appearance. Jesus said it is to the faithful, pure, and humble that the gifts of the Spirit are given (see Luke 16:10–12).

Archimandrite Sophrony said, "Of all ascetic practices the striving for prayer is the most arduous. Our spirit will be in constant flux. At times prayer flows like a strong current; at other times our heart will feel withered and dry. But the spells when we lose fervor should get briefer."

There Is No Salvation outside the Body of Christ

Salvation is communal by its very nature. The fierce individualism found in much of what claims to be Christianity is in opposition to the Orthodox understanding of faith. The Church as the Body of Christ is where we are united in Christ, becoming part of community. The ancient Greek word *ecclesia* means to be called into authentic community. It is within the Church that our personal transformation is intimately connected with the interaction we have with our fellow believers as we run side by side with them.

Ecclesia in modern usage refers to the Church and her role as a spiritual hospital, the place wherein we receive the healing that comes from Christ. This truth is demonstrated by the fact that we are called by the Scriptures to be at peace with our brothers and sisters before receiving the Holy Mysteries. We are asked to forgive others as we would be forgiven, and we are even called upon by Christ to love our enemies.

Our Christian faith cannot be lived in a vacuum, for our personal transformation requires working out our salvation within community. Even the confession of our sins takes place within this community, for each time we sin, we sin against the whole of the Body of Christ. When we receive the Body and Blood of Christ, we not only receive His Body and Blood, but also partake of the whole Body, the Church.

At the moment of our baptism, we are no longer defined as mere individuals but are united in the community of believers as one Body. Therefore, Orthodox believers understand that Christ, to whom we unite ourselves, is found in community—and this community is the Orthodox Church.

Holiness Comes Only to Those Who Are Watchful

Not an hour should pass without taking time to examine our heart, for the hour of judgment can come at any time, and we must be ready to give account to God for our lives. In the Gospel of Matthew, we read, "Blessed are the pure in heart, / For they shall see God" (5:8). It is clear that without a humble and contrite heart, we will not see God.

St. Isaac of Syria tells us, "No one has understanding if he is not humble, and he who lacks humility lacks understanding." The prescription given to us by all the Holy Fathers points out that discrimination and watchfulness are the path to achieving purity of heart. Someone who is proud and who has not rooted out the sickness within her heart will be unable to please God, for only holiness of life opens the doors to the paradise that awaits us.

We cannot make any spiritual improvement if we do not seek to please God with holiness of life; yet any good in our deeds must be attributed to God. "There is none who does good, no, not one," and "*there is* not a just man on earth who does good / And does not sin" (Rom. 3:12; Eccl. 7:20).

If we find we've neglected our spiritual struggle and acted with foolish abandon, we, in our weakness, must turn to God in repentance. This can happen only with an hourly examination of the heart. We must resolve to turn ourselves around, with God's help, and fight against the enemy of our souls, for holiness comes only to those who struggle.

AUGUST 15

The Battle with "Success"

Life is a constant battle with the material world. If you understand the tension that takes place on the spiritual level between what is transitory and what is eternal, you are better prepared for this spiritual warfare.

Many years ago I had given myself over to the acquisition of things. My position placed me in a field where most everyone around me, both colleagues and friends, judged success by what we owned, who we knew, where we vacationed, the car we drove, the clothes we wore, the restaurants we frequented.

With this as the basis of our collective lives, I'd become ever more aware that most of us were not very happy. Divorce was rampant, subtle sabotage of the careers of colleagues was not uncommon, infidelity was the norm, and bank accounts were never full enough. Success seemed like a dead end with a signpost that had misdirected all of us.

Having all the possessions, the money, the friendships, and the respect left me empty. My days became battlegrounds in a futile attempt at fulfillment and happiness. The things I'd been taught would bring happiness were not working. All my education and connections were not able to direct me to anything that made me feel like my life was worth the struggle.

My turning point was when I finally realized that the roadblock to that evasive happiness was my state of spiritual bankruptcy. My life had been given to me as a time of preparation for eternity, and I was squandering it by concentrating on the transitory.

When you abandon yourself to God, you find freedom, and victory is yours. Your life becomes His. Your struggles are His. Freedom is your trophy.

AUGUST 16

Advice to Orthodox College Students

The summer months are coming to a close, and many young people will be facing the prospect of heading off to college, some for the very first time. A scripture passage comes to mind: "Behold, I send you out as sheep in the midst of wolves. Therefore be wise as serpents and harmless as doves" (Matt. 10:16).

College professors almost universally enjoy challenging students to question authority, yet are taken aback when their own authority is questioned. They know they are addressing a class of impressionable minds and almost make sport of attacking the positions of their students.

My advice to Orthodox students is to refuse to be intimidated or discouraged. Most of these professors took years to acquire the knowledge and skill to successfully defend their belief system, or lack thereof, including atheism. Their pattern of teaching is nothing new, for there have been antagonists like them from before recorded history. Furthermore, their arguments are nothing new. They may be new to you, but suffice it to know these challenges to your faith have been answered by a great many apologists since the beginning of Christianity. The best advice I can offer the young Orthodox Christian heading off to college is this: The professor is a better debater than you, so don't place yourself in his scope. If you do, expect to be blown out of the water. Secondly, don't be embarrassed by your commitment to your Orthodox faith. Most students secretly wish to find a spiritual basis for the meaning of life. They may secretly envy you for your faith. My final advice is, "walk . . . with all lowliness and gentleness, with longsuffering, bearing with one another in love" (Eph. 4:1, 2).

Build a support system for yourself by gathering together with other college students to form a chapter of the Orthodox Christian Fellowship. Meet on a weekly basis for worship, study, and networking. Get to know your faith to the degree that you can stand up to the best of them when defending your beliefs. If you do, you may one day be the reason an atheist professor finds Christ and becomes an Orthodox Christian.

AUGUST 17

Freedom from the Fear of Death

Most Americans find the inevitability of death particularly difficult to face. We've become a people that eschew traditional funerals, preferring to "celebrate" the life of our loved one while disposing of the body and banning any sign of death from the memorial service. Yet our own eventual death is the very thing we should be thinking about if we want to be prepared for eternity.

When we live our lives focused on enjoyment, pleasure, and the acquisition of material goods, we enslave ourselves. Freedom from the bondage of this slavery, and the fear of death that comes with this bondage, can be found only in a relationship of love with our Creator. This love creates perfection and faultlessness, and when we think on our own death, we become free to perform every task for God.

In this relationship with God, our fallen and imprisoned heart is liberated. This love of God engenders a love that permeates our very essence, allowing us to love every person and every creature. Our heart burns with love. This love turns chaos into harmony; it is divine energy and divine strength that transforms us into the being God intended us to be. We are His children, deified and made whole, and the chaos of our lives is turned into harmony.

Wise Words on Judging Others

By all means, we should try to preserve peace of soul, and not be disturbed by offenses from others. For the preservation of peace of soul, it is also necessary by all means to avoid criticizing others.

St. Seraphim of Sarov

A man came to Elder Paisios of the Holy Mountain with a complaint about Greek priests hanging out in coffeehouses all day and not tending to their priestly duties. The elder responded by saying, "There are two types of people in the world, flies and bees. Flies know where all the dirt is, and where to find 'stink.' Whereas, bees know where all the flowers are, and know only that which smells beautiful."

The elder's words, together with the above words of St. Seraphim, are ones we should all live by. We spend entirely too much time looking for the faults of others, be they our bishop, our priest, or our neighbor, and not enough time looking for Christ in them. It is more profitable to judge only ourselves and to look only for what is lacking in ourselves.

A Smile Can Go a Long Way

Once I was sitting in a Seattle coffeehouse with my laptop open, working on some correspondence. Two college-age men were sitting at a table about two feet away. One of them made a rude remark that was obviously meant for my ear; he suggested to his friend that only a stupid old man would believe in God. I smiled at them and continued to work on my laptop.

Before leaving the café, I purchase two gift cards and asked the young woman to give them to the two young men after I left. About two weeks later I again visited the café. There they were, the two young men. They came to my table and asked if they could sit with me. I smiled broadly and said I would be delighted to have them join me.

One of the young men asked me why I'd purchased gift cards for them when I'd obviously heard their slam against me. I told them God had told me to buy them the gift cards and that the gifts were from God. One of the young men teared up and asked for my forgiveness. I told him I'd forgiven him the very moment he'd uttered those words, because Christ loved him. How could I not love them if God loved them, I asked.

Sometimes the most unlovable are the very ones who need signs of love the most. Who knows the difference a kind word or a smile can make in the life of an individual who is rude or abusive?

The most difficult people to deal with are often the very people who need our love and kindness the most. Being treated with respect and love, regardless of their behavior, can turn around the angry neighbor or coworker. They are the people who need our prayers.

God can change any heart, turning around the lives of the very worst people because of our prayers. Who are we to judge them? Perhaps they are there because we need to learn the lesson of forgiveness and charity.

AUGUST 20

How to Guard Your Heart

The lifeless things of this world offer no spiritual satisfaction, yet we often sell ourselves to things or people by giving them power over our hearts. It is easy to feel abandoned or hurt by those to whom we've given power. If we need affirmation from others, we take the chance that we empower demons who would use our personal needs to keep us from focusing on what is eternal.

Our need for affirmation from others can distract us from focusing on God. Ownership of our hearts should be reserved for God alone, for evil spirits use whatever means they can to make us feel abandoned, discounted, or unloved by those we've allowed to own our hearts. We can easily be distracted from our service to God if we allow ourselves to become envious of the recognition others receive. Recognition for a job well done can be nice, but not if it comes at the price of having lost our soul.

God's love must be sufficient, for only our relationship with Him has lasting and eternal value. Sometimes we have to pull ourselves back from others and enter into the silence. This self-imposed exile is the spiritual retreat that helps us focus on what we have in God. Then our relationships with others become healthy, fulfilling, and life-giving.

Open Wide the Doors to the Kingdom

The question recently came up among clergy of our diocese as to whether it is proper to allow a man to attend services while wearing an earring. It seemed to me that asking that he remove the earring would make him feel unwelcome, and unless it was causing undue distraction for other worshipers, the Church needed to accommodate these variations in style.

Style is style, and it is ever changing. Men of my generation were the first long-hairs in more than a century (yes, I was a hippie) and sported paisley bell-bottoms, tie-dyed shirts, and beads. The young have always experimented with their own generational style. That said, the Church has the duty to require those entering into the temple to dress modestly so as not to show disrespect to God's house or to distract other worshipers.

We are losing our youths, as statistics are clearly showing, so let us not make it even easier for them to leave by placing demands on them that are, ultimately, unimportant. I have worked with youths my entire monastic life, and they respond to me both when they come to the monastery and when I visit college campuses, because they sense I accept them just as they are.

I know a man whose neck and hands are tattooed with a barbed-wire design. He is now living out his repentance as a Benedictine monk because somewhere along the way he was made to feel welcome in a church. When I met him, I told him he would be a great example to youths of the truth that the door to repentance is open wide to all.

The great elder Archimandrite Sophrony of St. John the Baptist Monastery in Essex, England, once greeted the visiting daughter of a monk with great joy and sweetness, even though she had a large purple Mohawk. Love and acceptance open wide the doors to the Kingdom. We must love young and old into the Church just as they are.

Do We Think Ourselves Wiser Than the Church?

When the society around us regards the Church's laws and traditions unfavorably, we can easily give in to thinking the same thing and disregard them ourselves. If our work associates, friends, and even family members think our adherence to the periods of fasting is extreme, we can find ourselves giving in to peer pressure, just as children are known to do. If taking time out from work to attend special feast-day services is criticized by coworkers as being excessive, do we decline to ask for the day off for the next feast?

If we choose the traditions and societal structures of those around us in preference to the Church's traditions, canons, and laws, we will soon find ourselves betraying our Christian faith. Christianity was not meant to be easy; it is often compared to doing battle. If we desire the easy comforts and pleasures of this world, we will eventually lose the battle, and we will perish. If we prefer the laws of this world over the laws of the Church, in the end we will have lost what is most essential and eternal in value.

In times of turmoil and earthly hardship, we will find we have not built up the spiritual strength and fortitude to stand strong against the winds of destruction that lay hold of our lives. As we submit to mere human traditions and authority, we will find that a thief has taken the very treasure that is the Kingdom of God, and we will be left by the wayside, the gates of heaven having been closed to us.

If we revile the laws of the Church, we revile Christ Himself, who is the Head of the Church. This is true because the laws of the Church were given by the Holy Spirit through the apostles and therefore are not simply human traditions. Let us not think we are great teachers of our own souls, but let us humbly call out together with the wise thief, "Remember me, O Lord, in Your kingdom!"

Belittle No One

If we allow ourselves to belittle others, either because of their appearance or because of their state in life, we dismiss the truth that God can, in His divine providence, transform anyone into a saint. The person who seems to have succumbed to a worldly life, who is covered in tattoos and nose rings and has orange hair, could be in the process of coming into an awareness of God. Our judging her or shunning her could hamper this process. Human weakness can be changed by divine power. We must recognize this truth so that we never condemn or judge another.

We must always remember that it is God who has shown mercy to us, and it is this same God who wishes that all come to the knowledge of the truth and be saved. He is able to help all. St. Maximos the Confessor said, "And if in His providence He does not deliver all men together from their passions, yet like a good and loving physician, He heals with individual treatment each of those who are trying to make progress." If we judge others by their appearance or by their lifestyle, we forget that we belong to Christ because He first loved us. It was we who were lost but have been found.

Praying for Those Who Are Suffering

When we first become aware that someone we know is suffering, we must begin to pray for him. We must pray with much sincerity and with tears, knowing that our brother is being tormented and is filled with despondency. As Christians we must believe that intercessory prayer, when spoken with love and complete attention, leads to the intervention of the Holy Spirit, who brings healing of body and peace of soul to the person being tormented.

If you have a neighbor or coworker who despises you and is overcome with hatred whenever she sees you, start praying for her. Pray not that she would like you, but that she would find freedom from the anger and hatred that are ruling her life. If you have a relative who can never say anything nice about you, start praying for him, asking that God free him from the sin of gossip and infuse his heart with the understanding that he is a worthy person in his own right and need not divert the scrutinizing attention that would betray him by gossiping about another. If there are people you dislike, pray all the more for them, knowing that true love for them will grow in your own heart through the sincere act of remembering them before the throne of God.

Intercessory prayer is not just for monks but is a necessary component of every Orthodox Christian's life. For it is a wonderful way of remembering we are all connected as the children of the Most High.

Be Ready to Defend the Faith

All of us must be prepared to defend our faith in a challenging secular setting. Orthodoxy is not like any other form of Christianity. Only in Orthodoxy do we keep over half the year as periods of fasting. Only in Orthodoxy do we stand during our services, some lasting for many hours. Only in Orthodoxy are we expected to confess our sins to Christ frequently before a witness (the priest).

My point is that Orthodoxy is not "Christianity lite." The Orthodox Church has not attempted to reinvent herself every ten or twenty years. Her teachings, divine services, and way of life have remained virtually unchanged for two millennia and are not likely to change for the next thousand years. If it works, why change it?

Since the Church, ancient as she is, is still set in a modern world, her faithful need to be ready to live the life Orthodoxy expects of her faithful, regardless of the influences and temptations that abound around us. This is possible only if we strengthen our resolve to live our Orthodoxy in this secular environment by educating ourselves about our faith. Blind acceptance of the Church's practices and beliefs is simply not enough. We will ultimately fail in our adherence to our Orthodox Faith if we go through the motions without understanding.

Although the services impart the teachings of our faith (provided we understand the liturgical language being used), spiritual reading must also be a part of our daily routine. We must see spiritual reading and following the daily readings of the Church year as equally important with brushing our teeth. Reading books on prayer and the inner life should be as much a part of our day as having a nourishing breakfast. Feeding your soul is not just the job of your priest, for that would be like not expecting your children to do their homework.

The great ship of the Church is taking you on a wonderful journey into the heart of God. Be prepared for the storms that abound, that you not find yourself being tossed overboard.

The Jesus Prayer Banishes Anger

The very best tool to banish anger is the recitation of the Jesus Prayer. Calling upon the Holy Name of Jesus when under spiritual attack is a quick way to dispel the demon of anger. For example, when confronted with a driver who has cut you off on the freeway, uttering the name of Jesus by praying the Jesus Prayer is a sure way to bring peace to your soul and quench the fire of anger.

When you feel rage at someone overtaking your peace, saying the Jesus Prayer for that person changes your heart and opens you to the person who has enraged you. He becomes a child of God, even a brother, and is worthy of your prayers and love.

This prayer removes the memory of the perceived wrong done toward you and restores your peace. All malice is dispelled and replaced by the peace that passes all understanding. It is the peace that comes from the Prince of Peace, Jesus Christ, our Lord, God, and Savior.

Lord Jesus Christ, have mercy on me.

Lord Jesus Christ, have mercy on that person in the red truck.

Lord Jesus Christ, Son of God, have mercy on us all.

AUGUST 27

Experiencing the Reality of God

It is important to remember that our God did not create us as puppets, but rather as persons with the freedom to respond, or not, to His invitation to enter into communion with Him. I have been able to experience the presence of God because of the freedom I've been granted by a loving God who has reached out to me with grace and mercy. I, like everyone, can experience the presence of God through the joyful and awesome encounter with Christ while participating in the celebration of the Divine Liturgy.

I've experienced God while hearing a good confession and witnessing the results of the outpouring of God's grace upon the penitent sinner. I experience the presence of God while witnessing the wonder of discovery in the faces of college students who are hearing of the mystical theology of Orthodoxy for the first time. I experience the presence of God while visiting an old woman who has walked with God her whole life. I experience the presence of the Lord when witnessing the giggle of a child being hugged by his grandmother. I witness the love of God in the face of my confessor and the fellowship of my brother monks. I experience the love of God while concelebrating with my archbishop and my brother priests. I experience God in the early hours of the morning while I do my cell rule.

I experience God in the sunrise and in the sunset. I experience God in the freshly picked rose and the lapping of the water while standing at the seashore. I experience God as I taste the fresh corn from the stalk. I experience God in the purring sound of our cat, Hammi, while holding him in my arms. Finally, I experience God in the solitude of my heart.

Sin Is Illness, and the Church Is the Hospital

Our Orthodox faith defines sin as an illness that is in need of healing, not as a crime that requires punishment. The Church is a hospital for the soul whose therapists (priests) first sought therapy and then became therapists. As a healing institution, the Church is a place for broken souls. We come before Christ as tarnished images, far from what God intended. Yet this very Creator God is patient and loving, quick to forgive. He invites us to holiness, to be made whole. His grace is sufficient to lift us up out of our mire and into the height of a joy that is meant to be eternal. We need only humble ourselves and ask for help, and the Kingdom is ours.

Heaven and hell are not about location but about relationship. All that is needed is our response, followed by action. We say yes to God's invitation while seeking out the therapy that is ours within the life of the Church. Wholeness (holiness) is ours through this relationship with Christ, whose redemptive act upon the Cross, together with His conquering of death by death, delivers us from the depths of estrangement. We are lifted up to God, having been made whole, and eternal communion with God is our destiny.

A Defeatist Attitude Is a Prescription for Defeat

As Christians, we must believe that our ultimate welfare is in the hands of God and recognize that our life, although filled with many difficulties and struggles, is a journey in anticipation of the eternal life that is to come. Because this journey is not without sorrow and pain, worry and anxiety, it is easy to surrender to a defeatist attitude and act as though there were no hope.

Our attitude and our speech reflect on the health of our soul and are indicators of the wellness of our heart. If we are prone to complaining about our lives or about those around us, it is unlikely we will be prepared to choose a positive direction when the choice is before us.

The way we relate to others has an effect on their lives—and ours. If we make an effort to be positive and live our lives with hope and faith, those around us profit and become healthier in spirit and in heart. Giving ourselves over to anxiety and fear does nothing but bring us down, and it pulls those around us down as well. Allowing ourselves to speak negatively does nothing to promote well-being; in fact, it can worsen a situation. Approaching life with a defeatist attitude is a surefire way of being defeated in the end. "For the thing I greatly feared has come upon me, / And what I dreaded has happened to me" (Job 3:25).

The great King Solomon said, "To everything *there is* a season, / A time for every purpose under heaven: ... / A time to keep silence, / And a time to speak" (Eccl. 3:1, 7). Negative speech contributes nothing to the heart but death. Receiving everything that comes our way with joy is the only way to bring about the healing of the heart. Negative speech is a reflection of a heart that is in need of healing, but joyful speech is like water for a thirsty plant that brings forth fruit for all around.

AUGUST 30

How to Be Whole—Body and Soul

Unlike angels, who are entirely spiritual beings, we dwell in a material world. To be whole, we must worship God both in body and soul. This teaching is central to our Christian faith and is an affirmation of the sacramental nature of this material world. Because of this truth, icons have played a central role in Christian history, for they proclaim Jesus Christ's physical reality as God incarnate.

Icons depicting the Holy Virgin show the Christ Child with bare feet, reminding us that He walked the earth among us. He (the Logos), through whom all that exists was brought into existence, condescended to take on our flesh and walk among us. He joined His divinity to our humanity, that we might be icons of God.

The Lord Jesus Christ was born, lived, died, and rose from the dead in this material world. He broke bread with His disciples, ate fish with His friends, and invited His disciple Thomas to feel the wound in his side after His Holy Resurrection. Most of the miracles He performed were physical healings.

Because of the Incarnation, we must not allow our prayers to be based in our head. Using icons while praying, keeping our eyes open that we may behold the beauty of God's creation, brings our whole nature, both body and soul, into the material world into which we were born. This physical nature of prayer is what connects us to our true self, composed of both body and soul. This is where God reaches down to embrace us. Cutting off the physical world (keeping our eyes closed) does not bring us closer to God.

Icons are wonderful aids in our communion with God because they serve as bridges to Christ and links with the Holy Virgin and the saints. They are by no means necessary, for sitting on the top of a mountain or walking on the seashore with eyes open allows you to behold the beauty of God's creation and His love for you, His child. Both the beauty of an icon and the glory of God's creation can be windows for us into eternity.

AUGUST 31

Do Not Turn Right or Left

St. Basil the Great said, "The person who does not allow his thought to incline towards excess or deprivation but directs it to the midpoint, that of virtue, is upright in his heart." Virtue must be practiced. Just as those who desire to play the piano must concentrate all their energy and attention on the keys and the music, so must we give ourselves over to practicing virtues.

St. John Cassian tells us we should make every effort to strive "by humility to acquire for ourselves the good gift of sober-mindedness, which can preserve us unharmed by excess from both sides. For, as the Fathers say, the extremes from both sides are equally harmful—both excess of fasting and filling the belly, excess of vigil and excessive sleep, and other excesses."

Walking this Royal Way (or Path) means we do not give ourselves over to lukewarmness or indifference regarding our Orthodox faith, nor do we see strictness or correctness or even canonicity as the goal. If we are to live according to Orthodox teachings, we also cannot give ourselves over to living in step with the times or to making strictness or correctness the end-all.

As we strive to live our lives in balance, avoiding the extremes of excess on both sides, we must allow moderation to affect how we live our faith. By striving to live our lives in pursuit of virtue, we will walk the Royal Way in all sobriety, with humility and virtue as our rule and Christ as our compass.

Children Learn the Love of God from Their Parents

Most Orthodox parents want their children to grow up attending Sunday liturgies and staying active in the life of the Church throughout their lives. Yet few parents demonstrate the importance of having a relationship with God in front of their children. If you do not make God important, neither will your child. Children can see hypocrisy; they know when you are not following through with the teachings of the Church during the week. They hear when you take the Lord's name in vain. They observe when you don't make prayer central to your day. They notice if you only speak of God on Sunday mornings.

Making the sign of the cross, lighting candles, and burning incense only on Sundays teaches your children to compartmentalize their faith, thus leaving them defenseless in a world filled with temptations and distractions that lead them away from things of a spiritual nature. If you do not demonstrate the importance of prayer before your children, you will leave them defenseless in a world that hates Christ. Your children need to pray with you, read the Scriptures with you, be taught the Faith by you.

If you do not make your home a domestic church, your children will be lost to Christ, and Orthodoxy will not be lived out beyond your own grave in the lives of future members of your family.

What about Non-Orthodox Christians?

St. Silouan the Athonite was once traveling by train with an archimandrite who was quick to correct others about the True Faith. Coming upon a group of traveling Roman Catholics, this man proceeded to tell them that they must become Orthodox because their faith was without grace.

The saint asked him if it was indeed a fact that the Roman Catholics believed that Christ was true God and that He was present in the Eucharist. He also asked if it was true that these Catholics believed in the Trinity and venerated the Holy Virgin and the relics of the saints. The archimandrite answered yes. St. Silouan said he must rejoice in the knowledge they do have.

This does not mean we see the Orthodox Church as anything less than the Church Christ founded. It means we do not allow ourselves to think we have the right to correct or teach anyone. We must honor other people's beliefs. The truth found within Orthodoxy must be shared by living our faith in love, not by judging or correcting others. Truth, wherever it is found, is Orthodox truth. If other religions embrace some of these truths that are Orthodox, we must rejoice and give thanks for that.

People who love God and are trying to live holy lives pleasing to Him, according to the knowledge they have been given, are to be respected. They may not have the fullness of apostolic truth, but if they are believers in God and are trying to live a life pleasing to Him, they have God as their Father, just as we do. They can have the Church as their Mother only if they see the difference Orthodoxy has made in our lives.

That arrogant archimandrite could have shared the beauty of Orthodoxy had he embraced those Roman Catholics as fellow disciples of Christ. They would have seen Christ in him and known that Orthodoxy is a faith centered in love.

Making a Habit Out of Our Passions

All the Holy Fathers counsel us to do battle with the passions. Yet we continue committing the same sins over and over. Sometimes it is because we've allowed ourselves to fall into the habit of submitting to the same passions time and again. We stole an item from the office and got away with it, so the next time we think we need an extra pen, we take it. Perhaps we have twenty such pens in a large mug, sitting on the counter in our kitchen. Do we need all of them? Of course not. Yet we continue to collect them, because we've gotten into the habit of taking them. Do we think our job in a restaurant gives us the right to smuggle out food at the end of our shift, and do we think our low salary gives us an excuse to steal? Or perhaps we switch a high-end bulk coffee into the low-end store-brand bag so we can pay three dollars less per pound than we should.

Perhaps we snap at our spouse or our children, even when we are not angry. Or we drive aggressively, thinking we need to be ahead of someone driving the speed limit. Maybe we are verbally abusive with our employees because we have the power to be so.

To be freed from such passions, we can start by slowly returning the pens to the office, two by two, until they've all been returned. We can arrive early at the restaurant job and stay beyond our shift, paying for the stolen food with our extra hours of service. We can purchase a money order and anonymously pay back the grocery store the amount we've stolen from them over the year. We can choose to drive in the slow lane, leaving early enough to reduce the temptation to drive aggressively. As we drive, we can listen to a talk on Ancient Faith Radio, making the end-of-the-day commute a time of spiritual reflection.

Isolation Rules

We live in an age when families no longer eat dinner together, and children watch TV, play computer games, and text their friends from their bedrooms. People sit in a cafe with friends, all the while texting or talking to someone else on their cell phones. We have become a people living together in isolation.

I remember visiting my elderly grandmother. I'd walk into her kitchen and hear a radio, while in the living room I'd find her TV on, even though she rarely listened to either. I knew this was a sign that she was lonely; the noise kept her company. Yet when she did have someone there to visit, all the other sounds were shut off. On pastoral calls, I've had to ask people to turn off their TVs.

People don't often notice the distractions they've allowed to intrude into their homes, having become so accustomed to these invaders. Many husbands are shocked when their wives file for divorce, having failed to notice that the lines of communication between them and their spouses had been lost years earlier.

Children are no longer supervised with their homework because their parents are uninvolved. They trust their children are working on their homework, but the children are often watching videos while texting their friends.

Even in our spiritual lives we tend to live in isolation. Many reserve their prayers for issues revolving around finances or their health or that of a family member. They rarely think of the importance of corporate prayer with family and friends, apart from the Sunday Liturgy. Prayer is a private matter for them, rarely shared with others.

Entertainment has also taken on a central role in our lives, becoming so important as to replace visiting neighbors or friends. I remember the day when families would sit on their porches on hot summer nights, sipping lemonade and waving at passing neighbors out for a stroll. Now front porches have been replaced with private back patios, where no one can see us. Gone are the days of neighborliness. Isolation rules!

The End of Isolation

The Church is the Body of Christ and by her very nature is anything but an isolating institution. Yet we fail to involve ourselves with one another. The holy kiss Orthodox Christians pass on when we meet one another is one way we avoid the isolation that dominates the society in which we live. Kissing our priest's hand is another. So is staying for the coffee hour or the agape meal after the Sunday Liturgy as well as attending midweek services.

Taking children out for a Sunday afternoon drive, exploring the countryside with music and cell phones off, is a wonderful way families can reconnect. Taking grandmother on a family picnic to a local park is a good, old-fashioned way of introducing community to children. Letting them play with cousins in a park as the extended family gathers for a picnic can build family bonds that last a lifetime.

When was the last time you sat around with a senior member of your family and asked him or her to share memories? What a wonderful way to reconnect an aging grandfather to his youth and show him you value his life experiences. What an invaluable legacy you impart to your own children, letting them know they were not born in a vacuum but are a part of a long line of real people.

I am astounded when I think of how much my grandparents are a real part of who I've become. It is not just genetics they passed on to me, but memories of family history. Even parts of my personality were passed down from my great-grandfather, and filling my study with photographs, icons, and collectibles is a style I inherited from grandparents.

It just takes some commitment on our part to build family and community. What a wonderful thing it would be if every family had two hours each night when the house phone, the cell phones, the TV, and all other outside intrusions were banned—then they ended the evening standing before the icon corner, praying the Evening Prayers.

SEPTEMBER 6

A Reason for the Hope That Is in You

If we are attentive to all the Lord does for us, we can endure times when our prayers seem to go unanswered. That God is not always giving us just what we think we need in no way means He does not hear us. Our days are filled with gifts from God, most often in ways we do not even notice. When we pray in the Our Father "Give us this day our daily bread," we are asking God to give us what we need. It is not required of us that we be specific in our requests, for our loving Lord knows before we ask.

The Lord comes to us in the stillness of our hearts and provides for us in ways that are not even known to us. He loved us before our conception in the wombs of our mothers and is close to us even when we think He is far away. If we but allow ourselves to look closely, we will see His gifts abound in every breath we take, in every flower we pick, in every child we hold. Our hope is eternal, because God's love is eternal.

"But sanctify the Lord God in your hearts, and always be ready to give a defense to everyone who asks you a reason for the hope that is in you, with meekness and fear" (1 Pet. 3:15).

Becoming the Image of Christ to Others

To be true to our calling as the children of God, we must live in imitation of Christ. We must imitate His meekness and humility. We must love others just as He did. We must be willing to be transformed and made whole, that others might see in us the light of Christ.

We must closely scrutinize every hour, so that we make sure the image of the Savior shines forth as we interact with others. If we find ourselves growing angry toward a family member or a coworker, we must sincerely repent at that very moment.

Tomorrow is never early enough, for the day of our repentance must be today! If we see an old woman who needs help paying for her groceries, now is the time to reach into our own pocketbooks. If we see a woman being abused by her boyfriend, now is the time to speak out on her behalf or to call the police. If a clerk is rude to us, a smile must be our only response.

Church services, personal prayer, and fasting are all required components of the Christian life, but they are never enough if we wish to be saved. We must see ourselves as "our brother's keeper," for if we do not love our neighbor, we will not inherit the Kingdom of God. Only the Holy Spirit can ignite our souls with love for God and love for neighbor, but we must cooperate by working to make our hearts open to Christ.

Christianity is not meant to be an easy path, for how can anyone hear the words of our Savior that require us to love even our enemies, and not know how hard this journey is? Yet if we take up our cross hourly, we will have victory over our fallen nature, and we will be given the power to love everyone, even as we love ourselves. And the love of God will grow stronger in our own hearts as we remember these words of Scripture: "Without Me you can do nothing" (John 15:5).

Believing in God Is Not Enough

Many people believe God exists, but they do not know Him. It is one thing to believe in God, but quite another to have a personal relationship with Him. In John 14:8–9, the Apostle Philip asked Jesus to show the disciples the Father. Jesus responded by wondering how such a question could be asked: "Have I been with you so long, and yet you have not known Me, Philip? He who has seen Me has seen the Father; so how can you say, 'Show us the Father'?"

No amount of study can reveal God to us, for He is revealed to us by the Holy Spirit. No scientist or philosopher or theologian or historian can know anything about God unless the Holy Spirit has revealed it to him. Faith in God comes to us as a gift, and our response to this gift requires that we keep His commandments, for in doing so our faith becomes a relationship with God that is made personal. This faith transforms our lives and makes us whole. Entering into a personal relationship with Christ brings healing to a soul that has been darkened by sin and has no hope. In Christ that hope is restored, and we are brought into the Kingdom of God.

Complaining Bears the Fruit of Bitterness

Complaining seems to be such a little sin and nothing to worry about. Yet the impact of a complaining heart is spiritually ruinous, for when we complain, we bear bitter fruits that destroy our peace and the peace of those around us.

When we refuse to fill our lives with complaints, we preserve our inner peace. Some live as though avoiding complaining will make everything worse, because they would be ignoring the reality of negative things. Yet when we complain, we return evil for evil, giving the fallen spirits the very thing they thrive upon.

Complaining never changes a thing, but only strengthens the power of the evil that is the very basis of our complaints. When we face every bad situation with a positive response, we empower the heart to do good by diminishing the power of negativity. By keeping a positive mindset, we banish the sin of complaining from our lives, and everyone around us is bathed in a healing and healthy setting.

Instead of complaining, do something about your complaints. Make a difference in your life and in the lives of those around you by keeping focused on making a difference. If there is a reason to complain, change your complaint into a positive action that changes your perspective. Complainers never change a thing by their constant negativity, other than make those around them want to take a cab to the other side of town.

When God Seems Distant

There are times in our lives when God seems distant or even absent from us. These are usually times when your faith seems weak and you struggle to believe God really cares for you, or perhaps you begin to question whether God even exists. In Western Christian tradition these moments are often referred to as the dark night of the soul. God seems as though He's far removed from you, and you struggle with your faith.

In such times, it is good to remember that God is closer to you than your own breath; you only feel He's absent. God uses such periods as a way to make you work at your relationship with Him. As you struggle, you grow stronger. When God seems to withdraw Himself, He is like a parent who stands his toddler on his feet and moves a few feet away, encouraging the child to take his first steps alone. The parent is prepared to reach out, should the child fall, but letting her take that first step is necessary for her development.

Each time we are forced to work at this relationship, God's grace builds us up, making it possible for us to mature in the faith. Spiritual growth cannot happen unless we feel the need for God, since the Lord will not force Himself on us. The awareness of God's presence in our lives comes through struggle, and as long as we do our part, God's grace flows abundantly.

SEPTEMBER 11

Living in Expectation of Miracles

While just a little boy in the Lutheran Church, I asked the pastor why we didn't see miracles in the church like those in the Bible. He told me miracles had been used in New Testament times to jumpstart the church and were not needed now. I remember feeling cheated, for I wanted to see miracles; I felt we still needed them.

A Coptic man in Irvine, California, prayed for help from St. George the Great Martyr, and the saint appeared before him and gave him a wooden cross. Within a short time, this cross was gushing forth holy myrrh, which healed those who were anointed with it.

The Myrrh-Streaming Icon of the Mother of God of Hawaii also performs miracles of healing, both physical and spiritual. Before bypass surgery, I anointed myself with myrrh from this icon, and the cardiologist canceled the surgery right in the operating room because it was no longer necessary.

The scriptures tell us we can move mountains if we only have the faith of a mustard seed, yet many don't expect to see a miracle, even when they pray for one. I suspect it is because they don't think their faith is strong enough. We go about our lives as though there probably is a God out there, but He can hardly be interested in us.

If we begin to live each day with the expectation that God is not only there, but is actually interacting with us in a real way, we soon experience the truth of this. We begin to see with new eyes and hear with new ears how much God enters into each and every moment of our lives.

Faith must be built up little by little, much as a painter puts on layers of paint until one day, after layer upon layer, a beautiful painting is resting on the easel. Faith is formed through layers of learning to trust, so that one day we recognize the miracles that have been happening around us all along.

Don't React, Be at Peace

E ach day brings new challenges to the health of your soul. When a family member or coworker makes a remark that is meant to anger you, you need to guard your heart. When those around you are gossiping about someone, that is an opportunity for you to keep silent. The driver who just cut you off on the freeway, the woman who pushes her way in front of you in the checkout line, the rude neighbor—all give you an opportunity to take control and grow stronger spiritually.

Trials and temptations, when confronted with a peaceful heart, are conduits of healing and make the soul that much stronger and healthier. Reacting does nothing but bring paralysis of the soul, binding us to our fallen nature. Receiving all these temptations with a peaceful heart and not reacting to negative stimuli help strengthen you for the next round of trial and temptation. Little by little, you will find that the peace of Christ fills your every waking moment, bringing on a joyful spirit and a peaceful heart.

SEPTEMBER 13

The Mind inside the Heart

In the patristic tradition, the heart is the center of our self-awareness. This self-awareness is the energy of the mind inside the heart, something the Holy Fathers referred to as our "noetic faculty."

There is an important distinction between the Western and Eastern understandings of how we come to know God. The scholastic approach emphasizes the use of logic and reason in the acquisition of the knowledge of God, as seen in the teachings of Augustine of Hippo and Thomas Aquinas, and is unknown in the East.

In Orthodox theology, the mind and logic are not the same thing; logic functions within the brain, while the mind functions within the heart. Thus, the noetic faculty of the heart is the energy of the mind inside the heart. This important distinction results in the Eastern Church seeing herself not as a religious institution, but rather as a hospital of the soul, where one comes for therapeutic procedures that restore the health of the soul and allow it to progress toward the ultimate goal of union with God (*theosis*).

In the life of the Church, we enter into ascetic struggle like an athlete working out. We do this through fasting, prayer, and the reception of the Holy Mysteries (Holy Communion) in order to be made well. We are restored to health within the walls of this hospital of the soul, the Church, and trained in this athletic/ascetic dimension of living.

Our mishandling of the memory of God that led to the Fall is corrected and reactivated through the healing of the nous (the eye of the soul), and that memory is restored. This healing is not of a juridical nature, whereby an angry God has decided to overlook the evil and fallen nature of our souls by the bloodletting of His Son. Instead, it is through the cleansing of the nous that has been darkened, restoring us to health and wholeness. The memory of God is thus restored, and we are again in full communion with the Most High, freed from the permanence of death by the trampling down of the power of death through Christ's Holy Resurrection.

Arrow Prayers

Many Church Fathers taught the use of "arrow prayers," deliberately short prayers for personal devotion that were easily remembered and could communicate one's love for God while seeking His help. They are like arrows being shot into the air, wholeheartedly demonstrating our sincerity in asking God's help.

One of my personal favorites is an arrow prayer attributed to St. Gregory Palamas: "Lord, enlighten my darkness; Lord, enlighten my darkness; Lord, enlighten my darkness." This is the perfect prayer when seeking God's help in keeping His commandments and doing battle with habitual sins. By this prayer we are asking that grace abound and transformation take place. It is a prayerful plea for God's mercy, that He make us holy by coming quickly to our aid.

It is the perfect prayer to utter at the very moment we are receiving the Holy Mysteries of Christ's Body and Blood—the hot coals that burn within, bringing about healing of body and soul and illuminating our heart. In this prayer we confess before God that we are living in a state of darkness, and we are asking Him to dispel all the darkness that keeps us from attaining holiness and communing with Him.

St. Macarius the Great said, "There is no need at all to make long discourses; it is enough to stretch out one's hands and say, 'Lord, as you will, and as you know, have mercy.' And if the conflict grows fiercer say, 'Lord, help!' He knows very well what we need and he shows us his mercy."

The Role of Obedience in the Acquisition of Humility

In the Christian life there are two paths to salvation, and whichever road you choose you embrace with your whole being. Both marriage and monasticism allow the acquisition of a humble and a contrite heart. Unless we attain this, there is no salvation.

The salvific role of the institution of marriage and of the monastic vocation is the destruction of self-will. In marriage, the husband and wife are charged with being obedient to one another. The crowns used in the Orthodox marriage ceremony represent the crowns of martyrdom—death to self. The obedience a monk gives to his abbot is also a path to the destruction of self-will. The ego is the enemy, for just as Satan tempted Adam and Eve in the Garden, he uses the ego to keep us from communion with God.

When you are disobedient to your spouse or the rule of the monastery, God's grace departs from you. If you argue with your spouse or your abbot, pride and self-will rule over you, and you become the loser.

When you give yourself over to humble obedience, grace abounds. Each day you should begin with the prayer, "Lord Jesus Christ, help me to pass through this day without sin." The use of the Jesus Prayer throughout the day is a good way to keep yourself centered in that plea to Christ to help you through your day. "Lord Jesus Christ, Son of God, have mercy on me, a sinner."

The crushing of self-will takes effort and struggle, for our fallen nature is all about "me" and is in rebellion against God. Ascetic struggle—keeping the fasts, being strict in your observance of your prayer rule, making the services at your parish church the center of your week—contribute to your eventual triumph in your struggle for the prize: humbleness of heart.

God's grace abounds and is our ready helper. Like St. Paul, we can say that anything good we have done is Christ in us. God did not create us as robots but gave us freedom of choice. Choose wisely, and life with God is yours for eternity.

Joy Is an Infallible Sign of God's Presence

Although we have no written evidence that our Lord Jesus Christ laughed, I am convinced he did. How could He have shared in our humanity with perfection had he not had a sense of humor and shared moments of laughter with His disciples? Christ used humor when He depicted a camel struggling to get through the eye of a needle (Matt. 19:24). And we read in Proverbs 17:22, "A merry heart does good, like medicine."

Laughter is a precious gift, for it allows us to share circumstances in a special way. When we allow ourselves to enjoy funny events, we are able to put ourselves in proper perspective. Our ability to laugh at ourselves helps reduce our sense of self-importance.

That a Christian can laugh does not suggest it is proper to smile at dirty humor or to make light of another person's infirmity or failure. Our humor must never be based on ridicule or on the demeaning of another.

A sense of humor demonstrates to others that we live with joy and gladness in our hearts, because we have reason to be happy. We believe the gift of salvation is good reason to be happy, since the Lord's ministry did not end on the Cross but was followed by His Resurrection. Living with a joyful heart adds value to our faith because it makes others want to share in the joy they see in us.

We can laugh because we know that all will work out in the end because God loves us, and we believe His providential hand is at work in our lives. We believe God knows there is plenty of sadness, sorrow, and sickness in this life, but it will not prevail, because His plan for our salvation is at work.

The old Celtic saying, "Life is all about loving, living, and laughing, not about hating, dying, and moaning," has as its basis the Orthodox Christianity of the Celtic people. It is an oxymoron for a Christian to be crabby, grumpy, and whiny; joy is the infallible sign of God's presence.

SEPTEMBER I 7

The Cure for Our Disordered State

Humanity is in a perpetual state of disorder, far from the ordered life God intended for us. The cure for this disordered state is to be found in prayer. On the foundation of prayer we seek out the healing that will restore us to the image God intended at the moment of man's creation.

Prayer is the yearning of the soul toward the image of its prototype. When we are purified by God's grace, it is an attraction of like to like. We are deified by contact with the Creator, returned to an ordered state, and made whole.

We can achieve nothing by our efforts alone; yet if we commit ourselves to a prayer rule and stick with it, the Lord will reward us with an abundance of grace, and we will be restored to the ordered life we were intended to enjoy. Just as it takes two men, cooperating with one another, to move a broken-down car to the side of the road for repairs, so too must we cooperate with God if we are to be made whole.

Someone once complained to me that he wasn't sure there was anything to this "God thing," sharing he had real doubts as to whether any of the Church's teachings were true. I pointed out that he was hardly cooperating with the cure for his illness, since his church attendance was erratic and his prayer life nonexistent.

You don't enroll in a French class, not show up, and expect to learn French. Nor do you take a woman out for dinner, refuse to engage her in conversation, and expect her to accept an invitation for another date. Likewise, if we want to learn about the things of God, we will show up for services, read books on Orthodoxy, and otherwise avail ourselves of the healing that takes place within the Church. A relationship with God, like any human relationship, depends on our own commitment, for a relationship depends on both parties' active participation.

Humility Quickens Love for Malicious People

A man who is wrathful with us is a sick man; we must apply a plaster to his heart—love; we must treat him kindly, speak to him gently, lovingly. And if there is not deeply rooted malice against us within him, but only a temporary fit of anger, you will see how his heart, or his malice, will melt away through your kindness and love—how good will conquer evil. A Christian must always be kind, gracious, and wise in order to conquer evil by good.

St. John of Kronstadt

But how can we address such a person in love, when he has insulted us and spoken to us with disrespect? Love sprouts forth from our heart for such a person when our soul, seeing the meekness and humility of Christ, becomes humble. Then we will become like the Lord Himself, who loved even those who were spitting upon Him and crucifying Him, forgave them, and loved them to the Cross. It is in humility that we are able to love another who has this wrath, this sickness. It is through humility that we can love even the person who shows malice toward us.

Through Little Victories, Progress Is Made

The acquisition of holiness is not simply the result of having culti-vated virtues or of controlling oneself through asceticism, but rather of having an organic relationship with Christ. This organic relationship is the result of going through stages of repentance and purity, leading to a remarkable state of union with Christ, seen by the Church as deification, or theosis.

We can feel discouraged when we struggle to change our bad behaviors—to overcome sins that seem to follow us like bad debt. We feel overwhelmed and wonder if we will ever have victory. During times like these, it is good to remember the words of St. Peter of Damaskos: "It is through victories in small things that the fathers won their great battles."

Because this victory has as its foundation the gradual transformation of self, one must never think any sin too small to be confessed. The more we are truthful with our confessor, the greater the chance of victory over all our sins, including sins that seem incidental. These sins build up over time, helping submerge the will, so that even the big sins are excusable in our minds. The big battles are never won without the little skirmishes leading to victory.

Christian Pharisees

If your spiritual life is concentrated only on external practices and traditions and does nothing to bring about real change, you have gained nothing. Too many people think as long as they keep the fasting rules, say their prayers, and attend the services, they are good Orthodox Christians. Yet if there is no love, no charity, and no forgiveness of others, and your life is filled with gossip and judgment, your Orthodox Christian faith is worth nothing.

Christ condemned the Pharisees not because they kept the law and attended to the traditions of the Jewish faith, but because they did so while filled with pride and arrogance. Without sincere repentance and holiness of life, their encounter with God led to an emptiness of heart.

Because our Orthodox faith is one of tradition and liturgical structure, it is easy to fall into the trap of being nothing more than a Pharisee. Being strict in one's observance of Orthodox practices can easily lead to pride and arrogance. If you find yourself feeling better than others and proud of your piety, you have gained absolutely nothing. The external practice of the Orthodox Christian faith without heartfelt humility and repentance leads down the road of spiritual ruin.

The Church is the hospital of the soul, but healing can come only if we put effort into it. If your doctor prescribes a medication for your condition but you fail to follow your doctor's orders, you will not get well. The Church has all you need for spiritual transformation, but healing comes only if you cooperate with the healing process. The goal is holiness (wholeness), which is the direct result of our having submitted in all humility to a life of repentance. When you do this, Christ changes you. If you simply go through the motions of your Orthodox faith, you are no better off than the Pharisees whom Christ condemned.

We Inherit the Results of Adam's Sin, Not His Guilt

The doctrine of original sin as espoused in the West is foreign to Orthodoxy, yet this in no way suggests we do not need to be born again (born anew). We believe, as did the early Church Fathers, that we inherit only the results of Adam's sin, not his guilt. This is known as ancestral sin because the sin of our first parents, Adam and Eve, resulted in our inheritance of death, sickness, and an inclination toward evil. Christ's death on the Cross has its power, not in an atoning sacrifice, but in the conquering of the power of death. Death is trampled down by death. It is by Christ's Resurrection that a way was made for us to be transformed by contact with the living God, thus becoming His children by adoption.

Although we do not refer to ourselves as "saved," as do evangelical Christians, we nevertheless believe we are in need of salvation. Salvation is a process, not a one-time commitment. Our understanding of ancestral sin is distinct from the concept of original sin and the hereditary guilt that requires a substitutionary atonement sacrifice; this separates us doctrinally from Western Christianity.

Had the Fall never happened, the Second Person of the Holy Trinity, the Logos (Word), would still have become incarnate and taken on our nature. For it is through this condescension by our Creator God of taking on the nature of what He created that we are given the opportunity of being deified.

Our journey into the heart culminates in theosis, whereby we are joined in everlasting communion with the very God who created us. St. Athanasius of Alexandria said, "The Son of God became man, that we might become god." In 2 Peter 1:4, we read that we have become "partakers of the divine nature." St. Athanasius further says that theosis is "becoming by grace what God is by nature."

SEPTEMBER 22

An Invitation to Be God's Children

Many of us have been praying most of our lives, but do we ever think about what that means? Have we ever thought how incredible it is that our Creator God has invited us to speak with Him at any time? That the Lord of the universe has given us the right to speak with Him, to ask for help, to seek His mercy?

There is no greater honor given to humanity than the gift of being able to approach our God in prayer, any hour of the day or night, in every circumstance. In every season we can speak to Him. We can call upon God in our joy or in our anger, and from the depths of despair we can speak to Him.

It is beyond our human understanding that we have been assured that our God is always listening to us, yet it is true. Our Creator even condescended to join His divinity with our humanity, becoming incarnate in the flesh that we might see His face. In Christ, He has revealed Himself to us and has invited us to commune with Him forever.

Preserving Orthodoxy in Our Children

When parishes are forced to close, it is not just because the children have moved away and the old folks have died off. The problem is much greater than this. With increased numbers of immigrants joining parishes, often with the expressed desire to preserve their ethnic identity, we can easily fall prey to believing our churches are on solid ground and will thrive into the next generation. In our collective joy at seeing our churches packed for Sunday Liturgies, we forget about previous influxes of immigrants, whose children, upon growing into adulthood, became so Americanized that they saw the Orthodox Faith as relevant only for their parents and grandparents but meaningless to themselves.

The way to forestall another great exodus of our youth, I believe, is to wage a concerted effort to help our youth embrace Orthodoxy as their own. This means they must be able to understand the services, and since they are unlikely to learn Church Slavonic or liturgical Greek, we must admit that it is time to serve in English. The Ancient Church saw the language of the people as the vehicle for teaching the faith and passing Orthodoxy on to the next generations. Saints Cyril and Methodius helped the Slavic people receive Orthodoxy by translating the services into a language the people understood. Thus the Greek language did not remain the liturgical language of the newly illumined people of the Slavic lands.

The early missionaries knew the importance of teaching the faith so as to accommodate the local population and allow newly converted people to really know the Orthodox Faith. Our children must be able to understand the services and be taught the faith. They must understand why we do the things we do, why we fast, and why we worship the way we have worshiped for almost two thousand years. If this is not achieved by the local parishes, our youth will see Orthodoxy as nothing more than a quaint religion of a bygone age, meaningless to their own lives as modern Americans, and they will depart from the faith.

Works Are a Proof of Love

The very moment faith enters the soul, we turn toward God in repentance and recognize we cannot live without Him. As we grow in our faith, we come to realize we must remain in a continual state of repentance, for grace abounds in the heart of the person who is repenting. We come to see the truth that the saints are those who never ceased to call upon the Lord in repentance. Never did they think themselves worthy of anything but God's wrath, so their continued plea was for mercy.

This humility spawned God's love in the hearts of these saints, and works of love and mercy grew out of God's indwelling love within their hearts. Their works showed forth that their love and good works came out of that deep state of repentance, and their love was the proof of God's indwelling Spirit in their hearts. St. Gregory the Great said, "The proof of love is in the works. Where love exists, it works great things. But when it ceases to act, it ceases to exist."

If we do not do good works, love does not dwell in our hearts, and we have no faith. "But someone will say, 'You have faith, and I have works.' Show me your faith without your works, and I will show you my faith by my works" (James 2:18). The Liturgy reminds us that only those with faith and love may draw near to receive the Holy Mysteries. Our participation in the Body and Blood of the Lord provides each of us with the opportunity to be Christ-bearers in the world in which we live, and others will know we belong to Christ by our love for one another (John 13:35).

The World As Sacrament

*Everything that lives and breathes is sacred and beautiful in
the eyes of God. The whole world is a sacrament. The entire
created cosmos is a burning bush of God's uncreated energies.
And humankind stands as a priest before the altar of creation, as
microcosm and mediator. Such is the true nature of things; or, as
an Orthodox hymn describes it, "the truth of things," if only we
have the eyes of faith to see it.*

His All-Holiness Ecumenical Patriarch Bartholomew

These words ring so true to me, both as an Orthodox Christian and as
a man who has always loved the outdoors and found many opportunities to be out in it. Orthodoxy has never viewed the environment or
natural resources as being for plunder. It has historically viewed the earth
as a place to be nurtured, protected, and preserved for future generations.
The plunder of vast areas of Russia happened under the godless Soviets.
The great forests that surrounded Athens and Thessaloniki—cities built by
Greeks, who used stone for construction—were cut down by the Turks,
who built only with wood.

Our Church has special supplications and litanies for "seasonable weather,
for abundance of the fruits of the earth," and for protection in the case of
natural disasters. There is even a special prayer from the service said in times
of earthquakes: "The earth is without words, yet groans and cries: 'Why, all
people, do you pollute me with so many evils? The Master spares you but
chastises me entirely: understand and propitiate God in repentance.'"

Orthodoxy conveys a profound understanding of creation and of the role
of humanity as the priesthood of creation. As creatures who are able to alter
and reshape the world, we are bound by the Creator to be good stewards. As
the whole of the cosmos has worshiped the Creator, we have built churches
that represent a microcosm of this very universe. The promise of redemption
is for all of creation: the gift of salvation wrought by Jesus Christ.

Stay the Course!

Orthodoxy is not always easy, and many parishes seem to make living our Orthodox faith far more difficult than it needs to be. The lack of joy in some quarters is not true to Orthodoxy but reflects the fallen people who make up the Church. This is to be expected, of course, since the Church is a hospital for the soul and therefore home to a lot of sick people.

Don't ever let a mean-spirited parishioner or a harsh priest drive you from the Church. This is your home as well, and just as in a dysfunctional household, a lot of growth can take place here. Pray for your priest and for the people who have made you feel uncomfortable. Also pray to St. John the Wonderworker of San Francisco, who was a loving father and pastor, for help.

Although a good confessor and great preacher would be preferable to the priest who never has time for you, the Church is still your home. The priest may deliver lousy homilies, seem harsh as a confessor, and be devoid of people skills, but the reality is the Church is still the place for you.

Yet, if you and your children would benefit, by all means look into the possibility that another parish might be a better fit, a place where you can all grow in the faith. Better to leave a dysfunctional parish than to leave Orthodoxy. If you have no other options because your parish is the only Orthodox church in the region, make the best of it.

Ultimately, your life in the Church is all about Christ, and Christ is the same yesterday, today, and forever. He will not betray you, for He is the source of all joy and goodness. The Church belongs to Him, and the fact that we priests sometimes fail to be the light of Christ to our people in no way negates the fact that the Church is still the fountain of life and the place where we can receive healing of all that ails us.

Orthodoxy Is about Christ, Not Religion

Orthodoxy is not a religion, but a way of life that is centered in Jesus Christ. Orthodoxy, as a way of life, has the cure for what ails us and can return us to the state of wholeness that was God's original intent for humankind. Because Orthodoxy is not about religion, it can offer the transformation of the heart that comes with entering into a relationship with our Creator.

This transformation begins with repentance: the moment when we decide to return to the pure state of communion with God for which we were created. When we renounce ourselves, we are changed through the action of God's grace. Though we became corrupt because of the Fall, through repentance we are returned to the state for which we were created.

Elder Thaddeus of Vitovnica wrote,

> *One cannot say that Christianity is a religion. Christianity is a revelation of eternity and life. The angels rejoice greatly because God has revealed Himself mystically to His creature, man. Our human nature has become part of the mystery of the Holy Trinity, and that is a great gift which we do not even appreciate; instead, we have cleaved to the things of this world. We have been given the opportunity to prepare ourselves for eternity, to vanquish evil, and to always be with our heavenly Father.*[18]

How to Avoid Being an Obstacle to Prayer

You may know individuals who get dazed looks on their faces when the conversation drifts to a topic that does not center on them. I remember one such individual who always waited for a slight pause in the conversation when he could redirect it to be centered on him. There was no subject that could not afford him an opportunity to let you know what an authority he was on the subject or would not allow him to recall a moment in his life that he thought worthy of your attention.

Our prayer life should not be an occasion for us to behave in such a fashion with God. The Lord desires a relationship with us, and like the young man who is courting his girlfriend, showering her with attention and wanting to know everything about her, we too should be courting God.

This relationship with God started the moment we were conceived and began anew when we put off the old man at our baptism. The Lord has done all the work and simply awaits our response. Like any relationship, our communion with Christ must be one that we work on.

When we were created, we were given the gift of free will, which means it is an equal relationship from the very start. You would not have a deep relationship with someone if you felt obligated or forced. The relationship Christ offers us is based in love. He loved us first and has invited us into a relationship that is meant to be eternal.

Your prayer life should reflect the personal nature of this relationship. If you approach God like the person described above—not listening— your relationship will be shallow. God knows what you need and does not require you to present a daily list. Spend time in silent worship before the throne of God, and you will be rewarded with a joy that passes all understanding.

Anything Quickly Obtained Is Easily Lost

Americans are not a particularly patient people, as demonstrated by the fact that the fast-food industry began with us. We drive our car to a window, order our food, and expect it to be ready, without delay, at the next window. We expect a church service to end within one hour, on the dot. Our gardens are filled with flowers that come fully grown, are dropped into the soil, and look good from the first watering. No waiting around for the germination of seeds—we want instant beauty.

If an appliance breaks down, we buy a new one rather than wait a week for repairs. We throw ourselves into the latest fad diet that promises fast weight loss, only to see the weight come back after we've tired of the menu. We don't apprentice for a career, but walk out of a university expecting our career to begin on day one. Many of our young children are allowed to dress in adult pop fashion, and the precious sweetness of childhood is transformed into a sort of miniature adulthood.

Since we have grown accustomed to having everything happen without delay, we also expect our spiritual lives to be on the same timeline. We don't have the patience to build on the knowledge of the Holy Fathers, so we don't practice regular spiritual reading. Our church attendance is limited to the essential Sunday Liturgy, and even then we arrive late and leave before the thanksgiving prayers have concluded. If fasting is difficult for us, we don't fast at all. If keeping a prayer rule is tedious, we don't try to develop a set time for our prayers. If our mind wanders during prayer, we let it, avoiding even the least amount of struggle.

If we hope to make progress in the spiritual life, it is good to remember these words of St. Isaac the Syrian: "For anything that is quickly obtained is also easily lost, whereas everything found with toil is also kept with careful watching."

SEPTEMBER 30

Your Closest Friend Is Yourself

If you have never learned to accept and love yourself, you will never be able to love another person. If you don't learn to forgive yourself, you will never be able to forgive another person. You must learn to be your own best friend.

Loving yourself is not about narcissism, an excessive focus on oneself that can be a sign of serious mental illness. Rather, a healthy love of yourself is the love you have for what God has created. We recognize we have been created in His image and likeness, and we are worthy of love, because God Himself loves us.

Being our own best friend is a recognition that what God has created is good, and the invitation to commune with our Creator God has set us apart from the rest of creation. Being our own best friend is a way to kindle a grateful heart within ourselves and to open ourselves to the love God has for us. This gives us the ability to love God and to love others.

OCTOBER 1

Guarding Our Thoughts

Our thoughts really do have an impact on our world. Negative thoughts about family members or fellow employees change our relationships. If we dislike people at work and allow ourselves to think poorly of them, they are likely to fulfill our low expectations. If we pray for them and ask God to bless them, while asking the Lord to bless our interaction with them, they become changed for the good, and so do we.

We've all heard of the person whose cup is half empty and another whose cup is half full. The former is likely to go through life with unfulfilled goals, while the latter will see his world blossom as a beautiful garden. Even the weeds in that garden seem beautiful if we keep negative thoughts at bay.

I've counseled depressed individuals over the years to take a brisk walk every day for at least forty minutes while saying the Jesus Prayer. Their depression subsides within days, because the exercise, coupled with the prayer, pushes aside negative thoughts and sends depression into the abyss from which it originated.

Our negative thoughts keep us from the joy that is ours in Christ and keep that joy from uplifting others. If we fight off negative thoughts, we allow Christ to change us and those around us. St. Seraphim of Sarov said that if we acquire peace, a thousand around us will be saved. Negative thoughts do not promote peace!

The Saints: Models for Our Lives

Our Orthodox Christian life is not designed to be invented as we go. We are instructed to use as our models the lives of the saints who have gone on before us. Their lives are held up before us as examples of holiness. Their charity is to become our model of charity, their sacrifice our model of sacrifice, their asceticism our model of asceticism. Their humility must be the model by which we lead our lives. Their love of God and neighbor must become the supreme example for our own struggle to love God above all else and to love our neighbors as ourselves. Their willingness to suffer persecution for Christ's sake must be the model by which we are willing to face persecution, and even martyrdom, for our faith.

St. Syncletica, a fourth-century desert mother, said, "Imitate the publican and you will not be condemned with the Pharisee. Choose the meekness of Moses and you will find your heart, which is a rock, changed into a spring of water." The Pharisee was proud before God and people for his piety and accomplishments, even boldly standing in the temple in all arrogance, thanking God that he was not like other men. But the publican stood afar off, head lowered, beating his breast and saying, "God, be merciful to me a sinner!" (Luke 18:13). The Lord Jesus Christ told His disciples that the publican went away justified.

We must take care whom we set as the model for our own living, that we not take as our example a person who is worldly, self-centered, greedy, unloving, or devoid of any interest in the spiritual life. Rather, we must look to the saints as examples of how to live and how to love, that we, like the publican, will stand before God having been justified.

Giving Appropriate Correction

We have all witnessed embarrassing moments when someone loses his or her temper. The boss comes into the office with family worries and shouts at his secretary over something insignificant. We've sat uncomfortably as a hostess made a nasty remark to her husband in front of her dinner guests. We've suffered the unpleasantness of seeing parents correct their children in front of their little friends. And we have likely embarrassed others ourselves.

We may be justified in seeing the need for correcting employees or children regarding their behavior, but how much more easily would our message be heard if we delivered it in a soft voice and without anger. An angry voice immediately puts the other person on the defensive, so he or she is hardly able to hear what could be valuable correction.

As an abbot, I would be failing in my fatherly duties if I never corrected the behavior or the laziness of one of the monks under monastic obedience to me. Yet the kind tone of my delivery allows true progress, and the monk's knowledge of my love for him makes all the difference.

By letting those under our authority—be they our children or our employees—receive correction in a quiet, respectful tone, we enable them to know they are loved and respected by us, and that our expectation of excellence on their part is based on our respect for them. We also demonstrate excellence by making sure we ourselves keep those standards of performance. Then we will be amazed at their response, and we will, in turn, be able to keep our cool during moments when they disappoint us.

All this wonderful change begins with a simple apology on our part. If we truly desire others to do their part in making the household or the office run smoothly, we recognize the absolute necessity that we humble ourselves and ask forgiveness when we have spoken angrily, obscuring our intended correction and hurting those around us.

OCTOBER 4

Our Attitude toward Icons and Other Holy Things

One of the attributes of God is holiness. His holiness is reflected in His people and in physical objects that have been blessed by the Church for the use of His people in their journey toward Him. Therefore, reverence for these sacred objects and images is the manifestation of the relationship between us and God. "And you shall be holy to Me, for I the Lord *am* holy" (Lev. 20:26). Icons of Christ, His Holy Mother, the saints, and biblical events are not just art objects but vehicles for God's sustaining grace.

As Orthodox Christians, we should make it a rule never to have arguments or to engage in improper behavior before the images of the saints. And we should instill in our children, from the earliest age, reverence for the holy icons. Not only do we call upon the saints for their heavenly intercession, but their icons serve as reminders that Christ has called us to repentance and deification.

A holy item, even if it has lost its original appearance, should always be treated with reverence. Under no circumstance can an icon, even one that has not been blessed, be simply thrown away. It should be taken to the church, where it can be burned in a special place set aside for the disposal of holy things. Holy oils and any other blessed articles used in the home should always be treated with the utmost reverence, and, like the icons, never be improperly disposed of.

Your patronal icon should be held in particular reverence, for following baptism or chrismation, we each have a special bond with our personal saint. Parents should make it a tradition to bless each of their children with the child's personal icon as they set off for a new year at school or an extended journey, or when they marry. Family members should be sure to bring at least a few icons into the hospital room or the nursing home of their loved one, so a person's departure from this life can take place in the presence of his or her icons.

OCTOBER 5

A Culture Gone Mad

We have moved from a period in which we have said, "Speak, Lord, for Your servant hears" (1 Sam. 3:9) to one in which we say, "Listen, Lord, for Your servant speaks." Our American culture has become so enamored, even consumed, with the importance of self that we've made idols out of personal gain and fulfillment. Americans are ever seeking after the things of this world to the degree that we have, as a culture, forgotten the basic truths our ancestors took for granted. We have forgotten the importance of living altruistically, of living for the ultimate good of all, rather than limiting our scope to personal, materialistic gains.

We have forgotten the importance of making provision for future generations, whether it be in saving the environment for those who will follow us or in passing on the beliefs and values that make for a civilized society. Our children are no longer taught a value system based on the Christian concept that there is a truth that should govern our every action.

Our educational system has abandoned young people to moral relativism, leaving them rudderless in a sea of too many options. We do not teach our children the importance of living altruistically, where the good of the whole comes first. In doing so, we have failed to provide a foundation by which they can govern their lives in the light of the Gospels. Television programs, violent video games, easy access to pornography online, and movies filled with sex and violence have assaulted our nation like an enemy army, and we've failed to act.

As a nation, we are under spiritual attack and have failed to take notice. Our spiritual weapons gather dust while we hope for the best. But we do nothing to prepare our youths for victory. Relativism reigns while truth is forgotten, and our nation stands on the brink, having become powerless to withstand a spiritual attack it does not understand.

OCTOBER 6

Be Yourself

When we enter into communion with one another in the life of the Church, we come broken and far from the image and likeness God intended when He created us. Every one of us is in need of the healing that comes from a life in Christ. Yet we often hinder healing because we fear being who we are. This fear is sometimes based on what others may think of us or what may happen if we don't fit in. We fear being rejected for being ourselves.

Yet the Lord calls us to put aside our fear, because He loves us just as we are. In Christ there is no fear, because God is love—perfect and unconditional love. In our walk with Christ, we are healed and made whole. We don't have to shelve what makes us who we are, for we are being made whole.

Through total immersion in Christ and in the disciplines of the Church, the transformational power of God's grace changes us. We don't become a stamped-out version of everyone else, but are changed into the person God intends us to be. We are made perfect just as we are. "For we are His workmanship, created in Christ Jesus for good works, which God prepared beforehand that we should walk in them" (Eph. 2:10).

In our weakness we are made whole, for as Christ told St. Paul, "'My grace is sufficient for you, for My strength is made perfect in weakness.' Therefore most gladly I will rather boast in my infirmities, that the power of Christ may rest upon me. Therefore I take pleasure in infirmities, in reproaches, in needs, in persecutions, in distresses, for Christ's sake. For when I am weak, then I am strong" (2 Cor. 12:9–10).

Being a Christian is not about conforming to the image of other people, but rather to the image of Christ. You needn't shelve who you are, but take on the image of who Christ is.

As Metropolitan Anthony Bloom prayed, "Help me, O God, to put off all pretenses and find my true self."

OCTOBER 7

Love Your Enemies

It is a terrible temptation to wish for our enemies' destruction. Our Lord instructs us to love our enemies and to do good to those who hate us or persecute us. To wish their destruction is to ignore the love God has for us, even though our sins have made us His enemies.

Our salvation is not accomplished in a vacuum, for all of humanity is the beneficiary of Christ's redemptive act upon the Cross. Christ died for all of us, and our salvation is interconnected to that of all humanity. We should be just as concerned for the salvation of our neighbors as we are for our own.

When we see people filled with hate and far from God, we should pity them and pray for them. To wish ill upon them is not in keeping with our Lord's commandment. Love must reign in our lives, and the salvation of others must be a central theme in our own prayers.

OCTOBER 8

Avoiding This Present Darkness

Those who embrace the enjoyment of partying and entertainment, in an attempt to get a break from the hardships and struggles that make great souls, fail to embrace the essential element that makes their life journey salvific. They avoid the service of love God requires of us in enduring those difficulties that unite us to the love of Christ, and they sacrifice Paradise itself.

The Lord promised us the yoke would be easy and the burden light if we but unite ourselves to Him (Matt. 11:30). Christ opens the door to Paradise and fills our hearts with His divine love, and we become new creatures. But if we do not have Christ, we do not have love, and all our material gain will have led us down the road to a spiritual void that is darkness. If we do not have Christ, even our fasting, virtue, labor, and prayer will have been meaningless.

When we turn to Christ and let His embrace lift us out of the stagnation of this present world, rather than entertaining ourselves, we gain everything. Eternity will be ours, and love will fill the void that is this present darkness.

Pluralism Versus Absolute Truth

As our society has become more pluralistic, it has been easy for some to fall into the error of believing that it does not matter what you believe, as long as you are sincere. Just as we have seen the progressive moral bankruptcy of our society, we have also witnessed the wholesale sellout of traditional Christianity by much of America's religious community. The partial adherence of many of America's denominations to the traditional gospel call to repentance, forgiveness, and redemption through Christ has given way to a new kind of "salvation."

These "churches" are now more concerned with social idealism than seeing souls saved through entering into a relationship with Jesus Christ. They have ignored our Lord's own words, "My kingdom is not of this world" (John 18:36). They have shown forth for all to see that their loss of faith has led to a replacement of the Good News of salvation in Christ with a mandate to build a Utopian society where social justice and peace reign forever. They have forgotten that Christ said we would never attain this outside of His Kingdom, "which is to come."

What do we as Orthodox Christians do to counteract this insidious loss of traditional, otherworldly Christianity? Surely the answer is not less fasting, less prayer, and less penance. We must rekindle our zeal for Christ. We must give ourselves over to the joy that is ours in living a life in Him. It is not in the things of this world that we will ultimately find happiness, but in living a life rooted in Jesus Christ.

We have been given a great and holy gift. During each celebration of the Divine Liturgy, we sing the words, "We have seen the True Light, we have received the Heavenly Spirit; we have found the true Faith, worshiping the undivided Trinity, who has saved us." Let us commit ourselves anew to living this holy faith as true witnesses to the Lord. We have in our possession a great pearl. Let it be the inheritance we leave our children and the treasure we share with our neighbors.

The Need to Reunite a Society Divided by Age

Two major populations within our society are seeing a statistical rise in suicides: youths and the elderly. A whole generation of young people is without hope for the future; they are without hope of ever fulfilling their dreams. Meanwhile, many of our seniors feel discounted, and they have become an invisible segment of our society, as if they had nothing to offer.

Both of these populations are experiencing poverty, are marginalized from the job market, and are feeling an increased sense of worthlessness. Both have been disenfranchised and made to feel they have little to offer and no future.

A prerequisite to the empathy that would help alleviate the pain of our young and our old is that we pay attention to them. We must be compassionate regarding the despair experienced by our young and our old, and find solutions that unite all of us. We must find solutions that rekindle hope for a future that involves both our young and our old.

In past generations, these two segments of our society were interwoven in everyday life. The young experienced the love and support of senior citizens, who were valued members of our communities. The young knew they had a future, because the rest of society affirmed them, loved them, respected them, and offered them hope for the future. Such affirmation must begin anew.

Tuning in to the needs and feelings of another person is so desperately needed in these difficult times. The very old offer us the wisdom that comes with age, while our young offer hope for a future that will be better for all of us. Dismissing as inconvenient either of these generations dooms us to no future and a lost past.

To turn a blind eye to these two groups is simply to ignore that God created all of us in His image and likeness. We are as one family, even if religion or sociological differences seem to separate us. That even one member of this family would feel worthless reflects on our own failure to love.

OCTOBER 11

With Peace of Heart, Disappointments Are Meaningless

We often find ourselves disappointed. The job we really wanted is given to another person. An associate at work doesn't invite us to her dinner party. A person we'd love to have as a friend shows no interest, and we feel rejected. The music director at church doesn't allow us to join the choir. Someone much younger gets the promotion, along with an increase in salary.

You get the idea.

If we have peace in our hearts, all these disappointments are meaningless. Those who have peace give thanks to God for all things. We can embrace even illnesses and poverty if we see all as allowed by God because He loves us and grants just what we need for our salvation.

When we approach all that comes our way with a gladsome heart, we gain what is of the most profit. Nothing can take away the treasure that is ours—not even death. Glory to God for all things!

OCTOBER 12

The Principalities and Powers of Darkness

M any people are convinced we are living in the end times. They
look to changes in the Earth's climate, ever more disastrous storms,
failing economies, and political upheavals as signs of the end. Couple these
things with the increase in terrorist activity worldwide and the rise of
extremist Islam, and Christians are afraid. The truth is that we do not know
when the end is coming, for Jesus tells us that only the Father knows the
day and the hour.

We must remember that our battle is not with earthly enemies, but with
the principalities and powers of darkness. This is important to remember,
because the weapons needed to combat the enemy are not found in armies,
guns, tanks, and missiles, but in prayer. Our combat against the enemy
must be centered in the Church's services, prayer, fasting, spiritual pre-
paredness, and repentance.

Our enemies are not armies but demons who would demoralize us and
strike fear in our hearts. But in Christ Jesus we have all the strength to
overcome the powers of darkness that are set upon our destruction. There
is no need to panic when we have Jesus Christ by our side.

The end times will come when God decides. As for us, we must always
be prepared for the end, just as the disciples were. Fear is brought on by
the enemy of humankind: the devil himself. In Christ there is no fear.

Holy Scripture and Holy Tradition

The Bible can be understood only through the Church, for the Holy Scriptures came forth from the Church. The Protestant reformers dumped the papacy only to replace that institution with themselves as the ultimate authority. Since reason and logic ruled, there was no room for the intuitive, noetic nature of the heart. Thus the interpretation of the Bible became a debatable subject between believers, ending in new denominations proliferating like rabbits.

The Bible is the written account of the first Christians' experience with God. It was a living, oral tradition inspired by the Holy Spirit and put down in written form. The idea that it is therefore open to personal interpretation, apart from the Church from which it sprang, is the origin of over forty-one thousand different denominations today.

The Orthodox Church has kept the early teachings and liturgical traditions precisely because she has refused to interpret Scripture apart from what was always taught. Her divine services connect us to the early Church precisely because they are the same liturgical services used by the early Church.

Orthodoxy is increasingly becoming known in the West, and more and more people are being drawn to her. Yet we don't convert people to Orthodoxy by words and debate, but by the example of our lives. Judging others cannot be a part of our witness to the truth of Orthodoxy. Our witness to the transformational power of the Church is what convicts others of the truth of our faith.

We must pray for our friends and loved ones who do not yet know Orthodoxy, yet we should also give thanks for those who know Jesus Christ. It is a joy to have God as our Father and an extra benefit to have the Church as our Mother. But lest we forget, it is of no value whatsoever to be Orthodox if we do not have a personal relationship with Jesus Christ.

Replacing Temporal Joy with Lasting Joy

We all have certain things we feel passionate about. When I was a young man, long-distance running was my passion, and nothing gave me more joy than the run. Every day was organized around running. I even planned vacations around my runs, often heading to Vancouver, British Columbia, so I could run around Stanley Park. I'd stay in a cheap hotel near the park, figuring the room was needed for sleeping only, so why waste money on a nice hotel. Every morning and evening, I went out for a run around that magnificent park, and I spent the rest of the day touring the city on foot.

When I was teaching, I took two-hour lunch breaks and spent an hour and a half running. Sometimes I ran to work and ran home. My friends soon learned that any time spent with me was likely to be scheduled around a run.

Some years ago I had hip replacement surgery. My surgeon suggested I'd likely worn down the hip during all the years of pounding it had taken. Sometimes, when I see a runner, a flood of wonderful memories returns.

A friend once asked if I felt any bitterness over the fact that I could no longer run, age having slowed me down. I answered that the joyful memories of running are still with me, but now I have other joys that sustain me—central of which is my life in Christ. My only regret is that it took me so long to discover the depth of joy I've found in Christ, for this world offers only fleeting joy.

If I could, I would still run. But some things are meant to be temporal, confined to particular portions of our lives. The things of God are meant to be eternal and should be central to this life we are living now.

How Can We Possibly Love Everyone?

We are instructed by Christ to love our neighbors as ourselves—and even to love our enemies. There are always individuals we find difficult to like, let alone love. Given this, how do we follow the commandment of Christ to love everyone?

As Christians we venerate icons of Christ, among them those that show Him suffering on the Cross. When the priest or deacon censes the church during the services, he also censes the people, recognizing the image of God in everyone.

If we see everyone as Christ, we can still love those who are unlovable, unkind, hurtful, or even evil if we look upon them as Christ crucified. They, like us, are created in the image and likeness of God, yet their sin obscures the image. They, by their fallen nature and unrepentant lives, embody Christ crucified. They are loved by God, and we are commanded to do the same.

But how? This is where grace comes in. Like St. Paul, we can say that anything good we do is Christ in us. Loving one's enemies is perhaps one of the most difficult of Christ's commandments to keep, but with Christ all things are possible. As we struggle to love others, we must do so with a prayerful heart, asking that the Lord give us the grace needed to truly love others. It is the same grace from God that is needed to forgive those who offend or hurt us. God forgives us and loves us, so we can also forgive and love others. It is all about grace, for if we seek out the aid of the Holy Spirit, all things good can be ours, including holiness.

OCTOBER 16

Emotional Intelligence

Being critical of others is not an Orthodox trait, for being critical, whether of other people or of the way they approach their faith, can be a sign we are not centered in the heart. Holiness is about being made whole, and this wholeness depends on being centered in the heart, where we find the Kingdom of God. When we are in our head, we are more judgmental.

Emotional intelligence is the ability to be sensitive to the feelings and the viewpoints of others. It helps us avoid hurting another person's feelings and allows us to be open to how others might feel. It helps us handle interpersonal relationships judiciously and empathetically.

Orthodoxy opens us to possibilities that are often closed in other Christian traditions, for the image of the Church as hospital of the soul allows us to see ourselves and others as needing the healing that comes with a relationship centered in the God who loves us.

Whether the other person is an atheist or a believer, a Buddhist or a Muslim, a liberal or a conservative, she is not a threat to us, for we are secure, for we see ourselves and everyone else as patients in need of healing. As Orthodox Christians, we are able to see everyone, even unbelievers, as affected by Jesus Christ, the Word of God, through whom the cosmos itself came into being. We know this very Christ desires that all come to the knowledge of the truth and be saved. We love everyone because Christ loves everyone.

Emotional intelligence also enables us to work together for the common good. It enables us to see things through the eyes of others and to desire the best for them. It even enables us to further the salvific message of the Gospels, because we don't get in the way of the message. Others can experience God's love because the empathy we have for their feelings is imaged in how we interact with them and how we demonstrate our respect for their experiences, feelings, viewpoints, and beliefs.

OCTOBER 17

Being Orthodox in a Non-Orthodox World

In this pluralistic society, many Orthodox individuals have non-Orthodox family members. Sometimes these family members are not even practicing Christians, so the Orthodox person's struggle to keep to the traditions and practices of the Orthodox faith can be difficult. The Lenten periods can be especially hard when the whole family is eating meat, eggs, and dairy while the Orthodox member keeps the fast. Even the blessing prayers before each meal can be awkward when other members of one's household are not believers. There are also those Sunday mornings or feast days when some family members want to head for the beach, but you need to be in church for the Divine Liturgy.

The difficulty of being true to one's faith can be even greater if your family members hold to antireligious sentiments. I had an uncle who was so hostile toward religion that he forbade my aunt and cousins to attend church. Although he was an extreme example, there are many Orthodox Christians who struggle to live their faith in an environment that is not conducive to the spiritual life. For example, a good number of employers do not let Orthodox Christians take time off for holy days or even major feast days such as the Nativity of Christ.

When we are committed to Christ, we must not allow others to keep us from practicing our faith. Although it is not necessary to get in their face about our faith, it is important that we remember the example of the early Christians. They were so committed to Christ that they willingly faced martyrdom rather than deny their faith or compromise Christian principles.

OCTOBER 18

Politics Cannot Bring Forth the Kingdom

The gospel demands that Christians usher the Kingdom of God into this world, not by political ideology, but by the individual Christian's transformation of self. This command to usher in the Kingdom of God does not mean we should be neutral in the face of evil; rather it is a recognition that the Church is only the Church when she is there for others. The Church must be immune from any possibility of turning the message of Christ into anything that diminishes focus on the Crucified One, for her glory as the Church is in Christ crucified. St. John Chrysostom said, "If you cannot find Christ in the beggar at the church door, you will not find Him in the chalice."

Orthodoxy is the incarnation of beauty, while political extremism is devoid of poetry and art. Political extremism destroys beauty, while the Church embodies the very essence of beauty. The Church must never surrender to any political ideology, because she must always stand on the side of the weakest and poorest of society. When the Church aligns herself with one camp or another, she is in danger of being absorbed into worldly ideologies that obscure her beatific vision. Neither the democratic nor the socialist nor the monarchical form of government is needed for the Church to thrive, if she is committed to living out her biblical vocation of pointing to Christ Jesus, the Savior and Redeemer of the world.

The manifestation of the Kingdom of God cannot be brought forth into this world by any political movement, nor by force of arms, but by the changing of the hearts of men and women everywhere. Only when Christ is manifest in His people will the Kingdom take root, and peace and justice will reign in this world. The darkness cannot be overcome by any political movement, but only by the introduction of the light of Christ.

Creating a Christian Environment in the Home

Creating a Christian home begins with an icon corner. This bright corner is the center for every domestic church, where family devotions take place. This is also the family's way of declaring to visitors that theirs is a Christian home, where Christ is Head. Because the husband is a sort of domestic priest (a part of the priesthood of all believers), it is important that he be the one who leads the entire family in prayer.

All members of the family should have their own patron saint's icon. A wonderful practice from ancient times is to have a family icon written, with all the family's patron saints represented in the same icon.

The family should try to have dinner together every night of the week, and not while watching TV. The meal should be the time when the parents can talk to their children about school or other activities. In these modern times, there are often school- or work-related activities that don't always allow everyone to be together, but every effort should be made to make family dinner happen as often as possible.

The blessing of the food, with the father or mother making the sign of the cross over the meal with their fingers together as we do when blessing ourselves, should always be said. If we always say a blessing over our food at home, we are more likely to do so when at school or in a restaurant.

Television and the overuse of the internet are wreaking havoc on family life. Don't allow these foreign invaders into your home to replace Christ as Head of your household. Bad habits are hard to overcome, so replacing these diversions with communal time in the living room may be hard at first, but it is necessary as a basic foundation of a Christian home.

Guard your home from other invaders as well, such as reading material that is inappropriate for the Christian home. The music played in your home should also be uplifting. If you wouldn't want your priest to see or hear something in your home, it shouldn't be there.

OCTOBER 20

Family Times and Tasks

Regular family meetings where everyone has an opportunity to talk about things and where the atmosphere is loving, open, and safe help create trust and a sense of security for everyone. It is natural for parents to argue on occasion, but this should never take place in front of children. They need to feel secure.

Boys need to see their fathers as icons of Christ in the home, demonstrating the biblical image of a husband and father. For the sake of their children, men need to be examples in prayer and church attendance. Statistically, children whose fathers are churchgoers are far more likely to stay in church as adults. And spiritual instruction should not be left to wives. Men will be held accountable before the throne of God for their children.

By example, men need to teach their children to help around the house. In an age when both husband and wife often need to hold down jobs to make ends meet, a woman's work is not just household work. She should not have to come home from a job and do all the housework and cooking by herself.

Children should be given a small allowance (appropriate to their age) so they can learn to manage money. The biblical command to give ten percent of one's income back to God is almost never taught in the Orthodox Church today, which is why so many clergy are given such meager salaries and parishes have to hold church festivals. When we fail to tithe, we are stealing from God! A child who tithes ten percent of his allowance will grow into an adult Orthodox Christian who tithes.

These are basic suggestions for creating an Orthodox home. If you begin to implement them, the Lord will reward you with a family that stands strong, and your children will grow up as spiritually healthy Christians, grounded in biblical teachings and moral fortitude. Then your grandchildren will be raised with the same biblical principles, and you will be the most blessed grandparent on your block!

OCTOBER 21

When We Face Disappointment

Sometimes we find ourselves so caught up in what we want or think we need, we become despondent when we face disappointment or loss. We get so caught up in reaching our goals, we fail because we have not sought out what God planned for us.

Sometimes we rely on ourselves so much, we end up disappointed. And we blame God. This is when we need to give it over to God, let things be, and keep struggling in a quiet, prayerful way, enduring trials that, in God's time, make us stronger, more faithful stewards with the talents God has given us.

Hebrews 10:35–36 encourages us to be faithful: "Therefore do not cast away your confidence, which has great reward. For you have need of endurance, so that after you have done the will of God, you may receive the promise." And Romans 8:28 reminds us of our future: "And we know that all things work together for good to those who love God, to those who are the called according to His purpose."

When Charity Becomes Self-Worship

Food is a common problem for many people, for food often fills a void, becoming a way of comforting oneself when faced with the stresses that are a part of our modern, everyday world. But food is not the only addiction that can overtake a believer. The need for love and approval can be a form of addiction and can even replace a fulfilling relationship with God.

Being in service to others, such as volunteering for charitable causes, can be a way of seeking other people's approval and, in the process, making ourselves feel better. In serving others, we can sometimes find ourselves displacing God and making charity a form of self-worship.

This in no way suggests that what we do "for the least of these" is not a godly direction to take, for we are directed by Christ Himself to be in service to others. However, we want to make sure our charity is based on love of God and neighbor, and not on love of self.

We avoid this sin of pride by living in a state of constant repentance. When we notice pride rising to the surface, we repent. We always seek to make Christ the cause and foundation of our charity, not the praise of others. This can be done only if we are open with our confessor and squash our ego before it has a chance to take over.

Replacing Doubt with Faith

I n the Gospel narratives, we read that the Apostle Thomas told his fellow apostles he would not believe the Lord had risen from the dead unless he put his hand in His wounds. When He actually saw Jesus, he immediately said, "My Lord and my God," instantly believing without having touched his Lord (John 20:27-29).

Replacing doubt with faith starts with the desire to be a believer. We must choose to believe, for desire invites God's grace to abound. We turn to God, saying, "Lord, I believe; help my unbelief!" (Mark 9:24). Our willingness to voice our desire to believe is the beginning of faith. This faith is a gift from God, and our willingness to receive this gift is the beginning of a life that will be transformed by the living God, the Father of lights.

Anyone who wishes to play the piano or be a good golfer will not attain that goal without effort. Faith, if it is to sustain us and give us meaning in life, will remain dormant if we refuse to put any effort into it. Faith comes to us when we make the effort to reach out to God, confess our doubt, and invite faith into our heart.

As Elder Pavlos of St. Katherine's Monastery in the Sinai said, "When all is said and done, at the bottom line faith is a function of will—you must want to believe. The person who does not wish to—even if he sees God, he will not believe."

OCTOBER 24

Know Who You Really Are

We are all surrounded by fictional characters, inventions of film-makers, promoters, and even self-inventors. Ignorance of our true nature as children of God keeps us living as fictional characters, unaware of our own true purpose—the one God has chosen for us. When we stop relying on our own goodness and stop deluding ourselves into thinking we do not need God, we can cast our entire focus on discovering our true self.

The original meaning of the word *hypocrite* was "actor." Ignorance of our true nature is the root cause of so many living as though they are actors on a stage, afraid of what they might see if they were honest about themselves. True self-awareness can come when we are open to letting Christ into our lives totally. Continuing to live comfortably behind the mask of self-delusion, we are content to live in a carnal world, where we think happiness has its base in partying, making money, having sex, eating and drinking, living in the best house, and looking good.

We become like a Hollywood promoter, living behind the mask of our own invention, fearing we will be less interesting to others if we are outwardly religious. We fail to realize it is not enforced austerity and deprivation that is required, but a submission in love to Christ that brings us newfound freedom to be true to ourselves. Our new path leads to unspeakable joy and enduring peace.

OCTOBER 25

Waging War against Lust

U nlike the religion of Gnosticism—which teaches the separation of soul and body, with the physical world seen as evil and something to be overcome—historic Christianity teaches the unity of body and soul, with the physical world being transformed and made new in Christ. This means that, while caring about her soul, an Orthodox Christian must not leave the body without attention.

The body is given over to temptation, which is rooted in the mind. As Christians, we know that we must never play with temptations, for in doing so we have already fallen. Thus, an Orthodox Christian who takes her salvation seriously never partakes in seductive dances or enters into flirtation as though it were a sport, for she knows this is a dangerous game.

Temptations gain hold when we entertain thoughts and ideas, often because we allow our eyes and ears to partake of things that can overcome our will. It is much easier to stop a temptation in the beginning than to battle a seductive idea once it has gained entry. A person who wants to prevent a burglary makes every effort to keep a burglar from gaining entrance in the first place.

Many are convinced that sexual needs are so strong that they are impossible to resist. This is only the case when we habitually give in to the passions and avoid using the tools given to us by the Church to bring our body into submission. If we observe periods of fasting, especially the Wednesday and Friday days of abstinence, eat moderate amounts of food, avoid the overuse of alcohol, and say no to drugs, we have taken a big step forward in our struggle with lust. Remember, a healthy body contributes to the health of the soul.

It is good to take to heart the advice of St. Ephraim of Syria: "Think about the good so as not to think about the bad." Guard against spending time with people whose jokes and storytelling are occasions for sinful thoughts, and avoid bad company, for "evil company corrupts good habits" (1 Cor. 15:33).

Within the Fold but Without Love

That our Orthodox Church possesses the fullness of truth is a given, yet because of our weakness as believers, this obvious truth is often invisible to others. In our weakness as sinful people, we Orthodox clergy as well as the laity often fail to demonstrate the love and joy that would make our faith attractive to others.

When people visit an Orthodox temple for the first time, if they see beautiful ritual and a mystical interior but are not received warmly by the worshipers, they likely will walk away thinking this faith has no impact on the soul. Beautiful worship and sublime theology mean nothing if we don't live it out in love for others.

Grand services can be performed on any stage as reenactments of ancient Christian worship, complete with beautiful costumes and authentic images of an ancient faith. Yet these rites will be nothing but empty externals, devoid of meaning, if we Orthodox Christians make no effort to breathe in the faith and allow Christ to change our hearts and transform us into a holy people.

Only when we invite God to make us His holy people do the spiritual power of the services and the beauty of our temples become irresistible to others, and they become seekers themselves, by God's grace.

Faith without Action Is Dead

Although eternal life cannot be attained by works, for no one can do any good except by the power of Christ, faith without works is dead. Transformation is necessary for any of us to enter into God's kingdom, and this requires us to cooperate with God in our salvation.

The good news is that God provides the means by which we can live a life in action, ever moving toward holiness. Christ has done all the work, but we are required to do our part by cooperating with the action of the Holy Spirit, who provides the grace needed for this transformation.

This transformation takes place in the heart, for "the heart is not simply the physical organ but the spiritual center of man's being, man as made in the image of God, his deepest and truest self, or the inner shrine, to be entered only through sacrifice and death, in which the mystery of the union between the divine and the human is consummated."[19]

The means by which this transformation can take place are provided by God through His Church. By availing ourselves of frequent confession and the reception of the Holy Mysteries, we are given what we need to make this journey to the heart of God, being transformed into His likeness that we might be made worthy to spend eternity with Him.

OCTOBER 28

The Meaning of Salvation in the Ancient Church

According to Protopresbyter George Metallinos, dean of the Athens University School of Theology, "For [us] Orthodox the unique and absolute goal of life in Christ is theosis, our union with God, so that man—through his participation in God's uncreated energy—may become 'by the Grace of God' that which God is by nature (without beginning and without end). This is what 'salvation' means, in Christianity."[20]

As Christians we know that salvation is an ongoing process we are called to cooperate in. We are instructed to "repent, for the kingdom of heaven is at hand" (Matt. 4:17). The Apostle Paul made this clear when he told us to "work out your own salvation with fear and trembling; for it is God who works in you both to will and to do for His good pleasure" (Phil. 2:12–13).

Our faith is a free gift from God, not dependent on anything we can do. But the lifelong process of salvation requires that we cooperate with God's grace, that we might be transformed by the Holy Spirit and made holy. If we are to spend eternity with God, transformation must take place.

The sole purpose of the Church is the salvation of every human person, whereby we are united to Christ, transformed by Him in all holiness, and prepared for eternal life. This work of salvation is a gradual, lifelong process by which Christians become more and more like Christ. It begins the moment we commit ourselves to Christ, and within the abounding grace of the Holy Spirit, we are ever drawn closer in communion with God.

Theosis goes far beyond the simple restoration of people to their state before the Fall. Because Christ united the human and divine natures in His person, it is now possible for us to experience closer fellowship with God than Adam and Eve initially experienced in the Garden of Eden. Some Orthodox theologians go so far as to say that Jesus would have become incarnate for this reason alone, even if Adam and Eve had never sinned.

The Link between Repentance and Humility

In an age when self-focus is the rule of the day, and where the ego seems to reign, it is hard for people to see the value of humility. Many people, from politicians to rock stars, seem to climb the ladder of success by being anything but humble. In our darkened state, with sin dominating our lives and our bad habits seeming to be insurmountable, holiness seems to be only for saints, unattainable for ourselves. Stuck in our habitual patterns of behavior, we seem to have surrendered all hope for real change.

The antidote to this inertia can be found in one simple act: repenting. We fall down before our God, confessing our failure at keeping the commandments and asking for God's help in turning our lives around. We commit ourselves to crushing down the ego and to acquiring a humble heart. We take every opportunity to accept correction or criticism, without becoming defensive, for we know the truth in these words of St. John Climacus: "As with the appearance of light, darkness retreats; so, at the fragrance of humility, all anger and bitterness vanishes."

We refrain from judging anyone but only examine our own conscience, accusing only ourselves. St. Macarius the Great wrote,

> *Christians therefore ought to strive continually, and never to pass judgment on anyone—no, not upon the harlot on the street, or upon open sinners and disorderly persons—but to regard all men with singleness of intention and purity of eye, so that it may become like a fixed law of nature to despise no one, to abhor no one, to make no distinctions between them. . . . This is purity of heart, when you see sinners or sick people, to have compassion on them and be tenderhearted towards them.*

When People Don't Forgive

One of the Desert Fathers tells us of a young monk who came to his elder, complaining that he'd been wronged by one of his brothers. Following the Holy Tradition of the desert, the monk had gone to the one who had wronged him, asking for forgiveness. The erring brother refused, so the wronged brother wanted to know what he should do in response. The elder told the young monk that he had walked away justified in the eyes of God and there was nothing left for him to do except to pray for his erring brother.

This story makes it clear that we must always be quick to reconcile with others—even if they were at fault. We are not to remember the wrong done to us or to depend on others cooperating in the reconciliation. Their response is not required, for we will be held accountable only for our own response. Before God, we will be justified.

When another person refuses to accept our heartfelt apology, we must be willing to let it be and walk away, knowing that we've done our part. Abusive people such as these can, if we let them, prevent us from living our own life in Christ, for they keep our focus away from the forgiveness that comes from Christ. When we walk away from such negative people, we walk away having forgiven them, and we commit ourselves to praying for their repentance. There is nothing more we can do.

Keeping our focus on Christ, we do not react, do not resent, and do not lose our inner peace. The sickness that is at the basis of controlling, abusive people's attitudes must not be allowed to take away from the inner joy and peace that come from our personal relationship with Christ.

For your own soul's sake and for the soul of the abusers, continue to pray for them, but go your own way. "And the peace of God, which surpasses all understanding, will guard your hearts and minds through Christ Jesus" (Phil. 4:7).

OCTOBER 31

Reaping What We Sow

How could we expect there to be no consequences for a nation that has such a high number of our babies being aborted, has misused the resources given to us by God, advances wars for the sake of financial gain, and gives itself over to pride because of its scientific and technological advances? We have become a people that has turned away from the worship of God to worship material goods, sports, entertainment, and self.

St. John of Shanghai and San Francisco often expressed that absolutely nothing happens by chance and that human behavior leads to inevitable consequences, either good or bad. The horrible tsunami that hit Southeast Asia a few years ago killed thousands of people and devastated the area, which had grown comfortable with thousands of children being enslaved in a foreign sex trade, serving the perverted needs of pedophiles from all parts of the world.

God does not cause these devastating natural disasters; we do. God is in control of the forces of nature, but we are responsible for the results of the devastation that takes place. God does not send it upon us; it is we who bring it upon ourselves.

"Do not be deceived, God is not mocked; for whatever a man sows, that he will also reap" (Gal. 6:7). Let us use these natural disasters as a reminder to turn back to God and live our lives in repentance, and to turn away from our arrogance and contempt for the laws of God.

When We Are the Offender

We all have opportunities to bear the offenses and insults of others, which are occasions allowed by God to help us acquire the humility that everyone who would follow Christ must gain. Yet sometimes we are the ones who offend others, insulting family members, coworkers, or sometimes even strangers. The very moment we succumb to our ego, we fling aside Christlike humility, falling into the sin that led to the Fall. Like Adam and Eve, we sacrifice Paradise for a little moment of sin.

What are we to do in moments like this, when we find ourselves failing to live even a small portion of the Christian life? What are we to do with ourselves when we've allowed virtue to sink in the mire of our self-interest? We fall down as one unworthy even to kiss the sandal of our neighbor, and we ask the one we have offended to forgive us.

Then we start anew. Each time we fall, we keep our eyes on Christ. Each time we fall we reach out to the Lord, who is quick to forgive and who lifts us out of the darkness that would be our ruin.

NOVEMBER 2

The Temptation of Living Only for Today

The almost universal temptation of our time is to live only for the present moment. We want to enjoy ourselves now, to relax and be comfortable now, to have it all now. Our focus is, consequently, on a tiny slice of time. By focusing on such a short moment in time, we forget the importance of preparing for eternity.

Medical science has proven that teenagers often act without thinking of the consequences of their reckless behavior because their brains have not yet fully developed. They are not simply being defiant of the rules or taking chances with dangerous behavior, but have an inability to process the consequences of their actions. In other words, they don't recognize the possible finality of their behavior. For many of them, even death does not seem final.

When we focus only on the here and now, we are acting like teenagers. Our inner sense of the importance of preparing for eternity is shut down, and we don't think of the spiritual consequences of our short-term focus. We treat eternity as though it were a myth, and we put all our energies into getting what we think we need in the now.

By focusing on the acquisition of things and on being comfortable and fulfilled in this life, we forget the importance of spiritual preparation for what will be eternity. This life was not given to us by God for pleasure and the acquisition of things, but as a time for us to draw closer to the Creator God, who loves us and desires that we commune with Him for all eternity. Like the high school students who are preparing for their future lives by studying, so we must use this life as a time of preparation.

It's All about Me

When we closely examine our hearts, we must discern whether we are filled with a strong sense of self-importance or we see ourselves as the least of all. If we think highly of ourselves, that sense of personal importance can lead us to expect everything to go exactly as we think it should. We want to control the whole of our life. This sense of entitlement leads us to demand that everything be as we wish it, and we replace God's will with our own.

People who feel entitled because they are important tend to be easily annoyed with family members, neighbors, or coworkers. Their spouses and children are never good enough, and their friends are never sensitive enough to do the right thing for the friendship. Such people are always looking for signs that others are not doing the right thing by them, and they are easily offended.

Self-centered people ultimately complain to God and are unable to see the harm they are doing to their souls, for by demanding everything be according to their own will, they fall deeper into the abyss of self and into the land of the all-powerful ego.

If we recognize ourselves in this description, we need to make a good confession and embark on the journey toward acquiring a humble and contrite heart. This journey requires that we put other people first and become sensitive to their needs, putting those needs before our own. When we have accomplished this, we will be able to pray, as the Lord taught us, "Thy will be done on earth as it is in heaven."

The Role of Saints in Our Lives

Growing up Lutheran, I always believed the veneration of saints by Roman Catholics and Orthodox Christians was a form of idolatry. They were idolaters because they "worshiped saints." This worship of the saints was a major stumbling block for us Protestants, since worship was to be offered only to God. The distinction between veneration and adoration was unknown to us. (Adoration is reserved for God alone, while veneration is the respect we show to the saints.)

The historic Church has always venerated the saints, because the Church is undivided. The Church Triumphant in heaven and the Church Militant on earth are one. When the Church is at worship, the cloud of witnesses (those who've won the battle and are in heaven with God) is united in this worship before the throne of God with those on earth. When we enter into the communal worship of the Church here on earth, we are mystically united with the saints in heaven. Death does not separate us from those who've gone on before us, for in Christ there is no death.

When we venerate the saints, we are showing love and respect. Kissing an icon of a saint is much the same as kissing a Bible. When we kiss a photo of a loved one, we are not worshiping the person but demonstrating in a concrete way our love for the person. This is the very thing we are demonstrating when we kiss the icon of a saint.

When we are in need of prayer, we don't head for the nearest tavern and ask the man slumped over the bar to pray for us; rather, we ask for prayers from those who are close to God. No one is closer to God than those who've lived holy lives or who have died as martyrs, so we know they are alive in Christ and have His ear. We don't just ask a friend; we ask a saint to pray for us, because Christ is "glorified in His saints" (2 Thess. 1:10).

NOVEMBER 5

Love and the Acquisition of Holiness

As Christians, we know the struggle against the passions must be a daily one if we are to live according to biblical standards. This quest to defeat the passions is impossible without love, for a loveless heart desires nothing beyond supporting its own ego.

St. John the Evangelist tells us of the impossibility of loving God, whom we have not seen, if we do not first love our neighbor. Making this even more of a challenge is the fact that we are even charged by the Lord with loving our enemies.

Under the influence of Satan, because of his malice against us, we focus on self-love, and the battle against the passions remains dormant. Unless we seek out God's redemptive grace, we have no hope of letting love consume our hearts, and we remain locked in the darkness of sickness and death. Only through the power of the Holy Spirit and the accompanying acquisition of a humble and contrite heart does love gain the upper hand, and we are victorious in our struggle against self-will.

Without a loving heart, we cannot enter the Kingdom of God. Love is the key to holiness, and it comes only to those who struggle.

NOVEMBER 6

What Works Do—and Don't Do

When we respond to God's love with love, His mercy leads us into holiness, for entering into this relationship with our Creator transforms us, changes us. We were meant from the beginning to be in His image and likeness, and our positive response to the invitation to enter into divine communion leads to holiness.

We can do nothing good without God's grace, which is why St. John Chrysostom tells us, "Faith's workings themselves are a gift of God, lest anyone should boast." No man can call Jesus the Christ but by the power of the Holy Spirit, and the gift of faith implants in us the grace to do good works. Can good works save us? No! God's mercy and grace save us.

James wrote clearly about works and faith: "Thus also faith by itself, if it does not have works, is dead. But someone will say, 'You have faith, and I have works.' Show me your faith without your works, and I will show you my faith by my works" (James 2:17–18). Faith by itself, without good works, is indeed dead. Yet good works can only be done with God's grace (Christ in us).

James also wrote,

> *What does it profit, my brethren, if someone says he has faith but does not have works? Can faith save him? If a brother or sister is naked and destitute of daily food, and one of you says to them, "Depart in peace, be warmed and filled," but you do not give them the things which are needed for the body, what does it profit? Thus also faith by itself, if it does not have works, is dead. (2:14–17)*

If we claim Christ as our Savior yet have no love in us and do no good works, we delude ourselves, thinking we have Christ when in reality we simply have religion. Religion is dead, but Christ in us is alive! Works don't save us; Christ saves us. Good works are a sign that we are being transformed—made holy—because Christ dwells in our hearts. Anything good we do is because Christ is in us, and His grace abounds.

Purity Is Not Based on Age

It has been said that wisdom comes with age, and to some degree this is true. I've often had conversations with old college friends about how knowing what we know now would have made life so much easier; we'd have had fewer days of worry and stress over relationships, grades, and all the little things. After sixty-seven years of hanging around this planet, I'm far less likely to get stressed out about many things that would have overwhelmed me when I was a college student.

Yet one thing I know for sure: purity and passionlessness have nothing to do with age. They become part of our nature when we have gained humility. St. John of the Ladder taught that purity comes not because of our labors and certainly not because of our age, but only when we have humbled ourselves. And unless we have become humble, our passions will remain strong, and we will have made no spiritual progress. We will remain without wisdom.

Righteousness Is Not a Part-Time Job

Teachers and parents routinely remind children of the importance of refraining from giving in to peer pressure, knowing that good behavior can often be undermined by the desire to fit in with their friends and schoolmates.

We adults need to remember that we too are often subject to peer pressure. When we are surrounded by people who always take the moral high road, who are honest in their business practices, and who treat other people respectfully, our own adherence to the commandments of God is made easier.

What are we like when we spend time with that neighbor, friend, or relative who is fun to be with but shares off-color jokes or says horrible things about people we know? Do we give in to laughter because we want to fit in, or do we always take the high ground, keeping true to our Christian faith, regardless of the behavior of people we are with?

Bishop Nikolai Velimirovic wrote in *The Prologue from Ochrid,* "To be righteous among the righteous is a great and praiseworthy thing, but it is a far greater and more praiseworthy thing to be a righteous man among the unrighteous."[21]

Being righteous is not a part-time job.

NOVEMBER 9

Why Ask the Saints?

M ost Protestant churches reject all saintly intercession, citing passages such as 1 Timothy 2:1–5, which says that Jesus is the sole mediator between God and humankind, as well as Deuteronomy 18:10–11, which seems to forbid invoking departed souls.

Yet the Bible indeed directs us to invoke those in heaven and ask them to pray with us. In Psalm 103:20 we pray, "Bless the LORD, you His angels," and in Psalm 148 we pray, "Praise Him all His angels; praise Him all His hosts!" (vv. 1–2).

Those in heaven not only pray with us, they also pray for us. In the Book of Revelation, we read, "[An] angel, having a golden censer, came and stood at the altar [in heaven]. He was given much incense, that he should offer it with the prayers of all the saints upon the golden altar which was before the throne. And the smoke of the incense, with the prayers of the saints, ascended before God from the angel's hand" (Rev. 8:3–4).

And those in heaven who offer our prayers to God aren't only angels, but humans as well. John sees that "the twenty-four elders [the leaders of the people of God in heaven] fell down before the Lamb, each having a harp, and golden bowls full of incense, which are the prayers of the saints" (Rev. 5:8). The simple fact is, as this passage shows, the saints in heaven offer to God the prayers of the saints on earth.

Yes, we have Christ as our only Intercessor before the throne, but that doesn't stop our Protestant brethren from asking fellow believers to pray for them. We all, both those in heaven and those still on this earth, pray before the same sole mediator between God and humankind, Jesus Christ. It is Christ through whom we approach the throne of the Father.

Why would we not want to ask for the prayers of those who have already won their place in Paradise and are already standing before the throne of God, worshiping the Holy Trinity?

The Problem with "Bible-Based" Doctrine

Part of the problem for Protestants in accepting the veneration of the saints stems from their reliance on an approach to doctrine and practice that is Bible-only based. Proof texts are the norm for most Protestant debate about such issues.

However, the Orthodox Church bases its understanding both on our way of worship and on our doctrinal teachings on Holy Tradition and the Scriptures. Since the Bible comes out of the living, oral Tradition of the Church, the Scriptures can be properly interpreted only from within the life of the Church. In a nutshell, our understanding is based on what has always been taught.

The Orthodox Church proclaims as dogma what has been taught everywhere and at all times. What the Church teaches and the way she worships not only dates from apostolic times, but was everywhere taught and practiced in apostolic times. She is catholic (universal) because she is the same now as she was from the earliest times in her history. We rely on her Holy Tradition when interpreting the Bible, because it is from her Tradition that the Bible emerged.

Another point to think about is how Protestants interpret the concept of Christ as the "sole mediator." The Protestant idea assumes that mediator means "intercessor." But there is a more profound meaning: He is not merely an intercessor but the reconciliation of God and humans in the reality of the hypostatic union of God and man in the person of Jesus Christ. (The meaning of the Latin source of the word, *mediare,* is "to place in the middle.") Christ is certainly the sole mediator in that sense, but He need not be our sole intercessor.

Doesn't that make clear that the Protestant interpretation is missing the point? Once we understand that, the whole argument against the intercession of the saints has no basis.

NOVEMBER 11

The Church Must Not Become an Irrelevant Relic

When a priest makes a concerted effort to relate to his young parishioners by demonstrating a real interest in their lives, discovering
what is important to them, and taking the time to instruct them in the
Orthodox faith, there is a good likelihood they will remain pious Orthodox Christians for the rest of their lives.

A major problem for many young people (as many of our youths have
shared with me) is the language barrier. Most young people are simply not
interested in learning Church Slavonic, liturgical Greek, or Arabic, just
as they are not interested in studying church doctrine. Standing for long
services without understanding the message leaves them dry.

Priests cannot simply be liturgical functionaries without being one step
removed from wizardry. The divine services have to be more than form
and ritual, or the Orthodox faith will remain unknown to the people, and
personal, sustaining faith will not be imparted to them.

If we do nothing to help our youths to see the Church as more than
a vehicle for the preservation of ethnic culture and outdated religion or
something irrelevant to them, they will leave as soon as they leave their
parents' home. Bishops and priests of the Church must be willing to
interact with the society at large, dialogue with the thinkers of today, and
demonstrate that we actually believe Christ can change people's hearts and
bring healing to a culture that is falling into the abyss. The living faith that
is Orthodoxy will remain unknown if we fail to bring the gospel message
to this modern age. The Church will become an irrelevant relic of the
past—but only if we let it happen.

Heaven and Hell

Upon Christ's Second Coming, everyone who has ever lived will see Him in His uncreated light forever. For "those who have done good [go forth] to the resurrection of life, and those who have done evil, to the resurrection of condemnation" (John 5:29).

All will be separated at the moment of the final judgment, with the good experiencing Paradise as exceedingly good and radiant, while those who have rejected His love and whose lives ended without repentance will look upon Christ as hell, the "consuming fire" spoken of in Hebrews 12:29.

It is from Christ's Second Coming that the river of fire will flow. For the saints, this river of fire will be a golden light, encompassing them as an eternal joy. For the demons and the unrepentant, it will be as a burning hellfire. For this is the very reason we read in Luke 2:34 that Christ is "destined for the fall and rising of many."

Metropolitan Hierotheos Vlachos wrote, "Paradise and hell are not two different places. (This version is an idolatrous concept.) They signify two different situations (ways), which originate from the same uncreated source, and are perceived by man as two, different experiences."[22]

For those who reject the healing that has been offered, Christ will be their hell, their separation from eternal bliss. For the saints, Christ will be their resurrection into eternal life. This is why St. John of the Ladder wrote that the uncreated light of Christ is "an all-consuming fire and an illuminating light." This is why we say heaven and hell are not about location, they are about relationship. Heaven and hell are within the same realm, which is in the presence of God.

Pride and the Quest for Humility

Struggling with his pride, the monk focuses on bringing his own will into conformity with the will of God through monastic obedience. This obedience is not limited to obeying the directives of his abbot, but involves taking up a standard of humility that takes seriously his adherence to the 102 canons of the Sixth Ecumenical Council, including the garb he wears and refraining from cutting his hair and beard. The monk places his own will aside, taking up the tradition of the Church and making it his own.

Recognizing that false humility is almost wholly the product of self-righteous hypocrisy, the monk dedicates himself to a truth that is absolute and that transcends his personal opinion. It is precisely this humility that St. Paul reveals to us when, boasting of his sufferings and exploits, he tells us that they have meaning only in Jesus Christ.

The monk fights off the temptation to make his faith a form of ideology, for he knows that if the knowledge of Jesus Christ is transformed into an ideological and moralistic knowledge, it closes the door to others and turns Christianity into a list of requirements. This reduces the message of the Church to yet another worldly political force.

The monk refuses to let his Christian faith distance him from others, because he knows the monastic life is not a withdrawal from others but an embracing of all humanity through his intimate relationship with Christ, through whom all are united.

It is only through his immersion in a life of prayer that the monk's faith becomes something other than an ideology. Through uniting himself with the prayer of the Church, the monk loses himself, becoming one with Christ and with all Christians. His quest for humility comes through his having united himself to the humility of Christ, who condescended to take on our flesh in order to unite His divinity with our humanity.

Salvation: More Than Acquittal and Justification

Salvation cannot be explained using legalistic terms like acquittal and justification, for salvation is much more than simply being forgiven and getting into heaven. And works do not save us. But when works are placed in the context of a relationship, they do indeed have an eternal component.

Our works do not supplant the place of grace and faith in God but are part of the whole experience in our relationship with Him. St. John Chrysostom (349–407), one of the greatest of the Church Fathers, and perhaps the greatest preacher in the history of the Church, wrote,

> For Scripture says that faith has saved us. Put better: Since God willed it, faith has saved us. Now in what case, tell me, does faith save without itself doing anything at all? Faith's workings themselves are a gift of God, lest anyone should boast. What then is Paul saying? Not that God has forbidden works but that he has forbidden us to be justified by works. No one, Paul says, is justified by works, precisely in order that the grace and benevolence of God may become apparent.

The purging fire of God's presence is only a warmth for the one already purified with the good works done in this life. Yet those who waste this life, doing nothing to enhance their relationship with others through their good works, will experience the fire on Judgment Day as painful. For they who have not done good works in this life will have done nothing to promote a sound relationship with the God who has called us into a life of transformation.

Our works do not earn us salvation, but neither are works unimportant. According to the Fathers, works make our communion with God fuller and more complete. Our good works help us gain God's likeness in this life and bring us into a joyful communion with Christ. The more we become like Christ, the more joy we experience. Pain and suffering are the end result of our attaining less of God's likeness.

Spiritual Pain Control or Spiritual Healing?

S ince the Church is a hospital for the soul, it is important that we take
full advantage of all the resources she offers us for healing. Frequent
confession, where we bare our sins before God with a priest as the witness, is an important beginning to the healing process. Receiving the
Holy Mysteries of Christ's Body and Blood on a regular basis gives us the
grace needed for the healing of our souls, freeing us from the bondage that
comes from the sin that has weighed us down.

Keeping to a regular prayer rule given to us by our priest, confessor, or
spiritual father or mother also contributes to the healing process. Reading spiritually uplifting books as well as the lives of the saints also greatly
furthers the transformation that can be ours if we take our faith seriously.
The fasting rules of the Church are also designed to help us become whole,
promoting the healing process that began when we first made a commitment to live in Christ.

If we fail to follow these time-tested spiritual practices that are meant
to bring about healing of body and soul, we will not find the healing that
is available to us. Instead, we will find ourselves treating the Church as
though she were simply a pharmacy, where we get a quick fix for the pain
and sin that keeps us from becoming whole and find ourselves with short-
term results that only mask the sin and sickness that rule our lives.

It is up to us to decide whether we allow the Church to be a hospital
that brings about the cure or simply use the Church as a pharmacy so we
can mask our pain and sin. The choice is ours.

Sobornost: Divine-Human Oneness

S *obornost* means spiritual harmony based on freedom and unity in love. It is a necessary component in our membership within the Body of Christ, for if we are not bound together in love, our freedom becomes our enemy, separating us from others and ultimately from Christ Himself. This concept was so important to the early Christians that it was the basis for the agape meal, when Christians shared their food with one another after the celebration of the eucharistic banquet.

That the pre-communion fast would be broken after the Divine Liturgy with a communal meal (the love feast) clearly demonstrates the importance of community within the life of the Church. Sobornost is the divine-human oneness we experience as members of the one Body, the Church, and is the moment when we who are many become one. It is the image of the unity of the Holy Trinity, finding its expression among the believers.

Sobornost is not the same as fraternity, a submission to a brotherhood for benefit to the individual. Rather, it is akin to *kenosis* (the relinquishment of divine attributes by Jesus Christ in becoming human). Sobornost is when the individual gives up self-benefit for the community or *ecclesia*.

We cannot truly be one in Christ if we do not seek out oneness with our fellow Christians. Nor can we be one with Christ if we routinely reject sobornost for heights of spirituality that make us so conscious of self that they separate us from our neighbor.

Are You a Critic or a Doer?

It is easy to be critical of other people, finding fault with what we perceive they are doing, have done, or have not done. Yet those who point out how others have stumbled, finding fault in what they have not done and in what they could have done better, are, in reality, the ones who have stumbled.

The doer of the work may have stumbled or perhaps could have done a better job, but she must receive credit for having tried. This person still deserves credit, for she is the one who put forth the effort, whereas the critics have done nothing; knowing they have done nothing, they wish to take the spotlight off themselves and point it at the doer.

The credit belongs to the person who has erred and who perhaps comes up short again and again. He knows that without chancing some error or failure, he will never accomplish anything. This person takes up a worthy deed with great enthusiasm, in spite of the fact he may fail. The critics, fearing they will fail, do nothing. They will never know either defeat or victory.

NOVEMBER 18

The Capacity to Forgive and the Capacity to Love

The capacity to forgive is directly related to the capacity to love. In our act of forgiving others we find forgiveness. For in the turning away from our own self-concern and our own self-will, we begin to see that our salvation is directly linked to the salvation of our neighbor. To refuse to forgive our neighbor is to cease having the capacity to love, "for he who does not love his brother whom he has seen, how can he love God whom he has not seen?" (1 John 4:20).

Forgiving others requires work on our part, for we must cooperate with the grace that comes as a gift of the Holy Spirit. Since we have been forgiven much, we must forgive much. The Lord Himself told us we must forgive our brother seventy times seventy—no easy feat, to be sure. Yet it is this same Lord who gives us the power and the will to be quick to forgive those who have hurt or offended us. It is this very Christ who demonstrated the importance of forgiving others when He forgave those who were crucifying Him, saying, "Father, forgive them, for they do not know what they do" (Luke 23:34).

Helping the Vulnerable

When people are hurting and seeking professional help, they are vulnerable, and the trust they place in the professional makes them particularly open to exploitation. This is why we must have institutions and lines of authority that hold professionals accountable. We cannot allow anyone who is vulnerable—be it a child or an adult—to be exploited.

The bottom line is that we are all fallen and in need of redemption. None of us is beyond reproach, for we are all broken, and many in leadership roles are just as broken as those who seek out their help. The Church, as a living, healing organism, is the place where we can all be healed by Christ, the Great Physician of our souls and bodies. If we but humble ourselves, we can be made whole.

Those who hold positions of authority, be they police officers, teachers, clergy, physicians, psychologists, coaches, troop leaders, or just a friendly neighbor, must all guard their hearts, knowing they will one day stand before the Great Throne of God and give account. And pity the one who harms a child.

The Nativity Fast

During this period of prescribed fasting, we are to abstain from meats, dairy, eggs, cheeses, and all animal products. The Church does allow fish on the weekends during the Nativity fast.

Fasting is so important for the Orthodox Christian that many of the Fathers tell us we cannot consider ourselves to be Orthodox unless we keep the fasts. The spiritual discipline of keeping the fast is invaluable to the Christian life, for it helps make us lighter and more open to spiritual growth. We enter fasting periods because we want to go deeper into our life in Christ and gain strength in fighting the passions.

It is important to remember that fasting is not just about the foods we are to abstain from, but also about the quantity of food we eat. It is hardly a true fast if we eat the same amount of food we would normally eat when not fasting. Furthermore, if we avoid simple foods such as vegetables, breads, and vegan soups, and eat rich foods that are just as satisfying as non-fasting foods, we miss the point of the fast. It is hardly fasting if we consume a great variety of food in large amounts.

Being the Body of Christ

Every time we gather together in celebration of the Divine Liturgy, we are not just commemorating an event that happened two thousand years ago, nor simply reenacting the Last Supper Christ shared with His disciples. When we come together to celebrate the Eucharist, we are entering into an event already in progress.

Each and every Liturgy celebrated unites us with an event that is taking place in the here and now. Liturgy is not celebrated anew, for only one eucharistic banquet was celebrated, and that was when our Lord offered up the first Mystical Supper together with His disciples. Our offering is a rejoining of ourselves to that very moment in time when Christ is with His disciples.

At the moment of the eucharistic offering, we are made holy, just as the words spoken by the priest suggest: "Holy things are for the holy." In the Eucharist, we are made a holy people and set apart from the world. We become a people brought together in Christ, no longer apart and no longer alone. In each Liturgy we are rejoined to Christ and made as one Body, which is the Church.

The bread that has been set forth for the eucharistic offering becomes the Body of Christ and prepares us to be the Body of Christ. We are united in our celebration of the Divine Liturgy with the eternal eucharistic banquet that is ongoing in Paradise. As the faithful, we are brought together with all the saints who have gone before us. We will be united with them and our fellow Christians as one Body, which is the Church.

How Do We Keep Our Youths in the Church?

With all that has changed in our world—from access to information to moral norms to political polarization to crumbling family systems—is it any wonder young people are abandoning the Christian faith in droves? It is not enough to expect them to accept the authority of bishops, priests, and the traditions and teachings of the Church. We must demonstrate to our youths the difference between information and wisdom.

Wisdom is passed down and does not compete with worldly knowledge. It need not be in conflict with science, nor should it be linked to narrow-mindedness. Wisdom connects us not only to the best of human knowledge and experience but also to what is eternal. It gives our youths the ability to relate to our Creator, to our culture, and to others.

Nihilism has become the religion of countless youths, making life appear to be meaningless. The information age has driven God out of societal, cultural, and governmental prominence, resulting in mass disbelief. So we who are of the older generations must witness to the wealth of truth that is in the Church by demonstrating its worth in how we live. We can't simply teach the truth to our youths; we must live it in a way that makes it real for them. We must be patient with them, open to their struggles, and nonconfrontational when they disagree with us—or we will lose them forever to Christ.

If young people do not see a genuine living out of the Faith, they will look for truth in directions that will take them far from it. The Church will not draw our youths unless her members demonstrate holiness of life and reach out with love, patience, and understanding, offering something that is seen as real by today's young people.

Finally, our youths need to see joy in us. If we do not have joy, they will continue to wander in the wasteland of consumerism, materialism, and nihilism. And there will be no hope for the future of our planet.

Where Heaven and Earth Are United

As a priest, I bear the awesome burden of offering the Holy Oblation before the throne of God on behalf of all the people whose names are submitted to the monastery and who are Orthodox. I offer for my spiritual children and even for the whole world. I also commemorate my own beloved parents, Albert and Dolores, who converted to the Orthodox faith while in their mid-seventies and who lived many years in Orthodoxy before reposing in the Lord.

I remember my best friend in college, Russell, who, like me, converted from Lutheranism to Orthodoxy. He died at fifty-six in the pastoral care of my friend Archpriest Nicholas Letten.

I offer the Holy Oblation for the people who regularly attend the Sunday and holy day liturgies here in our monastery's temple. I offer, like all priests, the Holy Oblation for our nation, our civil authorities, and our armed forces. I offer the eucharistic sacrifice for our Holy Patriarch Kirill, Metropolitan Hilarion, Archbishop Kyrill of San Francisco, and Bishop Theodosy of Seattle.

I offer the oblation for all those who have no one to pray for them and for those who have died but are forgotten. I offer the Holy Sacrifice for all the clergy of the Seattle area and for my brother priests of the diocese.

And I offer the Holy Sacrifice for myself.

The whole of the cosmos is united in this heavenly offering, for it is the very source of life itself.

Orthodox Faith in a Multicultural Society

Multiculturalism has radically changed the face of many countries throughout the Western world, with immigration introducing many foreign religions into societies that were previously monolithic in religious tradition. Many countries in Western Europe and North America are now seeing the spread of Orthodoxy as never before, along with the introduction of Islam. This, together with the spread of secularism and atheism, has changed the religious map of many countries.

These changes have made the practice of our faith more difficult, since Western societies no longer culturally support the open practice of Christianity. No longer do we see the expression of Christianity in the public forum, except in Orthodox countries. Many people experience pressure to keep their faith private so as not to offend others by being "too religious." With pluralism dominant in the workplace and social settings, any display of our faith can be frowned upon.

This may work for some, but for a serious Orthodox Christian, this is problematic. How do we live Orthodoxy as our faith demands if we live it in a vacuum, shutting it off as a private practice only on Sundays? If we are truly to "put on Christ" and be transformed by the healing resources that are available to one who lives a committed Orthodox faith, we cannot allow ourselves to live Orthodoxy Lite.

We must be bold in our faith. As a monk who wears monastic garb everywhere, I can tell you it has a powerful impact on people. Even when sitting among friends who are not religious, I always bless my food. If I see a police car or fire truck pass by in downtown Seattle, I raise my hand in blessing. I wear a cross around my neck not only because I am a priest, but also because I am a believer.

I am not afraid to be public about my faith in Jesus Christ, for my faith demands it of me. Christ told His disciples that if they denied Him before men, so too would He deny them before His Father. Orthodox Christianity cries out to be lived publicly. Our very salvation demands it!

Don't Hide Your Faith

It has been my experience that many individuals who deny the importance of religion in their lives have simply been turned off to religiosity. They've seen a form of Christianity that is disingenuous and have therefore discounted Christianity altogether. Others see Christians as judgmental and self-righteous and are therefore turned off by any religious expression.

What to do?! First, we must not hide our faith under any circumstances. This does not mean we are preachy or self-righteous. A Christian who is grateful for the Faith is also compassionate toward those who have no faith. Giving a loving witness to Christ while following the dictates of our Orthodox traditions is a good starting point.

If we are seated at the dinner table with unbelievers, for example, it is important that we not be showy about our faith, but also important that we not hide the fact that we are Orthodox Christians. Making a simple sign of the cross over ourselves before we eat not only expresses our gratitude toward God for our food, but also gives quiet witness to our willingness to live our lives in open love of our Savior. The Lord said if we deny Him before men, He will deny us before the Father. Keeping the traditions of our faith, staying true to the fast periods, and making an effort to attend Liturgy weekly is absolutely necessary if we are to grow spiritually.

Most important, our dedication to our faith and a willingness to give witness to our love of Christ can have a huge impact on those around us. If our love of the Savior translates into love of family and neighbor, those around us will see that our God is real and that our Orthodox faith is truly a way of life—one that transforms our nature. When people see that we are filled with joyous living and not judging others, they in turn want what we have. The pearl of great price can be theirs as well.

Thanksgiving

It has become the practice in America for many Orthodox Christians to gather in our temples for the celebration of the Divine Liturgy on Thanksgiving Day, for what better way to give thanks to God than to celebrate the sacrament whose very name, Eucharist, means "thanksgiving." As we gather with friends and family, sharing in the traditional turkey dinner, we remember that this great country has set aside Thanksgiving Day, not as a day to overeat, but as a day when we come together as family.

The central service in the Orthodox Church is the Divine Liturgy, and since the word *liturgy* means "the work of the people," the centrality of this service is all the more important, for it involves us all in a most intimate way. The people of God, who make up the Body of Christ, come together to celebrate the Eucharist and receive the very Body and Blood of our Savior. Christ condescended to take on our flesh and condescends, again, to unite Himself to His creation in each celebration of the Divine Liturgy.

The Eucharist, by its very nature, is a meal of unity whereby we leave our isolated lives and come together around the table of the Lord. We are mystically joining in the heavenly banquet that is ongoing and celebrated in the heavenly realm. This celebration of the Divine Liturgy it is not an isolated event, but a meal of unity.

We Orthodox, perhaps more than most, understand the profound importance of coming together as one. We come together to celebrate the Liturgy, which is the work of the people, giving thanks to the Lord for yet another year of blessings.

Taking Orthodoxy beyond the Self-Congratulatory

Archbishop Averky of Syracuse of blessed memory once said of converts, "They are like envelopes; they have a tendency to come unglued." Many converts give themselves over to a zealotry that is without temperance. In their excitement at having found "the True Faith," they almost overnight take on external formulas that make them feel they are on the fast track to sainthood.

They notice when another parishioner seems careless in making the sign of the cross, so they demonstrate for all around them the proper way. They make a production of the fast periods, making sure their non-Orthodox family and friends know the seriousness of fasting. Their icon corners can be larger than that of the pious old woman who has been Orthodox all her life.

These people become spiritual gluttons; they take their newfound faith into a place of sensuality and pride that is miles from the holiness that comes from years of struggle. In their newness to Orthodoxy, they throw themselves into the externals and public displays, while preventing themselves from entering into the mystery of faith that comes only with the acquisition of a humble and contrite heart.

Our longing for drama and excitement can lead to spiritual pride rather than the holiness that comes with humbly receiving the faith by following the example of holy people. If our Orthodoxy is expressed primarily in the externals, we become followers of the Pharisee rather than imitators of the humble publican.

My spiritual father, Archimandrite Dimitry of blessed memory, gave me the best of advice when he said, "Little by little." Taking little steps, with the guidance and direction of one's priest or spiritual father or that pious little old lady whose face radiates the light of Christ, we will be able to enter into the Kingdom, having gained the humility and joy that do not necessitate being extravagant with the externals.

A War Plan for Repeat Offenders

In the Mystery of Confession, the priest stands in as the witness. After we have confessed before the Lord, the priest, acting in Christ's stead and by His authority, pronounces the absolution. Thus begins the process of transformation that leads to holiness. Regular confession is necessary if we are to triumph in our battle over sin, for only in confession do we face the reality of our fallen nature and confront the ego, seeking out God's help in conquering the passions.

The priest also guides penitents, helping develop a "war plan" by which we can learn to do battle with our fallen nature and find victory over our sins. The importance of confessing before the priest is evident in that it is difficult to gain victory over secret sins. We can travel through life dismissing our shortcomings when no one knows about them.

Since all sin (even that committed in secret) is against the whole Body of Christ (the Church), confession before the representative of the Church (the priest) is all-important.

When we find ourselves constantly repeating the same sins, over and over, having a regular confessor is especially valuable, for he can help us focus on ways to avoid those sins. Keeping a journal of our struggles can help us see patterns in our behavior that lead to habitual sins, thereby helping us to minimize the frequency of our falls.

It can be helpful if we remember that sin is what inhibits us from becoming holy—or whole. When we are whole, we are as God meant us to be. As people made whole, we become the very image and likeness God intended, gaining our inheritance.

When we find ourselves struggling with the same sins over and over, it is good to remember that we have but to give ourselves over to Christ, who promises us victory over our sins. The struggle for holiness is not about what we can do, but about what Christ can do in us.

A Prayer of Thanks

*We thank You, O Christ our God, that You have satisfied us
with Your earthly gifts. Deprive us not of Your heavenly Kingdom; but as You entered into the midst of Your disciples, O
Savior, and gave them peace, enter also among us and save us.
Amen.*

After-meal prayer

This prayer is one of my favorites, for it expresses concisely my need to
remember to give thanks to God for all He has given me. It connects
me to the ancient Church, for it allows me to recount the Lord's coming
in the midst of His disciples and granting them the peace I so desire. It
keeps me focused on the goal and remembering, throughout my day, that
the Lord is to be my focus.

This is a prayer many Orthodox Christians pray at the end of meals, yet
also a prayer that can be offered whenever we are feeling a certain gratefulness of heart or desiring God's loving mercy.

Prayers like this are easily memorized, allowing us to express our gratitude
to God without being wordy. The Lord knows our needs, and there is no
need to spell it out for Him. What is necessary is that we remember to give
thanks to God and let Him hear from us throughout the day. These short little prayers are perfect for keeping ourselves spiritually focused, as they express
our desire to make communion with God the central part of our day.

This is a wonderful prayer to say with children just before tucking them
in for the night, ending their waking hours by calling down God's peace
into their hearts. It also is a wonderful prayer to offer as we arrive safely at
our destination following the morning commute.

Just as an old couple who've shared a long life together don't need to say
a lot of words to demonstrate their love for one another, so too our prayers
don't need to be long and formal to let God know we love Him. But they
do need to be frequent.

Let Christ Increase While You Decrease

As we enter into the holiday season, our stress level tends to increase, leading to conflict. Worries about finances, interactions with certain family members who are not usually a part of our everyday lives, and holiday shopping and cooking obligations can lead to increased tension between members of families. Husbands and wives can find themselves arguing about petty things, children can become disobedient, and family arguments can overwhelm the peace that should reign during the holy season of the fast and the Nativity celebrations.

Sometimes one little remark of a visiting relative can open old wounds, leading to a family argument. Adult children can find themselves acting like angry teenagers, with one critical word leading to a meltdown and ruining a family dinner.

During the holiday season, you need to be vigilant, guarding your words and keeping your emotions under control. This season should be a time when you work harder at keeping the peace, guarding your heart, and letting Christ rule your words and thoughts. Don't let the celebration of the birth of our Savior be trampled upon by your ego. Make sure Christ is glorified in your speech, your actions, and your thoughts. Make this season one in which you treat all your family members, friends, and coworkers with extra respect and love.

May we let Christ increase in our hearts as we make ourselves decrease.

Do Not Let the Sun Go Down on Your Anger

Anger is by nature designed for waging war with the demons and for struggling with every kind of sinful pleasure. Therefore angels, arousing spiritual pleasure in us and giving us to taste its blessedness, incline us to direct our anger against the demons. But the demons, enticing us towards worldly lusts, make us use anger to fight with men, which is against nature, so that the mind, thus stupefied and darkened, should become a traitor to virtues.

Abba Evagrius the Monk

While getting into my car in a parking lot, I overheard someone taking God's name in vain. I saw that he was angry that he'd dropped something, and then I realized I knew him. He was a self-declared Christian who would have been horrified had he realized I'd overheard him. How sad I felt that he'd given himself over to the passion of anger to such an extent that he took the Lord's name in vain—the very Lord whose name he bears. There are many nonbelievers who guard their words better than many who profess Christ. The Fathers tell us that whenever anyone takes God's name in vain, the ramifications reverberate throughout the entire cosmos. However insignificant we think our secret sins may be, they affect the whole of God's universe. Redemption is not just about us but about the whole of the universe. My salvation and your salvation are connected.

St. Seraphim of Sarov said, "We must bear offenses from others with equanimity and accustom ourselves to such a disposition of spirit that these offenses seem to concern not us, but others. Such a practice can give quietness to the human heart and make it a dwelling for God Himself." And Abba Nilus said, "Prayer is the seed of gentleness and the absence of anger."

During this Nativity Fast, let us not only abstain from non-fasting foods, but let us more importantly abstain from all anger. If we truly are of Christ, we have the means to change, for it is because we have Christ in us that victory over the passions can be ours.

When God Seems Absent

We all have moments when we feel as though God is absent—or even nonexistent. Those times leave us feeling alone and abandoned, as though we were lost in an empty stadium. Or we feel as though we were on a boat that has been set adrift without an engine, floating further from shore and heading to an uncertain future.

Such occasions are not unlike those early days, while we were toddlers, when Mom would hold our hands while Dad reached out to us, just feet away, urging us to take our first step. We were not in any danger, but we certainly didn't feel that way as we felt Mom's hands separate from ours. We felt fearful, vulnerable. We felt as though we were going to fall, yet Dad's arms were reaching out, offering the security we'd always had, yet encouraging us to stand on our own, taking the first steps into independence.

God is like that with us. Those periods when He seems distant—or even seems to be a fictional being—are moments when He is actually closer to us than our own breath. These are the moments when God is drawing us out of ourselves and into communion with Him. His outstretched arms are there, even though we don't see them. These moments strengthen us and enable us to have a mature relationship with God, not unlike the mature relationship a child develops with her parents after taking those first steps alone.

DECEMBER 3

How to Be a Pious—Not Prideful—Orthodox Christian

I once noticed a young man standing in the front of the temple during Liturgy, making profound bows, together with frequent, almost exaggerated, signs of the cross. My first thought was that he must be a newly baptized Orthodox Christian; after embracing Orthodoxy, many people fall into the trap of exaggerated piety. I do not mean to diminish the importance of external piety or making the cross properly; liturgical correctness has its place. We just need to be careful to remember that our piety is not meant to be displayed before others.

I once knew a monk who always stood in the back of his monastery's catholicon, avoiding any public display whatsoever. He told me the temptation to be seen as a pious and holy monk was too strong. I am not suggesting everyone stand in the back of the church, lest everyone be doing battle for those few spots on a crowded Sunday morning. What I am suggesting is that we remember we are there for worship.

If you become aware that your motives for standing in front of others during worship arise out of pride, by all means move to the back. It is the Lord who should see us, and to Him our pious external acts of worship should give honor. Externals are meant to be an aid to worship, bringing our bodies into conformity with our hearts. We must guard the heart, making sure the externals are not temptations for pride.

The way to make sure our piety takes us deep into true worship is to express these external acts of worship in the privacy of our homes. Private Orthodox worship, expressed by standing before our icons, making the sign of the cross with care, and doing prostrations, instructs the heart in true worship. If we've established a true relationship with the Lord in our home, what we express in the temple publicly will be authentic.

DECEMBER 4

Procrastination

There is a story of a young monk who confessed to his elder that he was always struggling with procrastination. His elder told him his lack of faith made it impossible for him to see God everywhere and in all things, and for this reason he was careless and lazy about everything having to do with his salvation.

The Apostle Paul said, "'My [Christ's] grace is sufficient for you, for My strength is made perfect in weakness.' Therefore most gladly I will rather boast of my infirmities, that the power of Christ may rest upon me" (2 Cor. 12:9). In our weakness, we tend to put things off, especially those things that pertain to our salvation. We know the importance of keeping a prayer rule, of spending time each day with the reading of the Holy Scriptures, and of being productive in our spiritual lives. We know the importance of frequent church attendance, yet we put it off. Tomorrow, we tell ourselves, will be the day we will begin to take our spiritual life seriously. Tomorrow we will set our priorities—and keep to them. But tomorrow never comes.

Let me be clear that I am not addressing the form of procrastination caused by depression, as depression and procrastination often go hand in hand. I am referring to laziness but also to fear of failure, in which we fear we will not be good enough at a task at hand, so we put it off.

We only need to take that first step, remembering, "I can do all things through Christ who strengthens me" (Phil. 4:13). Procrastination has power over our lives only if we let it.

Procrastination stands in the way as we combat habitual sins that keep us from making spiritual progress. It can keep us from reconciling with family members or friends who've been estranged for years. It can keep us from making a good confession, thus unburdening ourselves of guilt that has been weighing us down.

DECEMBER 5

Sin Is the Sign of Our Illness

In our sense of guilt over our sinful nature, it is easy to look upon God as a judge. We, as sinners, are guilty, and we stand in the dock as one before a judge. Yet the truth of our situation is far more sublime. Our relationship with our God is not of a juridical nature; it is personal. God is not offended by our sin, just as a doctor is not offended by a sick patient and a mother is not offended by her sick child.

Because of the darkness of our nous (the eye of the soul), we have forgotten God's true nature as well as our relationship to our Creator. We have replaced God with idols of self and material things. We have replaced God with people, with music, with social engagements. And in the process, we have become pagans.

In a word, we have become ill, and we are in need of the cure. The symptoms of our illness abound, but God's grace abounds in greater amounts, and the doors of the hospital—the Church—are open wide for us.

DECEMBER 6

Walking Together Toward the Kingdom

I recently heard a wonderful story about a group of African children assembled before a large basket of fresh fruit. They were told the first child who could reach the basket would have all the fruit for himself. The Western adults who had set up this test stood in awe as the children linked hands and ran for the basket together. Arriving at the basket, they all reached out to touch the fruit at the same time.

When asked why they did not try to outrun the other children and claim the basket of fruit for themselves, they all cried out, almost as one voice, "We could not enjoy the fruit unless we could share it together."

This is how salvation works. We are all on the journey to God together. If we do not link our arms in love, none of us will enjoy the fruits of Paradise, "for he who does not love his brother whom he has seen, how can he love God whom he has not seen?" (1 John 4:20).

DECEMBER 7

The Importance of Confidentiality in Confession

The seal of confession is a hard-and-fast rule held throughout the history of the Orthodox Church. Since the priest, in Orthodox theology, is but a witness to the confession—the confession is given to Christ Himself—confidentiality is an absolute must.

Recently I had a man contact me by email, sharing his grief at not feeling he could trust his priest, who was known to have violated the confidentiality of this Mystery. He added that another priest refused to hear his confession, so he was feeling cast aside and devoid of joy.

Reading this man's words brought sorrow to my heart, for joy should be our common inheritance as Orthodox Christians. The ability to confess our sins and receive Christ's absolution is so central to our Christian faith and to our joy.

It is also imperative that the spiritual direction given by a priest in confession be for the penitent's ears only. If the priest is not permitted to divulge what the penitent says in confession, the penitent should not divulge what the confessor says. This does not mean that sharing what your priest said during your confession is as reprehensible as having your sins revealed by the priest. But it breaks the seal of confession and could easily lead to a friend revealing your confidentially shared words to another person and having them passed on as gossip.

Another good reason always to refrain from sharing what was said in confession is that your spouse will feel he or she has a right to ask what was said, fearing he or she might look bad in the eyes of the priest. If spiritual therapy is to result in healing, confession must be the one place where the penitent can always be up-front. Honesty has to be central to the confession.

As a final note, an Orthodox priest can never pronounce absolution in the case of murder, rape, pedophilia, or any other serious crime unless the person agrees to turn himself in to the police. An important element in confession for any person who is truly sorry for his sins is his willingness to accept the consequences of justice rendered.

Sharing the Truth in a World Devoid of Hope

If you wish to share the truth of the Orthodox Faith and of Christ, who is her Head, you must give witness to the love of Christ by loving everyone. Without Christ, Orthodoxy is just another religion, devoid of the power to transform and deify the human heart. Without Christ, the Church is nothing but a human institution, no different from a political party. For the Church to be herself, Christ must be visible in the love of her bishops and priests. He must be seen in the love of her people and in the charity and kindness that are displayed by all who call themselves Orthodox.

Without Christ, our world is devoid of hope, and for others to know this Christ, they must be able to see Him in us. The light of this very Christ must shine forth through the love of His Church and be made manifest in the works of His people. Without this love, there is only darkness upon the face of our world, and the world remains without hope.

Others cannot know they need Christ if they do not see Him in us. They will not know that Christ fills hearts and transforms lives if they do not see transformation in us. If we are fearful, angry, judgmental, arrogant, or aloof, the world will see nothing in our Christian faith worth seeking.

If others do not see in you a forgiving heart, how will they know there is forgiveness in Christ? If others do not see in you a heart filled with joy, how will they know they need the very Christ whom you proclaim as your Lord and Savior? If others see you as a judgmental, narrow-minded, unhappy person, why would they be drawn to the Orthodoxy you claim is the true faith?

Cooperating with the Physician of Our Souls

Although it's imprecise, we often use anthropomorphic language when speaking about God. For example, we say God is like a mother whose sick child is in need of healing and who is not offended by the child's sickness.

Yet we can also say that God is offended by our deliberate turning from the holiness and communion with Him we were created for. Our sickness is a clear sign of the presence of sin, and this sin grieves God. This same God does not merely offer an escape from the eternal bondage of death, but invites us to enter into life in Christ here and now.

Perhaps we can say God is scandalized with the state of our soul, as a doctor might be irritated upon hearing the news that her patient has not been taking his medication. Like the doctor, God has given us a prescription whereby the healing of the darkened nous can begin to take place. Yet our Orthodox Christianity does not hold to the notion that our guilt as sinful creatures translates into punishment for sin, but rather that confession and repentance are seen in therapeutic terms.

In our fallen state, we are not sentenced to punishment but invited to be spiritually healed, for salvation is not merely an escape from punishment. God, although He can be anthropomorphically described as a judge, is in reality our Physician. The cure He provides frees us from the eternal bondage of death and gives us entrance to life in Christ in the here and now.

We are invited to share in God's divinity through the action of theosis, in which the Creator condescended to take on our humanity and shares His divinity with us. Theosis is both the transformative process by which we become "partakers of the divine nature" (2 Pet. 1:4) and the goal of that process. The goal is the attainment of union with God and is brought about by the effects of the purification of mind and body.

Theosis is the very purpose of human life, and it is achievable only through a cooperation between humans' activities and God's uncreated energies (or operations).

Sexual Sins

Sins of a sexual nature are common. Much of the struggle is directly related to the fact that people do not take advantage of having a spiritual father or mother. If you are your own guide, your struggles with sexual passions can be beyond your ability to fight, leading to despair.

Our bodies are temples that have been bought with a price. We do not, therefore, own our own bodies.

The sixties mantra of the women's movement that laid claim to the right of a woman to abort her baby is the ultimate result of the misuse of human sexuality. Much justice came out of the women's movement regarding equal pay, equal opportunity, the end to discrimination, and the right not to be sexually exploited. But the idea that a woman can make the decision to abort a child (or a man pressure her into it, which often happens) is unjust, because such a belief ignores the right of a child to life.

That a man would see sex with a woman as a right because he took her out to dinner and a movie is another example of the wrongful view of the role of sex.

Our bodies belong to God, and our sexuality should be expressed only in ways that are sanctioned by God's law. Yet no one should be embarrassed by struggles with masturbation or falling into other temptations of a sexual nature.

Without the help of a spiritual father or mother, abstinence can seem impossible, especially given the powerful drive of our sexual nature and the pressures of our society to express our sexuality freely. For young men or women who are bombarded with the tales of the sexual exploits of their friends, the struggle for purity can seem impossible. This is one more reason we need to surround ourselves with friends who are committed Christians and who know the importance of living lives centered on Christ. Again, frequent confession with one's spiritual father or confessor is a tool that can make all the difference in our struggle to be free of sinful passions and triumphant in our goal of purity before the Lord, who loves us so.

The Purpose of Our Sexuality

O ur sexuality is a gift from God and is meant to feel good, but it is also a gift that has been given for a purpose. Through sexuality, our species increases, and through it a man and a woman become one. The sexual act between a husband and a wife is meant to unite them as one flesh, bringing them closer to each other in a bond of love. For this gift to be used in any other way is to trespass against God's intent.

Because our sexual drive is so powerful, it can be hard to control without the help of an experienced spiritual guide. In an age when sexual expression is seen as one's right and when many believe that people cannot be fulfilled if they are not sexually active, keeping oneself chaste can be a daunting task indeed. If everyone is doing it, how can it be wrong?

It is illogical for Christians to be selective about which commandments they are going to keep. We don't steal, because we know it is against God's commandments, and we don't murder another person, because we know all life is precious. Yet some of us think nothing of coveting another man's wife or sleeping with someone for the sake of personal pleasure. With such an attitude, an unborn child is dispensable because she is the inconvenient result of an evening of sexual gratification and would be costly to support.

Our human sexuality is a sacred gift from God. For the celibate monk or nun, this is a gift from God that we offer back to Him as a sign of our love and of our desire to be united completely to the Lord of lights. To the unmarried, sexuality is a gift saved for the marriage bed, where one gives of oneself to one's spouse.

DECEMBER 12

The Role of Suffering in Salvation

We should not forget that in our age of "sophistication" even little children are spiritually harmed by what they see and hear. As a result, purification is required, and this is only accomplished through bodily suffering. . . . You must understand that Paradisal bliss is granted to no one without suffering.

Elder Ambrose of Optina Monastery

We attain salvation through God's grace not only by our good deeds, but also by our patient suffering of various griefs, illnesses, misfortunes, and failures (Mark 8:31–38; Luke 16:19–31; Rom. 6:3–11; Gal. 6:14; Heb. 12:1–3). Jesus Christ gives us the power needed for transformation and prepares us to live with strength under the most difficult conditions, allowing us to have the peace that is eternal.

Heaven and hell are a condition of relationship with God that is either theosis or perdition. The lake of fire and heaven occur within the same realm, both being not about places but about relationship. The Orthodox Church teaches that heaven and hell are in the same realm, and that hell is not separation from God symbolically or physically; hell is a place chosen. For one who hates God, being in the presence of God will be eternal suffering.

The Western juridical misconceptions concerning sin have tended to distort a proper recognition of suffering and its connection to sin. In the Orthodox understanding, without suffering, we cannot join ourselves to the Cross, and when we do take up our cross in suffering, it is with our co-suffering Savior. Sickness and suffering are not given to us by a wrathful and punitive God because we have sinned, but rather are allowed by this loving God who co-suffers with us.

DECEMBER 13

Where Is God?

Many feel that God is a myth, a nice idea, but hardly believable. If this God they'd like to believe in were real, wouldn't He make it easier to see Him and seek Him out? If we are free to choose God, why doesn't He make Himself easier to find?

These are questions many people pose, at least to themselves. Many want to believe there is a God who cares for them and who is capable of making a difference in their day-to-day struggles, but they just can't quite surrender to belief. The nihilistic philosophy that has possessed the hearts of many young people today is based on the despair of an age that has seen so many wars, so much poverty, so many murders, so many children abused, and a seemingly hopeless future. How can there be a God when so much suffering abounds in this world?

Where is God? He is in the sunrise. He is in the glorious mountains and the vast sea. He is in the tender touch of a mother's hand. He is in the words of absolution pronounced by the priest after a confession. He is in the smile of an old woman at the sight of a young couple holding hands. He is in the wonder of the cosmos on a darkened night. He is in the giggle of a small child playing. He is in the warmth of a kitten held in the hand.

He is in the Cross that bore the Son of Man. He is in the bread and wine that become His Body and Blood. He is the transforming Spirit that changes hearts and makes people saints. He is closer to us than our own breath, more loving than a grandmother's embrace of a sick child.

He is everywhere, for there is no place He cannot be. He fills all things. He is everywhere to be seen, if only we look with open eyes and open hearts.

DECEMBER 14

Unwittingly Entertaining Angels

A ll of us meet someone in any given week who is in need of encouragement, love, and mercy. Consider mothers whose children are going to bed at night hungry because they cannot afford to buy food, or old women whose husbands are long gone and whose children are too busy to check in on them. The world is full of lonely people in need of comfort, kindness, mercy.

How about the college student down the hall in the dorm who has no place to go for Christmas, no caring family wanting to see him? Or the crabby old neighbor who is always frowning? Is it not possible that his frown masks grief for a lost wife or for a son who turned his back on his father? There's the police officer who pulled you over for going over the speed limit and was abrupt with you. Is there a chance she's having marital problems?

All these people can be in need of a word of kindness, a gentle smile, and a word of encouragement. Can you imagine the impact on the officer's day if you, after having been served with the traffic ticket, thanked her for making our roads safer? What if you sat down next to the old man and asked him how he was doing? What if you offered to take him to a café or baked a plate of cookies for him? What if you invited the lonely college student to celebrate Christmas with you?

What if you collected all your children's old toys and gave them to a shelter for abused women? What if you gave out one hundred dollars worth of ten-dollar bills to homeless people on the street? What if you made a pact with yourself to do seven acts of kindness each and every day, without judgment?

What if you entertained an angel? "Do not forget to entertain strangers, for by so doing some have unwittingly entertained angels" (Heb. 13:2).

DECEMBER 15

Standing and Falling before God

Standing before God has been the only acceptable posture for Orthodox Christians from the earliest of times. We recognize that a faithful
servant would never sit before his master, and the faithful are all servants
of the Lord. The Apostle Paul tells us, "Watch, stand fast in the faith"
(1 Cor. 16:13), and "stand therefore, having girded your waist with truth"
(Eph. 6:14).

As Christians, we must always be on guard spiritually, including as we
attend the divine services. By standing we subject our bodies in a way
that helps us pay attention to properly and fully worshiping God with all
our mind and soul. We subject ourselves before the Master as His humble
servants, being attentive to Him. When we become fatigued during long
services, we symbolically become offerings to the very God we worship.
St. Paul said, "Present your bodies a living sacrifice, holy, acceptable to
God, which is your reasonable service" (Rom. 12:1).

In addition to the ascetic practice of standing in worship, we Orthodox
can add the pious act of prostrations. Prostrations can be done when entering the nave from the narthex, before we venerate an icon in the temple,
or when saying the Jesus Prayer in the privacy of our homes. There are
times to sit (see the Kathismata, the sections of the Psalter read each day;
kathisma means "seated") and not to sit (the *Akathistos*: "not seated").

Monks commonly perform prostrations while saying the Jesus Prayer,
especially when fingering the beads that are spaced throughout a prayer
rope. Prostrations, like standing, help aid in purifying the heart, for in these
physical actions we bring the mind's attention back from wandering and
worship God with body and soul united.

Forgiveness Is a Two-Way Street

Psychologists have often made the observation that the one thing they lack when it comes to their profession as psychological healers is the ability to pronounce absolution. And many Orthodox Christians, after making a good confession and receiving absolution, feel as though they still need forgiveness. This is because, even though they have received the pronouncement that their sins have been forgiven, they act as though nothing had changed.

If we continue to be plagued by guilt, even after we have received the absolution of Christ through His agent the priest, we compound the very sin we've confessed. In clinging to our guilt, we act as though there were no forgiveness. Clinging to guilt is not a sign of humility but rather a sign of unbelief, for we turn a cold shoulder to the very forgiveness that has been pronounced, as though it were not true.

Christ's absolution is a two-way street, for having confessed our sin and being absolved of it, we must receive His forgiveness with great joy. We, like the woman at the well, must go and sin no more.

How Should We Pray?

At our monastery, we've had a number of people ask us to pray for them to win the lottery, promising that if they did, they'd donate a large portion to the brotherhood. The logic seems to suggest that if the monks are going to get some of the take, the Lord will be more than happy to tweak the numbers so they can win big.

I've often thought that if they won, they would likely lose their souls, succumbing to the temptation to go back on their promise to God.

I once prayed I'd get a certain job, thinking all my problems would be solved if only I had that job. I told myself that then I could get a better apartment and a new car, pay off my bills, and be set. When the job didn't materialize, I ended up going off to graduate school, which was the best thing I could have done for myself.

The Scriptures instruct us in how we should pray. In Acts 17:27–28, we read, "So that they should seek the Lord, in the hope that they might grope for Him and find Him, though He is not far from each one of us; for in Him we live and move and have our being, as also some of your own poets have said, 'For we are also His offspring.'"

Prayer is not about asking for things, but about relationship. It is the vehicle that takes us into the heart of God, where we find a peace "which surpasses all understanding" (Phil. 4:7). Prayer is our opportunity to show our love for God because of His great love for us.

An infant in the care of loving parents need not worry about food, clothing, security, or safety, for her parents know what she needs and freely give it in abundance. The Lord is like that with us.

If we trust the love God has for us, we trust that we need not ask for anything, but only offer worship and love, and give ourselves over to our heavenly Father. Like any child loved by his parents, we are assured of the love of the Father. Nothing else matters.

Darkness Is Just the Absence of Light

Our Orthodox Christian theology views evil not as a primeval essence that is coeternal and equal to God, but rather as a falling away from good. Evil does not exist in and of itself, and God did not create it. Our Orthodox Church rejects the gnostic teaching that the entirety of being is made up of two realms that have forever existed together: the kingdom of light and the kingdom of darkness.

This darkness does not exist in its own right, but is simply the absence or lack of light. Evil, according to St. Basil the Great, "is not a living and animated substance, but a condition of the soul which is opposed to virtue and which springs up in the slothful because of their falling away from Good. Do not, therefore, contemplate evil from without; and do not imagine some original nature of wickedness, but let each one recognize himself as the first author of the vice that is in him."

Nothing is greater than God, including evil. Evil results when the free will of God's creation is directed against God.

This is precisely what happened when the light-bearing morning star (Lucifer) fell away from the Source of goodness and became the evil one, Satan. By imposing his own will, Lucifer found himself in darkness. Since his power is based in falsehood, he can influence us only by convincing us that he is as powerful as God. Yet his power is finite, and good will eventually triumph on the Last Day.

That God would allow evil to exist in the first place is a mystery, for the Scriptures do not explain it. Yet we do know through the Scriptures that true love must express itself in action. And in the face of evil and suffering, a Christian is called to action by loving God and his neighbor. Evil then becomes but a simple practical problem, one the Christian finds ways to alleviate. As Christians, we are charged with bringing God's love and goodness into the world by our actions.

Taste the Presence of Christ

We all need a good dose of silent prayer each and every day. Finding that perfect place in your home that can become your cave, or prayer closet, will afford you sacred space where you can go deep into your heart and connect with God. It is the place where you can close off your family, your worries, your job, and your distractions, and go deep into your heart, where you will find the peace that comes from Christ.

The Jesus Prayer is the perfect prayer, for it is a prayer of adoration and praise, and a prayer that proclaims that Jesus is Lord and, as God, can grant mercy upon you. This simple prayer, which invokes the Holy Name of Jesus, can transform your life and take you into the very heart of God. This prayer is known as the prayer of the heart for the very reason that it is of the heart.

Lord Jesus Christ, Son of God, have mercy on me, a sinner. Said with the aid of a prayer rope (thus bringing your body into the action of the prayer), this prayer accomplishes St. Paul's admonition that we pray always. It takes you out of yourself and into communion with Christ. It is a prayer that can change your life because through it you can taste the presence of Christ beside and within you.

Let Your Prayer Arise As Incense

From Old Testament times, believers have burned incense as an offering when worshiping God. The ancient temple in Jerusalem even had priests whose sole duty was to keep the censer burning twenty-four hours a day.

Ancient pagan kings were often escorted with large fans of peacock feathers and burning incense when entering their palaces. Early Christians took both these symbols for their worship in recognition of Christ as their sovereign King and Lord. To this day, the Orthodox Church uses incense in most of her services. And large, circular fans, reminiscent of the peacock fans of ancient times, are held over the Gospel book during the proclamation of God's Word during the Divine Liturgy.

As a young man attending my very first Orthodox Liturgy, I was struck by the use of incense. The words of King David, "Let my prayer be set before You *as* incense" (Ps. 141:2), are chanted during every celebration of Vespers during the censing of the temple. During every service where there is a great censing of the whole church, the priest (or deacon) censes the frescoes and icons as windows into eternity, as the incense wafts upward as an offering of the people of God. The people are also censed by the priest in recognition of their having been created in the image and likeness of their Creator God.

Incense is so central in Christian worship that it is even used in the worship of the domestic church, where the family gathers in prayer around their own icons, reading the Scriptures together and offering their family prayers to the Lord.

Let my prayer arise as incense before You!

DECEMBER 21

When Ethnicity Becomes a Barrier

Over the years I have heard many grief-stricken parents and grand-parents lament the loss of their children and grandchildren from the Church. Sad as it may be, I'm not surprised, for over and over I've heard the sad truth behind this exodus. More often than not, these parents did not raise their children to be practicing Orthodox Christians. They may have had their infant baptized, but they went to church irregularly—and mostly just to keep ethnic links to the old country.

Parents often look upon baptism as the moment when their child is made Orthodox. But Orthodoxy cannot be seen as the ethnic link to a family's history any more than ethnic dancing and ethnic food make one Orthodox. It is fine to be proud of one's heritage and to want to preserve one's language and traditions. But our ethnicity does not save us. Being Greek or Russian or any other ethnicity does not save us. Only Christ saves us! We must not link ethnic preservation to our Orthodox Faith, for in Christ there is "neither Jew nor Greek" (Gal. 3:28). In Christ, we are one nation.

It is always sad to witness churches that are packed with Sunday wor-shipers who are there only because they want their cultural hit for the week. They want to get together with people from the old country who speak their language. But if these parishes place too much emphasis on cul-tural and linguistic ties, they are in danger of becoming nothing more than walled citadels of ethnic purity, keeping "outsiders" from entering into the gates of Paradise.

If we are not to repeat the mistakes of the past, which led to the exodus of the children and grandchildren of the last big wave of immigrants from the Church, we must teach our children and grandchildren. If they do not understand the language of worship, the faith will not become their own. And, if their friends are not made welcome in our churches, our children and grandchildren will eventually leave the Faith of their ancestors. And we will stand alone, wondering why our churches are empty.

If You Have No Spiritual Father

We cannot place all our dependence for spiritual nourishment on having a spiritual father. Most Orthodox Christians do not have one, and the average parish priest is not equipped, either with the time or the inclination, to take on the role of spiritual father to members of his flock. If we want to dedicate our lives to God on a full-time basis, but we don't have the needed guide to keep us on track, what do we do?

We can't just order up what God has for us, but we must make sure we are open to the movement of the Holy Spirit in our lives. Making life around the Church a high priority in our week can serve as a good start. Orthodoxy is by nature a faith that demands full participation and deep commitment; otherwise, it becomes just another religion, devoid of salvific, transformational value.

Unless Orthodoxy is something other than mere magic—with the priest as some sort of wizard who has the right formulas, thus allowing us to feel we've done all that is needed—it will have failed us. Do we read the daily prescribed Scripture readings? Do the lives of the saints influence our lives because we read about them? Do we prepare ourselves for regular confession by taking note of our sins and being ready to be accountable before God, with the priest as our witness? Are we holding up the Orthodox standard in our public life, or do we allow ourselves to be lost in the crowd, dismissing our obligations to God during the week?

The spiritual life is an adventure, full of pitfalls and great heights. Yes, it is best that we have a spiritual father or mother, and we should pray that God send us such a guide. But the road to Paradise must begin with a commitment to make the journey our main priority. We are on a journey, and it begins with that first step. Christ stands with us, ready to lift us up when we fall and even to pull us along when we stumble or grow fainthearted.

Why Attend Church?

Over the years I have met people who have not joined a church, choosing to "worship" at home. Some have convinced themselves that church is a waste of time and that they can be close to God while staying home on a Sunday morning. Others believe none of the churches teach the Bible according to their own interpretation, and worshiping at home ensures they don't have to hear any false teachings. Some people have chosen to stay away from church because of past conflict with a clergyman or because they got tired of hearing pleas for money and decided that giving to a charity was money better spent.

But God has given us the Church as the very place where we can grow spiritually while enjoying the protection and the blessings of being in weekly contact with other believers. Just as in an earthly family, we don't always enjoy everyone's presence, but it is often those difficult and uncomfortable moments that help us grow the most.

In Luke 4:16, we read that our Lord Jesus Christ was regularly in the temple, for "He came to Nazareth, where He had been brought up. And as His custom was, He went into the synagogue on the Sabbath day" (Luke 4:16). It was Christ's regular practice to go to a synagogue. If our Lord Jesus made it a priority to meet with other believers, how can we excuse ourselves from doing the same?

Perhaps the most important reason for weekly church attendance is that only in the church can we receive Holy Communion. And our Lord went so far as to say that unless we eat of His flesh and drink of His blood, we will have no life in us (John 6:53). In receiving Holy Communion, we receive the grace needed to grow spiritually, and we are empowered to live in all holiness and truth.

It's a Wonderful Life

One of the most beloved movies ever made is Frank Capra's *It's a Wonderful Life*. It tells the story of an optimistic young man who sets aside his own dreams to help others. After some of the money for his savings and loan company is lost, George finds himself struggling with the idea of committing suicide on Christmas Eve.

After George utters the words "I suppose it'd be better if I'd never been born at all," his guardian angel, Clarence, shows him all the lives he has touched and how different his community of Bedford Falls would have been if he hadn't been born.

Many of us have had moments when we felt we just couldn't go on, and suicide seemed like the only logical solution. As a young man, I experienced a terrible period of depression and despair, and I attempted suicide. Yet, when I hear from others how my daily blog and Ancient Faith Radio podcast have helped so many people, it is unfathomable that I was ever that despairing young man. Perhaps it is because I was that young man that I am able to sympathize with those who are suffering and to help them see that their dark time can be the very catalyst for a bright future.

We are all called, at some time or another, to be Clarence, that funny guardian angel who points out the worth of another person and reaches out with a loving embrace and soothing words of comfort. If, like Clarence, we pay attention to the fact that many people's high expectations for happiness during the Christmas season fall short and leave them lonely and despairing, our own acts of kindness, words of encouragement, and smiles of acceptance will make all the difference in the world. And we will become signposts pointing the way to a bright and happy future.

DECEMBER 25

Gratefulness Makes Us Happy

We all know that money can't buy happiness. And many gifts on Christmas Day can't bring happiness either. But do we know that practicing simple gratitude brings about happiness? Researchers testing gratefulness have discovered that it actually changes the brain and makes us happier. But gratitude changes more than brain chemistry, for it makes us better and kinder to others.

If we practice being thankful for the compliments we receive from our friends—for those dinners they treat us to, for the gifts they give us, or for just being there when we need them—we find that our gratitude brings about more friendships, for others are drawn to us.

Dr. Robert A. Emmons conducted a study on gratitude at the University of California at Davis that showed measurable benefits on the psychological, physical, and interpersonal health of subjects who practiced gratitude. He wrote, "Evidence on gratitude contradicts the widely held view that all people have a 'set-point' of happiness that cannot be reset by any known means."[23] This simply means that if we practice gratitude, we can be happier than we've ever thought possible.

Gratitude is an affirmation of goodness; we affirm that there are good things and good people in the world. Being grateful does not mean that everything in life is perfect, but that we look at life as a whole and receive with gratitude all the goodness in it. In turn, our gratitude becomes the foundation for building up those around us, for in being happy ourselves, we are more likely to bring about happiness in others. Being happy nurtures random acts of kindness and promotes goodness and kindness even among strangers. People love it when other people are good to random people.

There is nothing that brings about satisfaction like being grateful for our lives, for the lives of those around us, for the things in our lives, and for the love God has for us. Remember, it is not happiness that makes us grateful, but gratefulness that makes us happy.

Change Comes Little by Little

We often become frustrated with ourselves, wanting to change a bad behavior, but we seem to be incapable of doing it. The priest has heard the same confession from us, week after week; he could probably say our confession for us, having heard it so often. And there is a simple reason for our repetition: We don't struggle with the passions in a way that will bring about change.

People who stretch the truth are aware of their sin, but the habit is so strongly held, they find themselves lying before even realizing their confessed sin is being repeated. Overeaters make a commitment to lose weight, but make no attempt to empty the refrigerator of the leftover cake that was a temptation the night before. So, while they watch television, the thought comes into their mind that there is that one piece of cake remaining, and they rush to consume it. Then, almost like magic, there is another cake sitting on the counter by the next afternoon.

Our captivity to a bad behavior seems permanent and change impossible. Yet if we make a concerted effort to change, little by little, we find we can master those stubborn behaviors. Instead of beating ourselves up each time we fall, we take baby steps, and little by little, we make progress.

That cake we consumed becomes our last piece, because we don't go near the baked-goods aisle in the grocery store. We pass half a day without inventing a new story about ourselves, and before long, we are no longer confessing that sin. Little by little, we find we can change bad behavior.

St. Ambrose of Optina said, "A man cannot correct himself all of a sudden, but it is like pulling a barge—pull, pull, and let go, let go! Not all at once, but little by little. Do you know the mast on a ship? There is a pole to which is tied all of the ship's lines. If you pull on it, then everything gradually pulls. But if you take it all at once, you will ruin everything."

DECEMBER 27

Being Lazy about Church

O ur laziness and misplaced priorities regarding the Sunday and holy day services keep us from fulfilling our obligations to God and endanger our souls, for in keeping ourselves away from God's temple, we remain far from the cure that comes from participating in the Divine Mysteries. St. Gregory Palamas tells us that we "may remain uncured, suffering from unbelief in your soul because of deeds or words, and failing to approach Christ's surgery to receive . . . holy healing."

We cannot attain salvation in the privacy of our own homes, for our faith is a communal one, whereby we participate in the Body of Christ in a corporate way. It is in this life that we must participate in the communal life of the Church, for after death there is no treatment for what separates us from God. There is no repentance after this life, because all people share the same end. Each of us is destined to see the glory of God at the Second Coming of Christ.

Protopresbyter John Romanides tells us,

> *All people will see the Glory (Uncreated Light) of God, and from this viewpoint they have the same end. Everyone, of course, will see the Glory of God, but with one difference: The saved will see the Glory of God as a most sweet and never-setting light, whereas the damned will see the same Glory of God as a consuming fire that will burn them.*

Our laziness and our misplaced priorities keep us from the Divine Mysteries and deprive our souls of the healing grace that comes with an encounter with the living God. As the hospital of the soul, the Church has been established by Christ Himself as the place where we receive the cure, so that we may bask in the eternal banquet that awaits us in the afterlife. By depriving ourselves in this life of the grace-filled Mysteries, which are found only within the life of the Church, we separate ourselves from the very treatment that ensures eternal bliss in the next life.

Monasteries: Centers for Spiritual Healing

Although a primary duty of monasticism is worship and contemplative prayer, monks also have a long history as missionaries. Many of the great monasteries of Russia, for example, were founded in remote places but became centers of pilgrimage, attracting countless people. Whole cities often formed around monasteries, precisely because the monks had reached out with the gospel and worked among the people. Where there was a need, monks responded with charity and evangelical witness.

In these difficult times, when people are suffering economic hardship, loss of their jobs, and foreclosures on their homes, monks can bring a different perspective that can give hope to those who've lost all hope. People who've been struggling to find meaning can walk away with a new vision, gained through the interior work of the monks who've made themselves available as therapists for those who are hurting. Monasteries become centers of spiritual healing and empowerment.

Many see monasticism in a romantic way, with monks quietly and silently living out hidden lives; yet there are monks who work with people as spiritual fathers, preachers, and teachers, participating in an active way in service to the world. Each monk and each monastery is called apart for the service of God and His Church, as God wishes.

Although the Orthodox Church does not have religious orders as the Latin Church does, there are in Orthodoxy different styles of monastic life, both individually and in community. Generally, some monasteries are more liturgically oriented, while others are more ascetic; some have a certain mystical tradition, and others are more inclined to spiritual guidance and openness to the world for the purpose of care and counseling. These various styles of monasticism, which take both a personal as well as a corporate form, are the result of organic development under the living grace of God.

Yet all monastics share the vows of poverty, chastity, stability, and obedience, ever following the words of Jesus—the cornerstone for this life: "You shall be perfect, just as your Father in heaven is perfect" (Matt. 5:48).

Ways We Grow in the Church

It is important to remember that the Church, as defined by the early Church Fathers, is not a religious institution but a living organism that is the hospital for the soul. Her priests, who first sought therapy, became the therapists. Therefore, the frequent use of the tools given to us by Christ, through His Church, are of utmost importance to our spiritual progress. Frequent confession and weekly reception of the Holy Eucharist give us spiritual strength and enable us to live in the world without being of the world.

Whenever we meet a priest, we should ask for a blessing, remembering that it is not his blessing we are seeking but the blessing of the Lord Jesus Christ, whose priesthood the clergyman participates in. When writing to a priest or a bishop, whether by letter or by email, it is a good and pious practice always to ask for a blessing. This can be done by writing "Father, bless" to a priest or "Master, bless" to a bishop. Just before signing your name, write, "Kissing your right hand and asking your prayers."

This is not about the bishop or the priest; it is all about Christ, whose blessing we seek. It is much the same with the veneration of icons, for when we kiss the icon of a saint, we not only show our love and respect to the saint and seek his or her prayers, but we also are kissing Jesus Christ, who dwells in His saints.

Because Orthodoxy is holistic in nature, living it out should not be confined to Sunday morning. If we were pianists and made our living playing with an orchestra, we wouldn't think of going through a week without daily practice, for we would not stay in the orchestra for long. And a marriage that is not worked at on a daily basis is doomed to failure, for a relationship between two people requires work. If we expect to have a relationship with God and have Him dwell in our hearts and commune with Him, we have to treat our spiritual life as something important and something we are committed to. An occasional Liturgy does not suffice if we expect to grow in faith and wisdom.

What We Can Do to Build Community

Our choices are many when we consider where to put our energies in these difficult days. For example, we can volunteer in soup kitchens, tutor homeless kids, or work at childcare centers that give parents the freedom to find and keep jobs.

We can volunteer to be job counselors or deliver meals to those who are housebound. We can look in on the elderly woman next door or the young mother whose husband is fighting in Afghanistan.

We can volunteer to teach English as a second language to immigrant families or drive seniors to medical appointments. We can fill the gas tank of a struggling family at the next pump or pay for the groceries of the mother standing behind us in the checkout line.

When we see a person on the bus who is looking lost in worry, we can offer to pray for him or even invite him to church with us on Sunday. We can offer to sit with a sick relative to give the caregiver a few hours to get outside for some much-needed time away.

We can offer to take out to lunch a neighbor we know is going through some difficult times. We can buy a fistful of restaurant coupon booklets and give them to people who ask for handouts. As we hand them a booklet, we can ask them to pray for us. This allows them to pay for their food by their prayers. And by preserving their dignity, we make them feel less like beggars.

Whatever struggles we have on our plate will seem like nothing once we've given ourselves over in service to others. Even when we are struggling to make ends meet, the power of giving can change our lives for the better. When we become philanthropic and focus on others in need, our own problems seem less serious.

DECEMBER 31

From Fear to Boldness

Immediately following Christ's Crucifixion, His followers hid in fear for their lives. Yet after He arose, they boldly proclaimed the Resurrection despite intensifying persecution. Only a true resurrection could have accounted for a sudden change that would lead believers to give up everything, including their lives, to preach it.

One skeptic, Paul, was by his own admission a violent persecutor of the early Church. Yet after an encounter with the resurrected Christ, he underwent an immediate and drastic change from being a vicious persecutor of the Church to being one of its most prolific and selfless defenders. After his encounter with the risen Christ, Paul suffered impoverishment, persecution, imprisonment, beatings, and finally execution for his steadfast commitment to the Resurrection.

The sorrow we Christians experience during our Lenten journey is tempered with the knowledge that Christ is conquering death by His death and that His Resurrection is our resurrection. We look to the future with the faith of the saints and martyrs that have gone on before us, and we experience the truth of Jesus Christ's teachings, for our hearts are being transformed by the power of His message. Our sins have been forgiven, and we are guests at the eucharistic banquet, awaiting our time when the gates of Paradise will be opened to us. We fear nothing, just like the martyrs, because we know the truth of the Holy Resurrection of Christ our God.

Endnotes

1 http://www.pigizois.net/agglika/paisios/08.htm (accessed 9/16/14)

2 Ray Downs, *Christian Post Reporter,* December 26, 2011

3 St. Tikhon of Zadonsk, *Journey to Heaven* (Holy Trinity Publications, 1991)

4 St. John of Kronstadt, *My Life in Christ* (Holy Trinity Monastery, 1984)

5 Archimandrite Sophrony, *His Life Is Mine* (St. Vladimir Seminary Press), p. 72

6 Thomas Merton, *New Seeds of Contemplation* (New Directions, 2007)

7 St. Nikolai of Zhicha, *The Prologue from Ochrid* (Serbian Orthodox Diocese of Western America, 2008)

8 Herman A. Middleton, *Precious Vessels of the Holy Spirit: The Lives and Counsels of Contemporary Elders of Greece* (CreateSpace, 2011)

9 *The Wisdom of the Desert Fathers* (Cistercian Press, 2006)

10 Elder Paisios of Mount Athos, *Epistles,* quoted in http://www.fatheralexander.org/booklets/english/elder_paisios_mount_athos.htm (accessed 9/16/14)

11 Elder Thaddaeus of Vitovnica, *Our Thoughts Determine Our Lives* (St. Herman Press, 2008)

12 Abbess Thaisia of Leushino, *Letters to a Beginner on Giving One's Life to God* (St. Herman Press)

13 Elder Paisios of Mt. Athos, Epistle 4

14 *Eleftherotypia* (newspaper), December 23, 2001

15 St. Theophan the Recluse, *The Path to Salvation*

16 Elder Thaddaeus, op. cit.

17 St. John of Kronstadt, *Ten Homilies on the Beatitudes* (Cornerstone Editions, 2003)

18 Elder Thaddaeus, op. cit.

19 Kadloubovsky and Palmer, trans., *The Philokalia* (Faber and Faber, 1983)

20 George Metallinos, *I Confess One Baptism* (St. Paul's Monastery, 1994)

21 St. Nikolai of Zhicha, op. cit.

22 Met. Hierotheos Vlachos, *Life After Death* (Birth of the Theotokos Monastery, 1996)

23 Robert A. Emmons, *Journal of Personality and Social Psychology* 2003, Vol. 84.

The Very Rev. Fr. Tryphon is abbot
of All-Merciful Saviour Monastery
on Vashon Island in the Puget Sound.

Listen to *The Morning Offering* podcast at
http://www.ancientfaith.com/podcasts/morningoffering

Ancient Faith Publishing hopes you have enjoyed and benefited from this book. The proceeds from the sales of our books only partially cover the costs of operating our nonprofit ministry—which includes both the work of **Ancient Faith Publishing** and the work of **Ancient Faith Radio.** Your financial support makes it possible to continue this ministry both in print and online. Donations are tax-deductible and can be made at **www. ancientfaith.com.**

To view our other publications,
please visit our website: **store.ancientfaith.com**

Bringing you Orthodox Christian music, readings, prayers, teaching, and podcasts 24 hours a day since 2004 at **www.ancientfaith.com**